Henry VIII
in 100 OBJECTS

Dedicated to my headmaster who introduced me to the pleasures of the theatre and equipped me with the necessary writing and analytical skills that I would employ thirty years later as an author. Thank you for being such a kind-hearted, dedicated, charismatic, influential teacher. It was a joy and privilege to be one of your students.
Lionel Warne
1942–2020

And in loving memory of my dear friend and shipmate
Judith Brocklehurst
1973–2018

Henry VIII in 100 OBJECTS

The Tyrant King Who Had Six Wives

Paul Kendall

FRONTLINE BOOKS

Henry VIII in 100 Objects

This edition published in 2020 by Frontline Books,
An imprint of Pen & Sword Books Ltd,
Yorkshire - Philadelphia

Copyright © Paul Kendall, 2020

The right of Paul Kendall to be identified as the author of this work has been asserted by him in accordance with the Copyright, Designs and Patents Act 1988.

HB ISBN 978 1 52673 128 9
PB ISBN 978 1 52676 719 6

All rights reserved. No part of this publication may be reproduced, stored in or introduced into a retrieval system, or transmitted, in any form, or by any means (electronic, mechanical, photocopying, recording or otherwise) without the prior written permission of the publisher. Any person who does any unauthorized act in relation to this publication may be liable to criminal prosecution and civil claims for damages.

CIP data records for this title are available from the British Library

Pen & Sword Books Limited incorporates the imprints of Atlas, Archaeology, Aviation, Discovery, Family History, Fiction, History, Maritime, Military, Military Classics, Politics, Select, Transport, True Crime, Air World, Frontline Publishing, Leo Cooper, Remember When, Seaforth Publishing, The Praetorian Press, Wharncliffe Local History, Wharncliffe Transport, Wharncliffe True Crime and White Owl.

PEN & SWORD BOOKS LTD
47 Church Street, Barnsley, South Yorkshire, S70 2AS, England
E-mail: enquiries@pen-and-sword.co.uk
Website: www.pen-and-sword.co.uk

Or
PEN AND SWORD BOOKS
1950 Lawrence Rd, Havertown, PA 19083, USA
E-mail: Uspen-and-sword@casematepublishers.com

For more information on our books, please visit www.frontline-books.com, email info@frontline-books.com or write to us at the above address.

Printed and bound in India by Replika Press Pvt. Ltd.

Typeset in 10/14pt Adobe Caslon by SJmagic DESIGN SERVICES, India.

Contents

Introduction 7
Acknowledgements 9

1. Memorial Commemorating King Henry VIII's Birth, Royal Naval College, Greenwich 10
2. Eltham Palace 15
3. Henry VII's Tomb, Westminster Abbey 19
4. The Tower of London 23
5. Stained Glass Window Commemorating the Marriage of King Henry VIII to Katherine of Aragon, St Margaret's Church, Westminster.. 27
6. The Coronation Chair, Westminster Abbey 30
7. The Gatehouse, Richmond Palace 33
8. The Bronze Watch Bell from the *Mary Rose* 36
9. The Westminster Roll Depicting Henry VIII Jousting at Westminster 38
10. Two Tudor Docks at Woolwich Dockyard 41
11. Glass Slide of the *Henry Grace à Dieu* 47
12. Earliest known Portrait of Henry VIII, *c*. 1513 50
13. Oil Painting Entitled *The Meeting of Henry VIII and the Emperor Maximillian I* 52
14. Henry VIII's Tower, Tournai 56
15. Plaque Commemorating the Establishment of Trinity House 58
16. Parade Armet of Henry VIII 61
17. Cardinal Thomas Wolsey Statue, Ipswich 62
18. The 'Silvered and Engraved' Armour of Henry VIII, 1515 70
19. The Longbow 72
20. Letter from Henry VIII to Cardinal Thomas Wolsey, 1518 74
21. Greenwich Tiltyard 76
22. The Medieval St Paul's Cathedral 81
23. Portrait of King Henry VIII, *c*. 1520 84
24. Leeds Castle 86
25. Dover Castle 88
26. *The Field of the Cloth of Gold*, 1520 91
27. Henry VIII's Tonlet Armour, 1520 97
28. Thornbury Castle 100
29. Henry VIII's Portable Lock, Hever Castle 104
30. *Assertio Septem Sacramentorum Adversus Martinum Lutherum* by Henry VIII 105
31. King Henry VIII Gatehouse, Windsor Castle 107
32. The Round Table, Great Hall, Winchester 111
33. Charles Brandon, Duke of Suffolk and Friend of Henry VIII 113
34. Eltham Ordinances 115
35. Hever Castle 117
36. Henry VIII's Room 124
37. Henry VIII's Writing Desk 125
38. Love Letter Written by Henry VIII to Anne Boleyn 126
39. Treaty of Amiens, 1527 128
40. Bridewell Palace 130
41. The Black Friar 135
42. Hampton Court Palace 140
43. Remains of Whitehall Palace 142
44. A Surviving Tudor Cauldron 145
45. Emblems Celebrating the Marriage of Henry VIII and Anne Boleyn, Hampton Court Palace 147

46. Window Bearing Crests of Henry VIII and Anne Boleyn, Greenwich Palace 150
47. Queen's Stairs, Tower of London......154
48. Westminster Abbey 159
49. The Oath of Allegiance to Henry VIII and his Successors, 30 March 1534 161
50. Sir Thomas More Memorial, Chelsea 165
51. Lambeth Palace 169
52. Traitors' Gate 171
53. Bell Tower..174
54. The Act of Supremacy, 1534 177
55. Tyburn Memorial 181
56. Westminster Hall..............................183
57. Bishop John Fisher and Sir Thomas More, Execution Memorial Plaque, Tower Hill 187
58. Title Page of the Valor Ecclesiasticus 190
59. Portrait of Henry VIII, 1535 192
60. Tomb of Katherine of Aragon, Peterborough Cathedral...................194
61. Site of the Great Hall, Tower of London..201
62. Tower Green......................................208
63. Roundel from the Ceiling of the Great Watching Chamber, Hampton Court Palace 212
64. St James's Palace, London.................215
65. St James's Church, Louth 218
66. Pilgrimage of Grace Banner 225
67. Hussey Tower, Boston.......................230
68. Clifford's Tower, York 234
69. Portrait of Henry VIII, 1537 237
70. Nonsuch Palace Marker in Nonsuch Park, Surrey 239
71. Rievaulx Abbey.................................241
72. Design for a Henrican Castle on the Kent Coast...........................243
73. Camber Castle 247
74. Sandgate Castle 253
75. Glastonbury Abbey............................255
76. Portrait of Anne of Cleves 258
77. The Bishop's Palace, Rochester 261
78. Anne of Cleves Public House, Melton Mowbray..............................264
79. Tower Hill Execution Site 267
80. Surviving Wall of Oatlands Palace 272
81. Tudor Graffiti, Beauchamp Tower, Tower of London 276
82. Medieval Bishop's Palace, Lincoln 279
83. Pontefract Castle, Yorkshire.............282
84. King's Manor, York 286
85. The Chapel Royal, Hampton Court Palace.....................288
86. Ruins of Winchester Palace, Southwark, London..........................291
87. Guildhall, City of London................293
88. Model of the Medieval London Bridge, St Magnus the Martyr Church, London...................296
89. Block and Axe Postcard 299
90. Queen Elizabeth's Hunting Lodge................................301
91. Katherine Parr's Closet Chamber, Hampton Court Palace.....................303
92. Debased Groats 305
93. An English Cannonball Fired During the Siege of Boulogne, 1544 307
94. Queen Elizabeth's Pocket Gun, Dover Castle 309
95. Southsea Castle, Portsmouth 311
96. The *Mary Rose* 315
97. Bronze Culverin from the *Mary Rose* 320
98. The Rack...322
99. Statue of Henry VIII at St Bartholomew's Hospital and Smithfield Execution Site................325
100. King Henry VIII's Tomb, St George's Chapel, Windsor 329

Notes 333
Bibliography 339

Introduction

King Henry VIII is one of the most well-known English sovereigns. He made a significant impact upon the nation's history, attaining notoriety through his six marriages, his courage in confronting the Pope and Catholic nations in the creation of the Church of England and his ruthlessness as he governed by fear, executing anyone that opposed, challenged or defied his authority.

When Henry ascended the throne at the age of 17 in 1509, England was at peace and was part of a Europe in which Catholicism was the predominant religion. Henry wanted to be regarded as a great monarch at home and internationally from the beginning of his reign. During 1515, Francis I, aged 19, was crowned King of France and Charles I, merely 15 years old, became King of Spain. Charles would later become Charles V of the Holy Roman Empire, which was a conglomerate of German states, Bohemia and northern Italy. It was Henry's aim to compete with his kingly peers in Europe. Although he could sway the balance of power through his fickle allegiances and alliances with these countries, England was not as strong as them. If Henry had died through the sweating sickness or on the tiltyard, he may have been a forgotten king, but because of his determination to conceive a son, a male heir and his resolution to marry his mistress, Anne Boleyn, this chain of events would lead him to challenge and confront the Catholic Church and the European powers that followed that faith in order to achieve his aim. His struggle and his success to break away from the Catholic Church would immortalise and transform him into the most fascinating, renowned and notorious monarch that ever reigned over England, a sovereign that would have six wives. Henry was passionate and romantic when he fell in love, but brutal and ruthless, willing to dispose of his queen when she could not produce a male heir.

Henry owned more houses than any previous monarch and when he died, he had approximately seventy residences at his disposal, although most have not survived. Hampton Court Palace still remains in its entirety and is an excellent example of a Tudor palace, while there are remnants of a few others which can be visited today and are featured within this volume. The majority of the properties were situated in London and the surrounding Home Counties; several were positioned along the banks of the River Thames which enabled the king easy access by barge.

The accession of Henry VIII to the throne saw significant transformations in every aspect of English life and by the end of his reign he had bequeathed a lasting legacy for the nation which included a national religion, totally autonomous and separated from the Catholic Church. He would be the head of this new religion, but he also left a trail of ruined monasteries across the country which he had destroyed during the Dissolution. The wealth taken from the monasteries was used to fund his ambitions to fortify his country with castles, warships and soldiers to defend against the anticipated invasions from France and Spain, nations that opposed his rejection of the Catholic faith. Henry also laid the foundations for the Royal Navy and increased the number of warships from five to fifty-eight by the end of his reign. In addition, three dockyards were established at Portsmouth, Woolwich and Deptford to accommodate, maintain and replenish the English fleet. Henry was also responsible for the King's Mail which was established as a communications network across England that would carry the dispatches of the king; it formed the basis of the current Royal Mail. Self-made men were allowed to become socially mobile to the detriment of those from the aristocracy who were already made men through birthright. His most important achievement was his daughter Elizabeth, who would become a highly respected queen and whose reign would see great national achievements. Elizabeth would build upon Henry's Royal Navy, which brought triumphs during her reign that Henry had aspired to, but failed to achieve. When Henry died in 1547, he left his country bankrupt and a population that lived in fear as a result of his bloody reign of terror. Five-hundred years after the end of his reign tourists from all over the world visit Britain in order to follow in his footsteps and visit the places associated with him.

The format of this book is chronological, beginning with Henry's birth and featuring objects, including locations, paintings and documents, which represent various stages in Henry's fascinating, but turbulent life as well as providing a snapshot of significant events.

The narrative is interspersed with contemporary accounts from the period from various sources including Edward Hall, who chronicled the reign of Henry VIII. The *State Papers* of Henry VIII are also a valued source of information from the time. Among the important and unbiased testimonies are the reports of Eustace Chapuys, who wrote regular reports to his master, Charles V, the Holy Roman Emperor and King of Spain. Charles Wriothesley provides another contemporary account of the Tudor period. He had served as an officer of arms at the Royal College of Arms. As a herald he took part in the ceremony that established Anne Boleyn as Marquess of Pembroke in 1532 and a year later attended her coronation at Westminster Abbey. In 1540, his cousin Thomas Wriothesley was appointed the king's secretary.

William Roper's biography of his father-in-law, Sir Thomas More, provides compelling detail regarding his relationship with the king and about More's conflict between obeying his sovereign and maintaining his Catholic faith. Roper was Sheriff of Kent in 1521 and served as clerk of the pleas of the King's Bench. He had married Margaret More in 1525 and became a confidant of Sir Thomas More. Margaret died in 1544 and Roper wrote the biography of her father during the reign of Queen Mary. Roper died in 1578 at the age of 82.

The aim of this book is to detail key objects relating to Henry VIII and show readers where they can visit places associated with England's notorious king; some are known, but many are a revelation. It will be useful to people already familiar with the history of this infamous sovereign and for those who are looking for an introduction into this fascinating period in British history.

Paul Kendall
Folkestone, 2020

Acknowledgements

The project would not have been possible but for the help and assistance of Martin Mace, John Grehan and my partner, Tricia Newsome.

I would like to thank Revd Jane Sinclair, Canon of Westminster and Rector of St Margaret's Church, for kindly allowing me access to the altar of St Margaret's Church to take photographs of the stained glass window commemorating the marriage of King Henry VIII to Katherine of Aragon. I also thank Elaura Lacey for her help and assistance. I also thank Robert Mitchell for his superb work and assistance with images. I am indebted to Helen Francis at Hever Castle, Bethan Clark at the Royal Mint Museum and the Department of Digital, Culture, Media and Sport, for their kindness and generosity in providing me with images for use within this book.

All images used in this publication are from the author's collection unless stated otherwise.

For their support and assistance with images, I am grateful to the Dean and Chapter of Westminster Abbey and the Parliamentary Archives.

Memorial Commemorating King Henry VIII's Birth, Royal Naval College, Greenwich

Prince Henry, Future King Henry VIII, Born at Greenwich Palace

King Henry VIII was born on 28 June 1491 at Greenwich Palace, which once stood along the banks of the River Thames on the site of the Royal Naval College. A plaque commemorates Henry's birth there, as well as the births of his daughters, Mary, on 18 February 1516, and Elizabeth, on 7 September 1533. Greenwich is therefore of historic importance in relation to the Tudor dynasty. Henry VIII is recorded as having stayed 4,000 nights at Greenwich Palace between 1512 and 1530, more than at any of the other residences that he owned during that period.

Greenwich became a royal residence when Henry V gave this land to his brother, Humphrey, Duke of Gloucester, who subsequently built a house there, which he named 'Bella Court', in about 1433. He also constructed a large tower on the site of the Royal Observatory, which provided a good view of the eastern approaches of the Thames estuary and the City of London in the west. After Humphrey died, Margaret of Anjou and Henry VI expanded the building in 1447 and it became known as 'Placentia', or 'Pleasant Place'. Henry VII transformed this house into a red-brick palace with three large courtyards and renamed it Greenwich Palace. The king's chambers overlooked the River Thames; however, Henry VII did not spend much time at the palace.

The palace had strong connections with Henry VIII. He was born at Greenwich on 28 June 1491 and baptised in the adjacent Church of the Friars Observant. He married his first wife, Katherine, at Greenwich Palace in 1509 and spent the first two decades of his reign there, during which time he ordered further expansion, building a banqueting hall, forges, stables and a tiltyard where he enjoyed participating in jousting tournaments. He was able to pursue his passion for hunting in the nearby countryside and he could easily reach London, 5 miles west of Greenwich, by barge. The royal apartments were extended above a watergate to accommodate the king's library, which was the largest in England until it was superseded by a library built within Whitehall Palace later during his reign. The palace was in close proximity to the naval dockyards at Deptford and Woolwich, which enabled Henry to regularly oversee the construction of ships for his navy. Deptford could be seen from the palace, as this was west of Greenwich on the south side of the River Thames just as the river bends northwards along the western side of the Isle of Dogs. During the Tudor period Greenwich, Deptford and Woolwich were villages outside of London and were surrounded by rural countryside.

In 1514, Henry established a royal workshop, west of the palace, for the purpose of producing armour for his own personal use or to give as

MEMORIAL COMMEMORATING KING HENRY VIII'S BIRTH

Stone plaque commemorating the births of King Henry VIII, Queen Mary and Queen Elizabeth I at Greenwich Palace. This was unveiled in the Grand Square of the Old Royal Naval College in 2003. (Author's Collection)

Detail of the plaque commemorating the births of King Henry VIII, Queen Mary and Queen Elizabeth I at Greenwich Palace. (Author's Collection)

The Old Royal Naval College stands on the site of Greenwich Palace, which stretched along the southern bank of the River Thames. The tiltyard where Henry VIII competed in jousting tournaments was constructed along the south face of the palace where the Romney Road now runs between the Old Royal Naval College and the National Maritime Museum. (Author's Collection)

diplomatic gifts to European monarchs. Set up to rival armouries in Germany and Italy, the royal armourers established a reputation for being skilled craftsmen. Raw material for the royal workshop was obtained from a steel mill at Lewisham.

On 18 February 1516, Queen Katherine gave birth to Princess Mary at Greenwich Palace. When the young princess was aged 2 she was betrothed to marry the French Dauphin on 5 October 1518 in the Queen's Great Chamber at Greenwich Palace. The marriage was arranged to secure peace between England and France. The Doge, the leader of the Republic of Venice, elected by the city's aristocracy, from 1726–97, took an interest in the affairs of the Tudor court. The Venetian diplomat, Sebastian Giustinian, reported to the Doge on the festivities that took place at Greenwich Palace to celebrate the union of the two royal families and their respective nations:

On the 5th the bridal entertainments were celebrated at Greenwich: the decorations were sumptuous. The King stood in front of his throne: on one side was the Queen and the Queen Dowager of France. The Princess was in front of her mother, dressed in cloth of gold, with a cap of black velvet on her head, adorned with many jewels. On the other side were the two legates. Tunstal made an elegant oration; 'which being ended, the most illustrious Princess was taken in arms, and the magnificos, the French ambassadors, asked the consent of the King and Queen on behalf of each of the parties to this marriage contract; and both parties having assented, the right reverend legate, the Cardinal of York, placed on her finger a small ring, *juxta digitum puella*, but in which a large diamond was set (supposed to have been a present from his right reverend lordship aforesaid), and my Lord Admiral passed it over the second joint. The bride was then blessed by the two right reverend legates, after a long exordium from the Cardinal of York; every possible ceremony being observed. Mass was then performed by Cardinal Wolsey, in the presence of the King and all the others, the whole of the choir being decorated with cloth of gold, and all the court in such rich array that I never saw the like, either here or elsewhere.' All the company then went to dinner, the King 'receiving the water for his hands from three Dukes and a Marquis. The two Legates sat on the King's right: on the left were the Lord Admiral and the Bishop of Paris; and the Dukes of Buckingham, Norfolk and Suffolk were seated at the inside of the table. The other two French ambassadors, the Spaniard, one from Denmark,' and the writer, with others, dined in another chamber. 'After dinner the King and the Cardinal of York, with the French ambassadors, betook themselves into a certain room, to conclude some matters which remained for settlement; and all the rest departed'.[1]

The treaty committing the betrothal of Henry's first daughter to the French Dauphin would not last and the Princess Mary would be betrothed to other suitors, used as a political pawn to garner favour and wealth from other nations. In 1522, it was agreed that the Princess Mary would marry Emperor Charles V. Henry entertained Emperor Charles V, who was the nephew of Katherine of Aragon, at Greenwich Palace during a state visit.

Henry would continue to use Greenwich Palace as his principal London residence until 1530, when Whitehall Palace took prominence. Although Greenwich Palace was not used regularly as a residence, it still played a role during the latter part of Henry's reign, for it was here on 7 September 1533 that Henry's second wife,

Anne Boleyn, gave birth to Princess Elizabeth (the future Queen Elizabeth I). Unable to provide a son, Anne was arrested at Greenwich Palace on trumped up charges of treason and conveyed to the Tower of London in 1533.

It was at Greenwich Palace that Henry married Anne of Cleves, his fourth wife, on 6 January 1540. The Treaty of Greenwich was signed at the palace on 1 July 1543. This was a peace initiative offered by Henry VIII which aimed to unite England and Scotland. The treaty allowed Scotland to maintain its own laws and there was a subsidiary treaty which comprised a proposal of marriage between Prince Edward and Mary, Queen of Scots, a bid to unite England and the House of Tudor with Scotland and the House of Stuart. The treaty was ultimately rejected by the Scottish Parliament on 11 December 1543 which resulted in an eight-year conflict between the two nations.

The old Greenwich Palace was in a state of disrepair when King Charles II ascended the throne at the Restoration in 1660. Charles ordered it to be demolished so that a new palace could be built, designed by Sir Christopher Wren, and this building remains. Later it was used to house retired naval pensioners and between 1873 and 1997 it was the Royal Naval College. Now the building belongs to the University of Greenwich.

2

Eltham Palace

Childhood Home of Henry VIII

Eltham Palace was a royal residence from 1311, when King Edward II took possession after the death of its owner, Anthony Bek, Archbishop of Durham. Surrounded by a moat, it was much larger than Hampton Court Palace. Henry VIII spent his formative years as a boy at Eltham Palace away from court life. The Great Hall and the bridge that crossed the moat, built by Edward IV, are the only parts of the palace that have survived and would have been familiar to Henry VIII during the Tudor period.

During his childhood at Eltham Palace Henry lived with Elizabeth of York, his mother, Margaret Beaufort, his grandmother and his two sisters, Margaret and Mary. He was the third child of Henry VII and was not expected to become King of England. Henry saw little of his father, who was preoccupied with governing the country and protecting his power base against the threats posed by those who contested the throne. His elder brother, Arthur, the Prince of Wales and heir to the throne, resided at Ludlow Castle. Therefore, the young Prince Henry was surrounded by women,

The Great Hall, Eltham Palace was built by Edward IV during the period 1475–80. (Author's Collection)

Interior of the Great Hall, showing the impressive oak roof. (Author's Collection)

Lead oak leaves, *c.* 1528. These formed part of decoration on the choir stalls of King Henry VIII's chapel. Some are slightly crushed by earth, but they were originally gilded. (Author's Collection)

who showered him with love and attention. It is remarkable to think that this young boy, brought up in a female-dominated environment, would become a king who would mistreat and dispose of his wives in the way that he did.

Henry received his education during the days he lived at Eltham Palace up to 1502. While under the tutorship of the poet John Skelton, Henry learned to speak various languages, including Latin, and became a proficient musician, able to play the lute and organ. He could sing and write music and poetry. Henry was well educated and his character and standing were typical of a Renaissance man of his day. During 1499, William Blount, Lord Mountjoy, a courtier and tutor to Prince Henry who owned a house close to Greenwich, introduced Henry to the Dutch scholar, theologian and humanist Desiderius Erasmus and Thomas More. Mountjoy was a former student of Erasmus in Paris and Thomas More was a London lawyer and a friend of Erasmus. During this visit, Erasmus was impressed when the young prince was able to converse and correspond in Latin. Erasmus wrote of the visit to Eltham twenty years later:

Thomas More, who had visited me when I was staying at Mountjoy's country house, had taken me out for a walk as far as the next village [Eltham]. For there all the royal children were being educated, Arthur alone, excepted, the eldest son. When we came to the hall, all the retinue was assembled; not only that of the palace, but Mountjoy's as well. In the midst stood Henry, aged nine, already with a certain royal demeanour; I mean a dignity of mind combined with a remarkable courtesy. On his right was Margaret, about eleven years old, who afterwards married James, King of Scots. On the left Mary was playing, a child of four. Edmund was an infant in arms. More with his companion Arnold saluted Henry (the present King of England) and presented to him something in writing. I, who was expecting nothing of the sort, had nothing to offer; but I promised that somehow, at some other time, I would show my duty towards him. Meantime, I was a bit annoyed with More for having giving me no warning, especially because the boy, during dinner, sent me a note inviting something from my pen. I went home and though the Muses, from whom I had long been divorced, were unwilling, I finished the poem in three days.[2]

During those childhood years residing at Eltham Palace, Henry experienced family bereavement. His young sister, Elizabeth, died in 1495, Arthur died on 2 April 1502 and, within a year, his mother, Elizabeth, died at the Tower of London on 11 February 1503, nine days after giving birth to a baby who also did not survive. Henry was aged 11 when he lost his mother and during that same year he was further isolated when his elder sister, Margaret, married James IV and transferred to Edinburgh. This marriage was arranged by his father, Henry VII, in order to ensure peace with Scotland. Although he was elevated to the rank of Prince of Wales, Henry remained in seclusion at Eltham Palace until 1505 when his father moved him to Westminster Palace.

Eltham Palace was important during the early part of Henry's reign and he made improvements to the estate, including the building of a chapel and study. He even ordered the levelling of a nearby hill in order to improve his view from the palace. On Christmas Eve, 1515, he appointed Cardinal Thomas Wolsey as Lord Chancellor after the resignation of Archbishop William Warham while at Eltham Palace. Wolsey took the oath of office and was presented with the Great Seal of England within the palace. Ten years later Wolsey wrote the Ordinances of Eltham, an austerity measure designed to reduce waste and unnecessary expenditure within the Royal Household.

The Great Hall at Eltham was the scene of regular theatrical performances when the king was in residence. The chronicler Edward Hall recorded the Christmas festivities in 1515 when a castle was built within this space:

> After the parliament was ended, the king kept a solemn Christmas at his manor of Eltham, and on the seventh night in the hall was made a goodly castle, wondrously set out, and in it certain ladies and knights, and assailed the castle where many a good stripe were given and at the last the assailants were beaten away. And then issued out knights and ladies out of the castle, which ladies were rich and strangely disguised, for all their apparel was in braids of Gold, fret with moving spangles, silver and gilt, set on Crimson satin loose and not fastened. The men's apparel of the same suite made like Julius of Hungary, and the ladies clothes were after the fashion of Amsterdam, and when the dancing was done, the banquet was served comprising two Court dishes, with great plenty for everybody.[3]

Since Eltham was far from the River Thames, the journey to reach Henry's other palaces at Greenwich, Whitehall and Richmond was more difficult. Therefore, Henry stayed at Eltham less frequently during the 1530s and it became more of a stop-off point when travelling from London to the Kent coast or a place close to London to hunt. Eltham Palace was also used as a nursery for his children Princess Mary, Princess Elizabeth and Prince Edward.

The fifteenth-century moat bridge built during the reign of Edward IV. This was the entrance to Eltham Palace and would certainly have been used by Henry VIII to access the palace. (Author's Collection)

3
Henry VII's Tomb, Westminster Abbey

Death of Henry VII

After reigning for twenty-four years, Henry VII died from tuberculosis at Richmond Palace on 21 April 1509. The first monarch of the Tudor dynasty, he had brought peace and stability to the nation following the savagery of the Wars of the Roses. During the period 1461–85, five monarchs had ruled England. Henry VII also brought prosperity at the expense of high taxation and austerity, which was not popular among his subjects. In accordance with his wishes, Henry VII was buried in a vault beneath the Lady Chapel in Westminster Abbey in 1509. He had spent large sums of money to fund the building of the Lady Chapel, which began in 1503. The chapel was designed by Sir Reginald Bray, who had retrieved the crown of Richard III from Bosworth Field. Henry VII and Elizabeth of York were the first monarchs to be buried in a vault beneath Westminster Abbey. All previous monarchs buried within Westminster Abbey were buried in tombs above the floor.

On 9 May 1509, the embalmed corpse of Henry VII was drawn by chariot from Richmond Palace to St George's Field, south of the River Thames, where it was met by clergy. It was then transported across the old medieval bridge that spanned the River Thames and taken to St Paul's Cathedral where the Bishop of Rochester conducted Mass. The body was then taken to Westminster Abbey for internment the following day when a further ceremony was held. At the end of the ceremony a knight rode into the abbey wearing the late king's armour. The armour was removed by monks, who unbuckled it piece by piece and placed these upon the altar. Henry VII, the victor of Bosworth Field and the father of the Tudor dynasty, received the funeral of a warrior, buried alongside the symbols of medieval aristocracy.

During the first two years of his reign Henry VIII approached various artists to create a design for a decorative tomb to honour his parents. In 1512, Henry VIII commissioned the Italian sculptor Pietro Torrigiano for this purpose. Torrigiano learnt his craft alongside Michelangelo in Florence and was known for his volatile and an erratic personality. On one occassion he attacked Michelangelo, breaking his nose and claiming that this violent outburst was the consequence of some banter between the artists that went too far, a remark that irritated him. However, Giorgio Vasari, a friend of Michelangelo, attributed the assault to Torrigiano's rivalry with and jealousy of his contemporary artist's accomplishments. When Torrigiano accepted the commission to create a design for the tombs of Henry VIII's parents, he asked Benvenuto Cellini to collaborate with him on the project. Reluctant to work with the ill-tempered Torrigiano, Cellini refused the invitation.

Torrigiano conceived a design for the tomb in the Renaissance style and it took him four years to complete. Constructed of a black marble base, the tomb was decorated at each end with the coat of arms of Henry VII and Elizabeth of York, which are supported by cherubs. Six copper gilt medallions are decorated on the sides of the tomb depicting the Virgin Mary and patron saints including Edward the Confessor, Mary Magdalene, John the Baptist

Tomb of Henry VII and Elizabeth of York at Westminster Abbey. (Copyright Dean and Chapter of Westminster)

This image of Henry VII was painted on 29 October 1505 by an unknown artist from the Netherlands. It was commissioned by Herman Rinck, acting on behalf of the Holy Roman Emperor, Maximilian I. After the death of Elizabeth in 1503, Henry VII was looking for a second wife and this portrait was shown to the emperor as a potential husband for his daughter, Margaret of Savoy. It is believed that this portrait was painted as part of an unsuccessful marriage proposal. (Public Domain)

and John the Evangelist. Bronze, lifelike effigies of Henry VII and Elizabeth of York, lying horizontal and in a state of prayer, surmount the black marble tomb. The following words for Henry are inscribed in Latin on the tomb:

> Here lies Henry the Seventh of that name, formerly King of England, son of Edmund, Earl of Richmond. He was created King on August 22 and immediately afterwards, on October 30, he was crowned at Westminster in the year of Our Lord 1485. He died subsequently on April 21 in the 53rd year of his age. He reigned 23 years eight months, less one day.

Elizabeth of York died during childbirth on 11 February 1503 and her loss would have a profound effect upon the young Prince Henry. The inscription for Elizabeth of York reads:

> Here lies Queen Elizabeth, daughter of the former King Edward IV, sister of the formerly appointed King Edward V, once the wife of King Henry VII, and the renowned mother of Henry VIII. She met her day of death in the Tower of London on the 11th day of February in the year of Our Lord 1502, having fulfilled the age of 37 years [the date is given in Old Style dating, now called 1503].

Around the edge of the tomb the following words are inscribed:

Henry VII rests within this tomb, he who was the splendour of kings and light of the world, a wise and watchful monarch, a courteous lover of virtue, outstanding in beauty, vigorous and mighty; who brought peace to his kingdom, who waged very many wars, who always returned victorious from the enemy, who wedded both his daughters to kings, who was united to kings, indeed to all, by treaty, who built this holy temple, and erected this tomb for himself, his wife, and his children. He completed more than fifty three years, and bore the royal sceptre for twenty four. The fifteenth hundredth year of the Lord had passed, and the ninth after that was running its course, when dawned the black day, the twenty first dawn of April was shining, when this so great monarch ended his last day. No earlier ages gave thee so great a king, O England; hardly will ages to come give thee his like.

The tomb not only serves as Henry VIII's tribute to his parents, but it symbolises the union of the Houses of York and Lancaster and the end of the Wars of the Roses. England had been torn apart by thirty years of bloodshed, but after Henry VII defeated the Yorkist Richard III at the Battle of Bosworth on 22 August 1485, in an attempt to unify the nation and prevent further conflict he married Elizabeth of York on 18 January 1486. The tomb is a visual emblem signifying the birth of the Tudor dynasty and the legacy of Henry VII, a legacy that Henry VIII wanted to maintain and continue. A legacy that could only be continued by a male heir.

4

The Tower of London

Royal Power Base

After the death of Henry VII, his heir apparent, Prince Henry, arrived at the Tower of London on 22 April 1509, remaining within the fortress until his father's funeral. The White Tower stands in the centre of the Tower of London. It was built in about 1080 on the orders of William the Conqueror. Its upper floors were used as royal apartments by monarchs including Henry VIII. It is called the White Tower because in 1240 Henry III ordered that the walls be whitewashed.

The Tower of London was associated with sadness for Henry because his mother, Elizabeth of York, died during childbirth within its royal chambers in 1503. On 21 April 1509, Henry VII died at Richmond Palace and during the following day, the 17-year-old Henry and his courtiers were secretly taken from Richmond to the Tower of London. The death of Henry VII remained a secret for two days while courtiers prepared for the succession. On 23 April, St George's Day, Henry was proclaimed king and became the first sovereign since 1421 to inherit the throne instead of attaining it through violence or usurpation. It was possible that he was taken to the Tower of London as a place of safety, to ensure that no one attempted a coup to seize the Crown.

The Tower of London had a sinister reputation as a prison and place of execution during the reign of Henry VIII. On the same day the young king arrived there, Sir Richard Empson and Edmund Dudley were also conveyed to the fortress, arrested for treason on his orders. These two unpopular ministers were accused of extortion during the last days of his father's reign. They held a reputation for indicting citizens on obsolete laws and statutes in order to incarcerate them in prison from where they could extort money from ransoms and fines for the royal coffers in exchange for their liberty. Dudley was tried in London on 18 July 1509 and convicted of treason. Empson's trial took place in Northampton Castle during October 1509. Despite his youthful age, Henry demonstrated that he was assertive, aware of court matters, mindful of public opinion, conscious of potential enemies and was not afraid to exert the law of the land to punish those who committed crimes against the state and to appease his subjects on the first day of his reign. This act showed that Henry was determined to protect his father's legacy and strengthen his own standing as king. Empson and Dudley were eventually executed at Tower Hill on 17 August 1510.

Henry remained in the Tower until the king's funeral and burial at Westminster Abbey on 10 May 1509. During the first ten weeks of his reign, Henry's grandmother, Lady Margaret Beaufort, Duchess of Richmond acted as regent until Henry's 18th birthday.

It was tradition that monarchs would stay at the Tower of London prior to their coronation. Henry maintained that ritual and returned to the White Tower on 22 June 1509 with Queen Katherine, two days before for their coronation. Henry 'ordered twenty-six honourable persons to repair to the Tower of London on 22 June, to serve him at dinner, where those who are to be made knights shall bear dishes "in token that that they shall never bear none after that day"; and on 23 June, at the Tower, they are to be made Knights of the Bath.'[4]

The Tower of London viewed from the south bank of the River Thames. St Thomas's Tower and Traitors' Gate can be seen bottom left. The White Tower dominates the fortress. (Author's Collection)

THE TOWER OF LONDON

During his reign Henry VIII used the Tower of London for diplomatic purposes and visiting ambassadors from Europe could marvel at the various wild animals kept within the grounds and view England's armaments stored there. Henry VIII allowed foreign diplomats to see England's military assets and used it as an opportunity to posture, to show his strength as monarch and to demonstrate that he was willing and able to defend the country as well as embark on wars overseas. Pietro Pasqualigo, Venetian Ambassador to the English court, recalled such a visit on 30 April 1515: 'Have seen the Tower, where, besides the lions and leopards, were shown the King's bronze artillery, mounted on 400 carriages, very fine; also bows, arrows and pikes for 40,000 infantry. They say they have a like store at Calais and a place near Scotland.'[5]

Yeoman Warders were a detachment of the King's Bodyguard and were established during the reign of Henry VII. Their scarlet attire was worn throughout the period of the Tudor dynasty, and has continued to be worn over the ensuing centuries. When Henry VIII ascended the throne in 1509, he took twelve of the least fit Yeoman of the Guard and established the Yeoman Warders to guard the Tower of London. They came to be known as Beefeaters during the seventeenth century because they were allowed to consume as much beef from the king's table as they required.

The White Tower at the Tower of London. During Henry VIII's reign the White Tower was extensively renovated. In 1533 the domes and weathervanes were installed above the four turrets as part of the preparations for Anne Boleyn's coronation. (Justin Black/Shutterstock)

Stained Glass Window Commemorating the Marriage of King Henry VIII to Katherine of Aragon, St Margaret's Church, Westminster

The Wedding of Henry VIII and Katherine of Aragon

In the east window of St Margaret's Church, Westminster, there is a Flemish glass window which commemorates the marriage on 11 June 1509 of Henry and Katherine of Aragon, who are the kneeling figures featured in the bottom left and bottom right-hand corners. It is believed that the window was created in Holland in about 1526 and features the crucifixion of Jesus Christ.

Katherine, the daughter of Isabella I of Castile and Ferdinand II of Aragon, had married Henry's elder brother, Prince Arthur, in 1501, but he died five months later. In order to maintain and secure Anglo-Spanish relations King Ferdinand II offered their daughter in marriage to Arthur's brother, Prince Henry, who was six years her junior. A treaty of marriage was agreed at Richmond Palace on 21 June 1503 and was authorised on 3 March 1504 when King Henry VII signed the treaty which specified that betrothal of Henry, who was aged 12, and Katherine, aged 17, would be sanctified on 28 June 1505, when Henry turned 14. It stipulated that Ferdinand II would pay a second instalment of the marriage dowry, in addition to the payment relating to her marriage to Arthur. There was a problem, however, because canon law was based on a verse from Leviticus in the Bible which stated that 'if a man shall take his brother's wife, it is an unclean thing, he hath uncovered his brother's nakedness; they shall be childless' (Leviticus 8.16). Although Pope Julius II in Rome granted a special dispensation allowing Henry to marry Katherine, Henry VII kept her in limbo, living in a state of penury. He was saving his son for a marriage to another royal princess, where an alliance could be forged that would be politically and financially more advantageous and affluential. It was on his deathbed that he commanded his son to marry Katherine. In a letter written by Henry VIII to Margaret of Savoy, daughter of Emperor Maximilian, on 27 June 1509 he wrote:

> True it is, . . . that for the consideration which we are bound to have for the treaty and appointment that was a long time made, promised, accorded and sworn between the late King our lord and father and our father-in-law and mother-in-law, the King of Aragon and the Queen of Spain, his consort, concerning the marriage of ourself to the Lady Katherine their daughter, and considering also the betrothals that were afterwards made between us and her *per verba pruescenti* [contract of marriage]; we being come to full age, as well among divers wise counsels, honourable instruction and behests

Stained glass window commemorating the betrothal of Henry VIII to Katherine of Aragon. (Author's Collection)

According to Hall, after Henry VII's death, counsellors recommended that before the coronation Prince Henry should marry. The motivation for the marriage was based on it being 'honourable and profitable to his realm . . . least she having so great a dowry, might marry out of the realm, which should be unprofitable to him'.[7] Also, there was an urgent need for an heir to the throne to be born to ensure the line of succession, preserve the Tudor dynasty and prevent a civil war on the scale of the Wars of the Roses, which had been fought during the previous century. Henry VIII also wanted an alliance with Spain in order to confront France. Thirteen days before his coronation, the king married Katherine of Aragon in the Queen's Closet at Greenwich Palace in a private ceremony officiated by William Warham, Archbishop of Canterbury on 11 June 1509.

Although the marriage was arranged and intended to preserve Anglo-Spanish relations, there is evidence to suggest that Henry married Katherine for love. In a letter to King Ferdinand II, dated 26 July 1509, Henry wrote of his strong feelings of devotion for his wife, in the third person, intimating if he was not obliged for political reasons, he would have married her anyway: 'The bond between them is now so strict that all their interests are common, and the love he bears to Katherine is such, that if he were still free he would choose her in preference to all others.'[8]

Detailed image of King Henry VIII within the stained glass window. (Author's Collection)

that the King, our said late lord and father, gave us when he summoned us before him, he being then upon his death bed, he gave us express command that we should take in marriage the Lady Katherine, in fulfilment of the said treaty and appointment of the said betrothals.[6]

6

The Coronation Chair, Westminster Abbey

Henry VIII Crowned King of England

The Coronation Chair was made under the orders of King Edward I to enclose the Stone of Scone, which had been taken from Scotland and transferred to Westminster Abbey. It was built of oak and completed in 1301. This throne was used during the coronation of thirty-eight English monarchs including the coronation ceremonies of Henry VIII and Katherine of Aragon on 24 June 1509.

On the day before the coronation, Henry VIII, on horseback, and Katherine, in a litter, travelled in a procession from the Tower of London, through the streets of the City of London to Westminster. Edward Hall described Henry's demeanour and appearance during that journey:

> The feature of his body, his goodly personage, his amiable visage, princely countenance, with the noble qualities of his royal estate, to every man known, needed no rehearsal, considering, that for lack of cunning, I cannot express the gifts of grace and nature that God hath endowed him with all; yet partly, to describe his apparel, it is to be noted, his grace wore in his finest apparel, a robe of Crimson Velvet, furred with ermine, his jacket or cote of raised gold, the placard embroidered with Diamonds Rubies, Emeralds, great Pearls, and other riche Stones, a great Bauderike about his neck, of great Balasses.[9]

Tapestries and Arras cloth were hung from the buildings along the procession route. As the royal cortège passed through Cheapside, Hall recorded that 'every occupation stood, in their liveries in order, beginning with base and mean occupations, and so ascending to the worshipful crafts: highest and lastly stood the Mayor, with the Aldermen'.[10]

During the morning of the coronation, the royal couple walked to Westminster Palace and then towards Westminster Abbey upon cloth. After walking on this cloth, the crowd cut pieces from it as souvenirs, because, according to Hall, the 'clothe was cut and spoiled, by the rude and common people, immediately after their repair into the Abbey'.[11]

Once in the abbey, Katherine sat on a lower chair, while Henry sat on this throne. The coronation ceremony was conducted by William Warham, Archbishop of Canterbury, in the presence of noblemen and the general public from all walks of life. When this crowd was asked whether they would receive, obey and accept this noble prince as their king, Hall recorded that 'with great reverence, love and desire, said and cried ye, ye'.[12]

It is believed that the crowns of King Edward the Confessor and his wife, Edith, were used during the joint coronation. It was a joyous occasion, which was celebrated by a banquet in Westminster Hall and further festivities, including jousting in the days that followed. After years of political uncertainty and economic austerity during the reign of Henry VII, the accession of the youthful Henry VIII brought hope and optimism across the nation.

THE CORONATION CHAIR, WESTMINSTER ABBEY

The Coronation Chair, Westminster Abbey, on which King Henry VIII sat as he was crowned on 24 June 1509. (Copyright Dean and Chapter of Westminster)

A sixteenth-century woodcut of the coronation of Henry VIII and Katherine of Aragon showing their heraldic badges, the Tudor rose and the pomegranate of Granada. (Author's Collection)

Thomas More applauded the coronation in a letter a poem entitled 'Coronation Ode of King Henry VIII', proclaiming that 'this day is the limit of our slavery, the beginning of our freedom, the end of sadness, the source of joy, for this day consecrates a young man who is the everlasting glory of our time and makes him your king'.

Katherine of Aragon and Anne Boleyn were the only wives of Henry VIII to be crowned at Westminster Abbey. Jane Seymour was not crowned as queen due to the plague, which was rife in London during 1536, and maybe because Henry was reluctant until she bore him a son. Henry's marriage to Anne of Cleves was annulled before her coronation and so she was never crowned. There were no coronations for Henry's fifth and sixth wives, Katherine Howard and Catherine Parr.

7
The Gatehouse, Richmond Palace

Royal Residence of Henry VIII in the Early Years of his Reign

All that remains of Richmond Palace, which was built along the southern bank of the River Thames, is the Outer Gateway and a small part of the house known as the Old Palace which is on the western perimeter of Richmond Green. The gatehouse formed the principal access to Richmond Palace on the landward side. It comprised a sizeable opening which once held a pair of large doors (the surviving hinge pins still exist) and a now-blocked entrance to the right of the gatehouse. The arms of Henry VII, restored in 1976, are carved above the entrance. Of great significance to the Tudor dynasty, a plaque on the wall confirms 'Richmond Palace. Residence of King Henry VII, King Henry VIII, Queen Elizabeth I'.

Richmond had been used as a royal residence since the reign of Henry I when there was a manor house on the site. Edward III transformed this

The Outer Gateway, Richmond Palace. (Author's Collection)

Coat of arms of Henry VII above the landward entrance to Richmond Palace. (Author's Collection)

were inspired by the Burgundian court. When construction was complete, Henry VII named it the Palace of Richmond, which was the earldom held by him before his accession to the throne. Henry VII died here in 1509 and Henry VIII made use of this residence during the early years of his reign and spent his first Christmas as king there.

The Christmas feast was followed by jousting which took place outside these gates on the site of Richmond Green on 12 January 1510. Henry VIII had always been fascinated by jousting, but he was forbidden to engage in it by his father. After the passing of Henry VII, Henry was able to pursue this interest and this Christmas tournament was the first that he took part in, although he did so anonymously. Some of the courtiers knew that Henry was participating in this joust and when Sir Edward Neuell knocked William Compton from his horse, and nearly died, one of those courtiers thought that the king had been injured. Edward Hall recorded:

> Diverse gentlemen freshly apparelled, prepared themself to joust, unknown to the King's grace, whereof, he being secretly caused himself and one of his privy chamber, called William Compton to be secretly armed, in the little park of Richmond; and so come into the jousts unknown to all persons and onlookers. The King ran as never openly before, and there were broken many stakes, and great praise given to the two strangers, but specially to one, which was the King; howbeit, at a course of misfortune, Sir Edward Neuell Esquire ... did run against Master Compton, and hurt him sore and he was likely to die. One person there was, that knew the King and cried, God save the King, with that all the people were astonished and then the King discovered himself, to the great comfort of all the people.[13]

building into the Palace of Shene, where he died in 1377. When Anna, the wife of his successor, Richard II, died here in 1394, the king, distraught at his bereavement, ordered the destruction of the palace. Henry V started construction of a new palace, which was completed by Henry VI. This palace became a favourite residence of Henry VII but it was destroyed in a fire at Christmas 1497. The king immediately ordered the construction of another palace on the same site. During the four years it took to reconstruct the building, Henry VII and his family lived at Eltham Palace. The new palace was built of red brick and featured courtyards and galleries that

Richmond

Richmond Palace drawn by Wenceslaus Hollar in 1638. (Author's Collection)

On New Year's Day, 1511, Katherine gave birth to a son at Richmond Palace. Henry was euphoric, for the heir that he wanted was born. Five days after his birth, the new prince was christened Henry and proclaimed 'Prince of Wales'. On 23 February Prince Henry died within the palace.

In October 1515, Henry VIII returned victorious from the war in France and in haste went to Richmond Palace to present to Katherine the keys to the cities that had been captured by the English. In his absence Henry had entrusted the governing of the country to Katherine, whose actions led to the defeat of the Scottish at Flodden in September 1515. When the sweating sickness epidemic was sweeping through London during the spring 1517, Henry relocated his court to Richmond Palace.

With his increasing yearning for privacy, Henry VIII ordered the building of long galleries in his palaces at Hampton Court, Greenwich and York Place (later known as Whitehall Palace), for which he alone owned the key where he could walk in complete privacy, or discuss matters of state with his ministers and courtiers. As a consequence, he became disinterested in Richmond Palace and it became a residence for Princess Mary. The palace was later given by Henry VIII to Anne of Cleves on 24 June 1540, as part of their divorce settlement, but she later returned it to Edward VI.

8

The Bronze Watch Bell from the Mary Rose

Construction of the *Mary Rose*

Threatened with invasion by France and Scotland, Henry VIII ordered the construction of the Mary Rose *within a year of his coronation. Henry named her Mary after his sister and she was built in Portsmouth dockyard (close to where she is now displayed) during 1510. The ship's bell of the* Mary Rose *was cast in 1510 and is one of the few objects that remained with the ship throughout its career which spanned thirty-four years until she sank in 1545.*

Henry VIII ordered the renovation of the ship *Sovereign* and the construction of two new vessels that were named the *Mary Rose* and the *Peter Pomegranate* (referred to as the *Peter Granade* during that period) in Portsmouth dockyard. The first record of the *Mary Rose* appeared in state records on 29 July 1511, a payment to 'Robt. Brygandyne, clerk of the King's ships, for the conveyance of two new ships, *The Mary Rose* and *The Peter Granade*, from Portsmouth to the Thames.'[14] This reference probably related to the maiden voyage of the *Mary Rose*, commanded by her first master Thomas Spert. Further payments were made to Brygandyne in September 1511 for expenses relating to these vessels, once they had arrived in the River Thames. In October 1511 payments were made relating to stocking ordnance aboard the *Mary Rose* and the *Peter Granade*.

In 1512, the *Mary Rose* displaced 600 tons and was manned by 120 sailors, 251 soldiers and 20 gunners, 2 pilots, 5 trumpeters and 36 servants. She was armed with 43 heavy guns and 37 small guns. She was rebuilt in 1536, weighed 700 tons, carried 71 guns and was able to fire broadsides and was classified as one of the first sailing wooden warships.

The ship's bell from the *Mary Rose*. (Author's Collection)

The *Mary Rose* participated in two battles, at Saint-Mathieu, near Brest in 1512, which was possibly the first battle fought at sea where guns were fired through gun-ports, and the Battle of Solent in 1545. The vessel became a

THE BRONZE WATCH BELL FROM THE MARY ROSE

Model of the *Mary Rose*. (Author's Collection)

favourite of Henry VIII and accompanied him as escort when he sailed across the English Channel on his journey to meet King Francis I of France at the Field of the Cloth of Gold in June 1520.

The *Mary Rose's* bell was cast in Malines, near Antwerp, and remained with her throughout her service. Made of bronze and weighing 5kg, the Flemish inscription skirting the top of the bell states, 'I was made in the year 1510', as the *Mary Rose* was being built. Its primary purpose was to alert the ship's company to the time to enable them to know when to change watch and to give an indication of time during that watch. For instance, at 8am the bell would be rung eight times on that hour, and would be rung every half an hour until the end of the watch at midday. At 8.30am it would be rung once, followed half an hour later with two rings, then three rings on the next half an hour until midday when eight bells were rung, denoting the end of the watch and the process would begin once again for the following watch. The bell was also regularly used in fog to alert other nearby ships of the ship's presence.

The Anthony Roll was compiled in 1540 and is a list of all Henry VIII's vessels within the navy, recording the names, tonnage, dimensions and crew members of each vessel. This is the only contemporary image of the *Mary Rose*, showing a carrack design with high castles fore and aft. Despite the fact that the position of the gun-ports and the number of guns is not entirely accurate, this is a reasonably accurate interpretation of the *Mary Rose*. (Public Domain)

9

The Westminster Roll Depicting Henry VIII Jousting at Westminster

A Tournament to Celebrate the Birth of Prince Henry

Jousting was a spectacle of the English court and a sport enjoyed by royalty and the nobility. The Olympic Games are the modern-day equivalent of the jousting tournaments held during Henry VIII's reign. Two knights, dressed in armour, would charge down a tiltyard towards each other at great speed, armed with a lance, which they would use to either break the opponent's lance or knock him off his horse. The opposing knights on horseback would be separated by a wooden wall, known as the tilt, which ran the full length of the tiltyard. During each run or course, points would be awarded according to where the lance struck upon the opponent's body. A strike to the head would receive

Henry VIII jousting at Westminster in the presence of Katherine of Aragon. (Courtesy of the College of Arms)

THE WESTMINSTER ROLL DEPICTING HENRY VIII

higher points. Success on the tiltyard would bring fame, fortune and political favour.

Henry VIII excelled in jousting tournaments, enjoying the opportunity of demonstrating his courage, his physical strength and his horsemanship skills. The armour he wore for jousting was used to display his style and wealth. These jousts were held to celebrate prestigious events where he could posture and parade in front of his subjects and foreign diplomats. As the royal family were avid specators at such tournaments, this was the only opportunity for the masses to come into contact with them.

The first child of Henry and Katherine, Prince Henry of Wales, was born on 1 January 1511 and six weeks later a jousting tournament was held in honour of Katherine and the heir apparent in the tiltyard at Westminster Palace on 12 and 13 February 1511. The Westminster Roll, comprising thirty-six vellum membranes sewn together and measuring 60ft in total, depicts this jousting tournament. It was commissioned by King Henry VIII, who was proud of his own prowess on the tiltyard, to commemorate the tournament. This part of the roll (Membranes 24 to 27) shows the challengers on the left and the answerers on the right. Queen Katherine, her ladies-in-waiting and courtiers observe the joust from a pavilion. Katherine lies in a bed, recovering after giving birth to Prince Henry. Henry VIII is depicted as a challenger riding a charger that wears a protective bard bearing the queen's initial 'K'. A wooden wall, the tilt, separates the two jousters, preventing them from crashing into each other. Henry is seen galloping along the tiltyard as his lance breaks upon striking his opponent's helmet, which attains him the highest score in the tournament.

Valiente Desyre, alias for Sir Thomas Knevet, riding for the challengers, and Richard Blounte, for the defenders, were awarded prizes worth 200 crowns by Queen Katherine on the first day of the tournament. King Henry riding as Coeur Loyal, for the challengers, and Lord Edmund Howard were victorious during the second day of the tournament and were awarded similar prizes.

Henry took an enormous risk in participating in such a dangerous sport – wood splinters could get in the eye and subsequently cause blindness, there was risk of being knifed in the groin or under the arms which were not protected by armour, and this would result in certain death for doctors were unable to treat such wounds during the Tudor period.

Celebrations for the birth of Prince Henry ended when the heir to the throne died on 23 February 1511, ten days after the tournament was held at Westminster.

10

Two Tudor Docks at Woolwich Dockyard

Henry VIII's Navy

Henry VIII is regarded as the father of the Royal Navy and at the beginning of his reign he recognised the benefits to the nation of a permanent naval force. The navy would defend the sovereign shores, protect established trade routes, act as platforms for artillery, transport soldiers and heighten the king's prestige, allowing him to assert his power and authority and promote England as an affluent nation. He inherited five warships from his father and towards the end of his reign he commanded approximately fifty-eight vessels. Henry established a Navy Board to deal with the administration of the navy and ordered the construction of new dockyards to build warships. These two surviving dry docks formed part of Woolwich dockyard which was expanded in 1540 and known as the King's Yard.

After the completion of the *Mary Rose* at Portsmouth, Henry VIII was keen to monitor carefully the progress of further ships built for his navy. He therefore established a dockyard at Woolwich in 1512 and one at Deptford in 1513, which were close to his palace at Greenwich and the armouries at the Tower of London which could supply these vessels with arms, munitions and provisions. Wood required to build ships at Deptford and Woolwich was sourced from forests and woodlands in Kent and Sussex. Large storehouses were put up at these dockyards to accommodate the vast amounts of stores required for the vessels under construction and that were operating from the dockyard. London was deficient of skilled shipwrights and it was necessary to recruit qualified men from ports in Devon, Kent, East Anglia and Yorkshire, and consequently further buildings had to be constructed close to the new dockyards to accommodate these craftsmen. As well as their wages, free accommodation and food was provided.

Woolwich is 4 miles east of the site of Greenwich Palace which enabled Henry VIII to make regular visits to oversee work on the building of his warships. This included the *Henry Grace à Dieu*, which was the first vessel to be built at Woolwich, work commencing in 1512. She was built at Bell Water Gate which is where the car park for the Woolwich ferry terminal is situated, east of the two surviving dry docks.

There is evidence to suggest that Henry took an interest in ship design and worked with shipbuilders. The *Mary Rose* and *Henry Grace à Dieu* were the first ships in the navy to be equipped with watertight gun-ports with hinged flaps, which enabled heavy bronze cannon to fire a broadside on both sides from these ships. It also meant that these guns could be positioned on lower decks, just above sea level, to fire at enemy ships and stabilise the vessel. The Imperial Ambassador, Eustace Chapuys, had no reason to praise Henry VIII but he acknowledged his involvement in shipbuilding in a report to Charles V on 16 July 1541: 'The King has also sent to Italy for three shipwrights expert at making galleys, but Chapuys thinks he will not set them to work as he has begun to make ships with oars of which he himself is the architect. London.'[15]

The Eastern dry dock (No. 3) at Woolwich dockyard, looking south from the Thames Pathway. This dock is one of two from the surviving Tudor dockyard. It was rebuilt during the reign of Queen Victoria between 1844 and 1846. (Author's Collection)

TWO TUDOR DOCKS AT WOOLWICH DOCKYARD

The *Mary Rose* regularly visited the River Thames throughout her career and was moored at Woolwich at the beginning of 1513. There exists a reference to payment of a passage from London to the West Country and back to Sandwich in Kent during 1513 which confirms that the *Mary Rose* began that journey from Woolwich, 'The charges of the good ship called the *Mary Rose* from 14 March to 16 July, viz. at Woolwich (18 March) Sandwich (25 March), Dartmouth, Plymouth (10 May to 23 May), Hampton (4 June), Portsmouth (8 June) and Sandwich (22 June to 15 July)'.[16] It was during this voyage that the *Mary Rose*, as part of the English fleet, encountered some French warships and during a brief battle Admiral Sir Edward Howard was killed.

Woolwich dockyard continued to be used for the construction and repair of ships in Henry's navy throughout his reign. In November 1518, there exists record of a payment in the Navy Accounts 'For bringing *The Great Nicholas* out of her dock near Woolwich, and into her dock at Deptford.'[17] In an inventory of how many ships belonged to the monarch in October 1525, the dock at Woolwich was mentioned: 'The *Sovereign*, 800 tons, in a dock at Woolwich. She must be new made from the keel upward; the form of which ship is so marvellous goodly that great pity it were she should die, and the rather because that many things there be in her that will serve right well'.[18] The *Sovereign*, inherited by Henry from his father, had participated in the Battle of Brest in 1513 and was neglected. This reference

Another view of the Eastern dry dock (No. 3 Dock) at Woolwich dockyard, looking northwards towards the Thames Pathway. (Author's Collection)

A view of the Western dry dock (No. 3 Dock) at Woolwich dockyard. This formed part of the old Tudor dockyard which was rebuilt between 1838 and 1841. (Author's Collection)

Western dry dock (No. 3 Dock) at Woolwich dockyard. This image was taken from the Thames Pathway looking south. (Author's Collection)

One of two slipways, possibly from the reign of Henry VIII, that can be seen along the Thames Pathway between the Woolwich ferry pier terminal and the two docks. (Author's Collection)

The entrance to Western dry dock (No. 3 Dock) at Woolwich dockyard. The dock can be seen to the right of the photo. The Woolwich ferry pier terminal is visible on the left of the image. This was the site of Bell Water Gate where the first Tudor docks at Woolwich were built and where the *Henry Grace à Dieu* was laid down in 1512 and launched in the presence of Henry VIII in 1514. The dockyard expanded from the site of the Woolwich ferry pier terminal to where the two twin docks are situated in 1540. (Author's Collection)

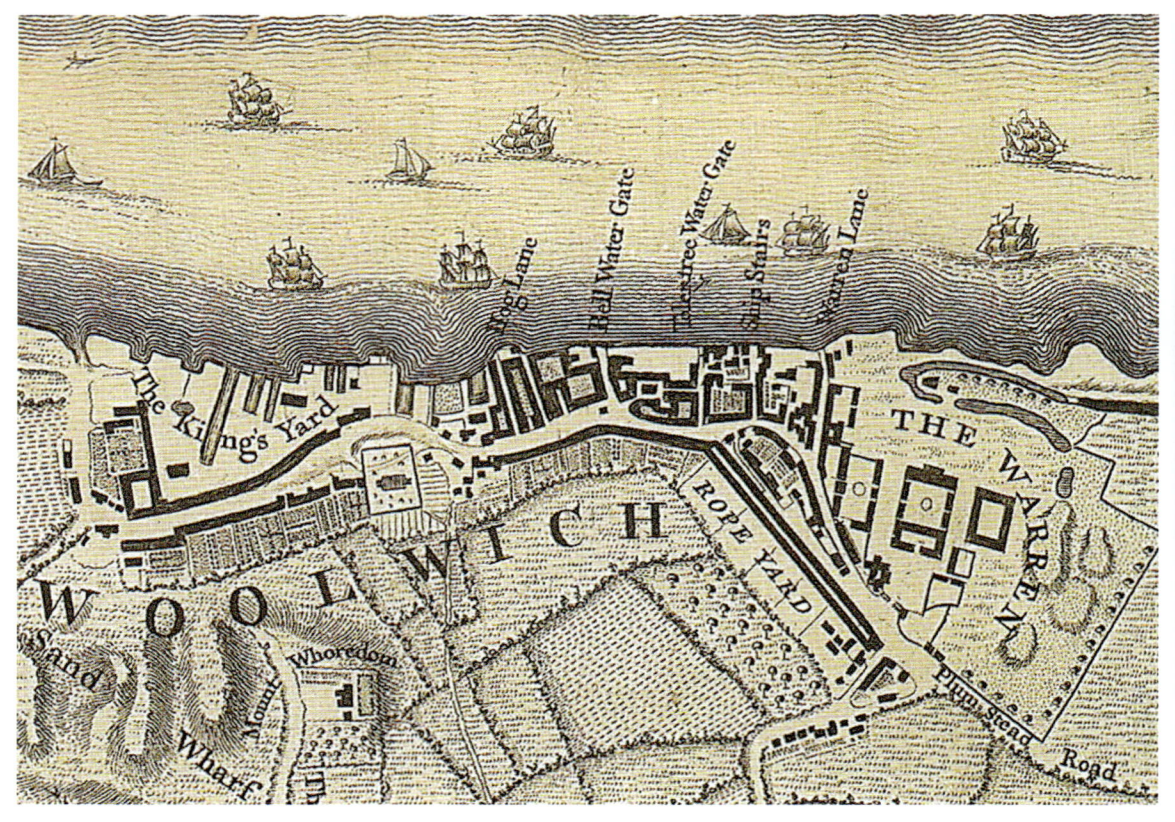

Detail of an eighteenth-century map of London. Engraved by Richard Parr and surveyed and published by John Rocque in 1746, this map shows the King's Yard (left) and old Woolwich (centre). (Author's Collection)

indicates that she was going to be rebuilt in 1525, but the plan did not come to fruition and she was left abandoned at Woolwich. The remains of the ship were found in 1912 along the river bank during construction of Woolwich Power Station.

The Royal Navy used the facilities at Woolwich dockyard for over 350 years until its closure in October 1869. The *Sovereign of the Seas* was built at Woolwich during the reign of Charles I in 1637. HMS *Beagle*, the vessel used by naturalist Charles Darwin during his voyage around the world between 1831 and 1836, was launched at Woolwich dockyard in 1820. Queen Victoria and Prince Albert were present at the launch of HMS *Trafalgar* on 21 June 1841 and the launch of HMS *Royal Albert* on 13 May 1854 at Woolwich dockyard.

The two docks, situated along the southern bank of the River Thames, are a visual testament to the legacy of Henry VIII and his role in the establishment of the Royal Navy. The photos of the two docks today were taken during 2018, shortly before the construction of nearby apartments commenced.

11
Glass Slide of the Henry Grace à Dieu

Flagship of Henry VIII

The destruction of the English ship Regent *by fire during the engagement with the French at Pointe de Saint-Mathieu, off the Brittany coast, on 10 August 1512, prompted Henry to order the construction of a replacement vessel that would rival the construction of the* Great Michael *which was being built by King James IV of Scotland. The vessel commissioned by Henry was a 1,500-ton carrack, named* Henry Grace à Dieu (Henry Grace of God) *and was laid down at Woolwich dockyard in 1512, at a cost of £8,000 (approximately valued at £5 million in 2019).*

Henry played an active role with shipbuilders in designing his warships and vessels, his focus being to create the largest vessel of its day in order to impress other nations, instead of concentrating on practical value at sea. Among the oversights in the design process was that the *Henry Grace à Dieu*'s large draught meant that it was unable to dock in the harbours at Dover and Calais. It was considered top heavy and to be unstable. Although spectacular to look at, it was expensive to operate on a daily basis.

Once completed, the *Henry Grace à Dieu* was launched on 13 June 1514 at Woolwich dockyard in the presence of King Henry, accompanied by Katherine, his sister, Princess Mary, and courtiers and ambassadors. Among the ambassadors were Gerard de Pleine and John Colla. In a letter to the Emperor Maximilian, they reported:

> Went with all diligence to the King. Found him, on Tuesday, in his new great ship of 1,500 tons, which was that day dedicated with great triumph. Met the Queen, the Princess Mary, the Pope's ambassadors, several bishops, and a large number of nobles. Were most honourably received, and conducted by the King through the ship, which has no equal in bulk, and has an incredible array of guns. In the scuttle on the top of the mainmast are eighty serpentines and hackbuts. The ship contains seven tiers, one above another. On the ambassadors leaving the ship, a salute was fired from all the guns.[19]

It was fitted out at the naval dockyard at Erith in 1515. Henry VIII was affectionately known among his subjects as 'Great Harry' during the early years of his reign and this vessel was also known as the *Great Harry*. Regarded as the largest ship of its day, it displaced approximately 1,000 tons. Its firepower was awesome because the *Henry Grace à Dieu* could carry a total of 80 guns, including 51 heavy guns and 29 swivel guns positioned on upper decks, including a 4-deck foc's'le. The ship's complement of *Henry Grace à Dieu* amounted to 700 personnel including 420 soldiers, 260 sailors and 40 gunners. Sir Thomas Wyndham was her first commander.

The *Henry Grace à Dieu* had to wait three decades before she fired her guns in anger and for much of her career she was mothballed in port during peacetime. She was solely used for diplomatic purposes and was an asset that Henry VIII enthusiastically showed off to foreign dignitaries. In 1520, she formed part of the fleet that escorted Henry to Calais, on his journey to meet King Francis I of France at the Field of the Cloth of Gold.

Glass slide depicting Henry VIII's carrack the *Henry Grace à Dieu*. This is how she would have appeared after she was rebuilt. (Author's Collection)

Henry VIII was proud of his navy and when he welcomed Charles V at Dover during his state visit on 26 May 1522 he gave him a guided tour of his fleet, including the *Henry Grace à Dieu* and *Mary Rose*, which were moored outside the harbour. Hall recorded:

> The King brought the Emperor aboard on his new ship, called the *Henry Grace à Dieu*, a ship of xv. C. and rowed about to all his great ships which then lay in Dover rode,

the Emperor and his lords, much praised the making of the ships, and especially the artillery, they said, they never saw ships so armed.[20]

In an account dated 4 June 1522, Vice Admiral William Fitzwilliam, 1st Earl of Southampton rated the *Henry Grace à Dieu* and detailed in a report to Henry VIII how she performed in turbulent seas in the English Channel on 30 May 1522 after the state visit of Charles V.

GLASS SLIDE OF THE *HENRY GRACE À DIEU*

The *Henry Grace à Dieu* sailed as well and rather better than any ship in the fleet. She weathered them all, save the *Mary Rose*; and on a wind, there would be a 'hard chose' between them. The galley was next them, but if she 'may veer the ship, she will go from us all'. All yesterday the wind blew 'sore and strainably'; but the *Henry* rode as still and gently at anchor as the best ship in the fleet.[21]

The *Henry Grace à Dieu* served throughout Henry VIII's reign and was rebuilt in 1539. On 19 July 1545, she fired her guns during the Battle of the Solent. After the king's death in 1547, it was renamed the *Edward*, after Henry's son and heir, however she was destroyed by fire at her moorings in Woolwich dockyard in 1553.

A nineteenth-century depiction of the *Henry Grace à Dieu* by Antoine Léon Morel-Fatio. (Public Domain)

A picture of the *Henry Grace à Dieu* from a series of images entitled 'Ships that have made history'. (Author's Collection)

Seizième siècle. — Le Grand-Harry. (Voy. 1838, p. 305.)

12

Earliest known Portrait of Henry VIII, c. 1513

Young Henry

This portrait of Henry VIII was painted by Meynnart Wewyck in 1513. It depicts a slender, beardless, handsome prince which presents the monarch in a different perspective in comparison with later paintings which showed a disgruntled, angry and aggressive king, bearded and obese.

This image of the youthful Prince Henry depicted in this portrait corresponds with a description written on 30 April 1515 by Pietro Pasqualigo, Venetian Ambassador to the English court, who met the king at Baynards Castle in London. As well as describing his appearance, he mentions the king's ability to speak various languages, play musical instruments, sing, handle a bow with skill and his competence at jousting:

> The King is the handsomest potentate I ever set eyes on; above the usual height, with an extremely fine calf to his leg, his complexion very fair and bright, with auburn hair combed straight and short, in the French fashion, and a round face so very beautiful that it would become a pretty woman, his throat being rather long and thick. He was born 28th of June 1491, so he will enter his twenty-fifth year the month after next. He speaks French, English and Latin, and a little Italian; plays well on the lute and harpsichord, sings from book at sight, draws the bow with greater strength than any man in England and jousts marvellously.[22]

The earliest known portrait of Henry VIII. (Berger Collection, Denver Art Collection)

The painting shows Henry wearing a red robe with brown fur edges. The sleeves reveal that the robe is lined with gold cloth on the inside. He wears a chain of balas rubies, a red gemstone, across his shoulders. An ensign, or cap badge, which depicts scenes of the Old Testament is worn on his head. In his right hand he holds a Tudor rose, symbolising the continuance of the Tudor dynasty.

Henry was aware that his reign was vulnerable to Yorkist supporters who would like to see him overthrown and he was therefore determined to preserve the Tudor dynasty. He was also keen to wage war upon France in order to bolster his prestige upon the international stage and gain the respect of other European monarchs. Andrea Badoer, a Venetian diplomat, reported on 21 April 1509 that 'this new King is magnificent, liberal and a great enemy of the French'.[23] Another diplomat's account on 26 April 1509 confirmed that 'the King swore immediately after his coronation to make war on the King of France. Soon we shall hear that he has invaded France.'[24]

In 1513, the year when this portrait was painted, Henry VIII sailed for Calais on 30 June to launch a campaign against the French. He proclaimed Queen Katherine as regent and before departing ordered the execution of Edmund de la Pole, the Earl of Suffolk, who had been incarcerated in the Tower of London since 1506. The French King Louis XII was prepared to acknowledge Pole as King of England. Henry therefore acted to eliminate the threat of a Yorkist usurpation of his throne. Roberto Acciaiolo, Florentine Ambassador in France, wrote on 20 May 1513, 'nothing is heard of the English except that they have beheaded the Earl of Suffolk, because his brother is in the French Court, and is called rightful heir of that realm'.[25] Despite his youthful, effeminate appearance in this painting, Henry VIII was a ruthless sovereign who was determined to secure his throne.

13

Oil Painting Entitled
The Meeting of Henry VIII and the Emperor Maximillian I

Henry VIII's Territorial Ambitions

Early during his reign Henry VIII held aspirations to reconquer land in Normandy and Aquitaine, France that had once been controlled by England and had been lost towards the end of the Hundred Years War in 1453. When Henry VIII succeeded his father in 1509, Calais was the only part of France that remained under English control and he wanted to emulate the victory of Henry V at Agincourt with his own military accomplishments, yearning for glory on the battlefield.

An opportunity arose in 1511 when Louis XII of France challenged the authority of Pope Leo X. Henry VIII joined a Holy League of European Nations that included King Ferdinand II of Aragon and the Holy Roman Emperor Maximilian in a bid to defend the Catholic Church against France. In January 1512, Parliament voted for funds to finance an invasion of France and war was declared in April 1512. In June 1513, Henry sent the English army into northern France and surrounded the town of Thérouanne (sometimes known as Terouenne). On 27 June, 500 English soldiers and 100 waggons transporting vital supplies to replenish the English siege were attacked by French troops near Ardres and the provisions taken to Boulogne. John Taylor, Clerk of the Parliaments, recorded in his diary 'that 200 Englishmen were slain in the encounter, that the French had carried off their dead, whose number could not be ascertained, had stripped the bodies, and so mutilated their faces that it was difficult to tell which were English or which French; nevertheless 20 fine horses of the French were found dead on the field.'[26]

After Henry had designated his wife, Queen Katherine, as regent, responsible for governing England in his absence, Henry VIII ventured to Calais to join his army, comprising approximately 13,000 troops, to regain control of northern France and Thérouanne. Henry arrived in Calais on 30 June and spent the following month assembling his troops and preparing for the campaign. He was joined by 8,000 German mercenaries before heading to Thérouanne.

During that campaign, Henry met Emperor Maximilian I, head of the Hapsburg Empire and Holy Roman Empire. That meeting is depicted in this oil painting entitled *The Meeting of Henry VIII and the Emperor Maximilian I* in a series of four horizontal bands which show the main events during the campaign. The bottom band shows the Hapsburg Emperor Maximilian I on the left, shaking the hand of Henry VIII, on the right, at their initial meeting on 11 August 1513 at Ayre. According to Edward Hall, 'the king was in a garment of great riches in jewels as pearls and stone, he was armed in light armour'.[27] Maximilian was wearing black because he was mourning the recent death of

THE MEETING OF HENRY VIII AND THE EMPEROR MAXIMILLIAN I

The Meeting of Henry VIII and the Emperor Maximilian I. (Royal Collection/Public Domain)

his wife. The meeting was short because of the heavy rain and strong gales. A tent woven of gold and purple which was intended to house the reception between the king and emperor was damaged by the bad weather. It was during this same day that Henry received a message from a herald sent by King James of Scotland declaring his intention of invading England if Henry continued his invasion of France.

The next band above shows the two leaders, on horseback and dressed in armour, in conversation on 12 August 1513. State papers reveal that their discussion was secret and the painting depicts them alone while their soldiers stand observing them. It also shows their respective tents bearing their coats of arms. Henry was flamboyant and revelled in pageantry. Maximilian, however, was not that way inclined, as recorded in the diary of John Taylor, Clerk of the Parliaments, '[the] Emperor visited the trenches and returned the next morning to Ayre. He is of middle height, with open and manly countenance; pallid complexion; has a snub nose, and a grey beard. Is affable, frugal, an enemy to pomp. His attendants are in black silk or wollen'.[28]

In the top right corner of the painting is the town of Thérouanne, which was besieged by English forces from June 1513. When Henry and Maximilian met close to the town, they brought with them reinforcements which gave the Anglo-Burgundian alliance an advantage over the French who were fortified within the ramparts of the town. French reinforcements were confronted by Anglo-Burgundian cavalry and forced to flee on 16 August. This engagement at Bomy, known as the Battle of the Spurs, is depicted in the third band. It was reported:

> Yesterday morning, after he [Henry] and the Emperor had crossed the Lys, which passes before Terouenne, towards Guinegate, news came that all the French horse at Blangy were moving, some toward Guinegate, the others to the place where Lord Talbot was stationed before Terouenne to cut off supplies. A skirmish took place and there were taken on

his side 44 men and 22 wounded. The French, thinking that the English were still beyond the Lys, considered they would not be in time to prevent them revictualling the town. The English horse however passed by Guinegate and confronted the French, who were three times their number. Several encounters took place and men were wounded on both

Albrecht Dürer's portrait of Maximilian I, Holy Roman Emperor. (Kunsthistorisches Museum)

sides. After this, in the Emperor's company, advanced straight against the French, causing the artillery to be fired at them, whereupon they immediately began to retire, and were pursued for ten leagues without great loss to the English. Nine or ten standards were taken and many prisoners, among whom are the Duke of Longueville, Marquis of Rothelin, Count de Dunois, Messire René de Clermont, Vice Admiral of France, and others whose names are enclosed. It is said that Lord Fiennes is killed, for his horse is in the English camp. The standard bearer of the 'grand escuyer de France', Count Galeace de St. Severin, is also taken. De La Palice is said to be either wounded or killed. The Emperor has been as kind to him [Henry] as if he were his real father. At the camp at Gynegate before Terouenne, 17 Aug. 1513.[29]

On 23 August, the French forces holding Thérouanne capitulated and gave up the town to Henry VIII and Maximilian I. Laurent de Gorrevod detailed the surrender in a letter to Margaret of Savoy:

At 9 am was concluded the treaty with the French in Therouenne, under which, about midday, they left the town, under safe conduct, with bag and baggage, mounted and armed, lance on thigh and ensigns furled (*ployées deans les fourreaux*). The foot likewise. Those townsmen who wished to go with them went, with their goods. The rest of the inhabitants will make oath to the King of England and be treated as his subjects. The Emperor and the King of England were in arms with most of their army both horse and foot, ranged, the horse on the one side and the foot on the other, while the French passed between, by two and two, the baggage going first, then the French foot, 3,000, then the lansknechts who numbered 200 men of arms well mounted and armed. Those who understand such things and have viewed the town say that if the French had had the courage to defend it, it could not have been taken by assault. By order of the Emperor and King, the Count Tallebot has entered the town with 2,000 English foot, both to keep it and prevent pillage by English or Burgundians, and has closed the gates. The Emperor returned to sup and sleep in the abbey of St. Jehan, in his lodging, and the King and his army returned to camp. To-morrow morning the Emperor and King will be at mass in the great church of Therouenne. Has twice to-day solicited the Emperor to write to her his pleasure as regards the gentlemen with her, but he answers that he will write to-morrow. 'Madame vous ne veistes oncques gens si gorgias que le roy d'Angleterre et son armée ont esté aujourd'huy; car ce n'estoit tout que drap d'or et campanes d'argent dorées a plusieurs.' To-morrow the Emperor and King will settle what to do with this town. Would like now to return, as she orders, but it is impossible until the affair of the King Catholic is settled, which the Emperor has put in charge of him and others. The Emperor and King of England have been nine hours on horseback, and I with them. Abbey of St. Jehan, Tuesday, 23 Aug., about 6 pm.[30]

Control of Thérouanne was passed to Maximilian who ordered its destruction on 26 August, when it was set alight, except for the cathedral. The left-hand corner of the painting shows the town of Tournai, the next objective after Thérouanne, under siege.

It is believed that paintings such as this were commissioned to record the significant events in a monarch's reign, and this particular painting was displayed in Whitehall Palace, together with another painting representing the Battle of the Spurs.

14

Henry VIII's Tower, Tournai

Tournai Held by the English

Henry VIII captured Tournai from the French in 1513. This circular tower was built at Tournai on the orders of Henry VIII during the five years it was occupied by English troops between 1513 and 1518.

After the capture of Thérouanne, Henry VIII turned his attention to Tournai. By 15 September 1513, the English army had surrounded the Belgian town, which was affluent due to its production of rich textiles. It was during this period that Henry received confirmation that King James VI of Scotland had executed his threat to invade England if Henry did not withdraw from France. The Scottish army crossed the border and overwhelmed and destroyed Norham Castle. However, Queen Katherine had mustered a force led by Thomas Howard, Earl of Surrey which confronted the invaders, defeating them at Branxton Moor in an engagement known as the Battle of Flodden on 9 September, when King James VI and 13,000 men were killed.

Buoyed by this successful victory at home, Henry continued to besiege Tournai. When heavy guns were brought forward to support the siege, the occupants of Tournai surrendered. John Taylor, Clerk of the Parliaments, reported:

> To batter down the iron gates and stone towers of Tournay, guns came from Lille of immense magnitude, enough to conquer by the very sight of them. On the 21st, before they were tried, the city submitted, and next day handed over the keys. Lord Lisle, chief marshal of the army, was made Governor. On the 24th, the King entered it, met by the chief men of the city – their horses and mules having the English ensigns painted on paper before them. At the first gate, the King passed under a canopy of gold and silk prepared by the citizens, and carried by six of the principal burgesses – others attending bearing wax torches conducted him to the Cathedral, where, after service, the King made several knights. After dinner in the market place a deputy chosen by the citizens offered the city, its inhabitants, and their goods, to Henry, on which the people shouted *Vive le Roi*.[31]

Before returning to England in October 1513, Henry ordered that the defences of Tournai be strengthened. All that remains now is the keep, which was known as Henry VIII's Tower. Although Henry returned home in triumph, his accomplishment of capturing two towns in northern Europe was deemed insignificant, given the expense incurred in financing the campaign, for the war bankrupted England. Ferdinand II and Maximilian abandoned the campaign to attack France and Henry was left isolated. The capture of two French-held towns did not constitute a major victory and Henry had to make peace with Louis XII.

Cardinal Thomas Wolsey, who was a royal secretary serving the Privy Council, negotiated a peace treaty with France where King Louis XII offered to pay Henry an annual pension and Henry promised to give back Tournai, on condition that they did not interfere with Anglo-Scottish relations. Tournai was eventually

Henry VIII's Tower at Tournai. (Courtesy of LimoWreck)

returned to French control in 1518. In order to cement the alliance between France and England, Henry's younger sister, Mary, married Louis on 9 October 1514. Mary was aged 18 and Louis, who was embarking on his third marriage, was 52, thirty years her senior. Mary was not happy about the marriage, but she put duty and her country before herself, but she was only Queen of France for three months as Louis XII died on 1 January 1515.

15

Plaque Commemorating the Establishment of Trinity House

Origins of Trinity House

Trinity House is responsible for the provision and maintenance of buoys, lighthouses and lightvessels to aid seaman around England, Wales, the Channel Islands and Gibraltar, as well as providing experienced navigators to act as pilots for vessels operating in North European waters. The organisation was established after a guild of mariners from Deptford raised a petition expressing their concerns about unregulated pilots operating on the River Thames and the lack of experienced pilots.

Henry VIII was a keen sailor, a competent navigator and had a deep understanding of tidal behaviour. He was aware of the importance of this knowledge and the benefits of keeping sailors and their vessels safe. On 19 March 1513, in order to address the issue of the deficient navigational skills of his mariners, Henry VIII issued the following grant which was the first action to establish an organisation that focused upon training pilots who would assist masters of vessels to avoid the dangers of the coastal shores. It was the birth of Trinity House, its name derived from the Holy Trinity and St Clement, the patron saint of mariners. The grant stated:

> The Navy. Licence to the Masters, Rulers, and Mariners of the King's Navy in the Thames and other places to found a guild, in honour of the Holy Trinity and St. Clement, in the church of Deptford Stronde, for reformation of the Navy. The long and curious petition prefixed states that practise of pilotship in rivers, by young men who are unwilling to take the labour and adventure of learning the shipman's craft on the high seas, is likely to cause scarcity of mariners; 'and so this your realm which heretofore hath flourished with navy to all other lands dreadful' shall be left destitute of cunning masters and mariners; also that Scots, Flemings and Frenchmen, have been suffered to learn as loadsmen the secrets of the King's streams, and in time of war have come as far as Gravesend 'and fette owte English ships to the great rebuke of the realm'.[32]

The pilot was a highly skilled individual aboard a ship, with the responsibility for navigating the vessel, especially into harbour. He was required to know where the danger spots were located at sea, such as rocks and sandbanks; and had to ensure that the vessel under his pilotage avoided these hazards. He also had to possess an understanding of tides and weather. It would take years for a pilot to gain sufficient knowledge through apprenticeship to become a proficient pilot. This meant that Henry VIII had to rely on foreign pilots to pass on their navigational skills and knowledge to English mariners. A Frenchman was appointed England's first Hydrographer in 1544 and by 1545, Henry VIII employed approximately sixty French pilots to navigate English vessels.

PLAQUE COMMEMORATING THE ESTABLISHMENT OF TRINITY HOUSE

Trinity House at Tower Hill. The establishment of Trinity House is among the many legacies of Henry VIII's reign that benefit our nation today. (Author's Collection)

Trinity House has been a leader in maritime safety and navigation since Henry VIII presented a Royal Charter on 20 May 1514. Sir Thomas Spert, the master of the *Mary Rose* and *Henry Grace à Dieu*, was appointed first master of Trinity House. The organisation evolved during the reign of Henry's daughter, Elizabeth I, when in 1566 through the Seamarks Act she empowered Trinity House to establish 'so many beacons, marks and signs for the sea . . . whereby the dangers may be avoided and escaped and ships the better come unto their ports without peril'.

Plaque commemorating the granting of the charter for Trinity House by Henry VIII in 1514. (Author's Collection)

16

Parade Armet of Henry VIII

A Gift from Emperor Maximillian I to Henry VIII

An armet was a helmet that enclosed the entire head. This particular armet, known as the 'horned helmet', formed part of a piece of armour commissioned by the Holy Roman Emperor Maximilian I as a gift for Henry VIII. The emperor had forged an alliance with England against France at the beginning of Henry's reign and, as discussed previously, had won victories against the French at Thérouanne and Tournai in 1513.

In 1511, Maximilian's court armourer Konrad Seusenhofer in Innsbruck, Austria received the order to construct this armour. It was delivered to Henry during 1514, along with another piece of armour that Henry had commissioned independently. The helmet has a bizarre appearance, with protruding eyes, a fixed grimace revealing teeth and stubble on the chin, and is adorned with ram horns riveted to the upper sides. The armet provides protection for the skull and hinged cheek pieces cover the face. The armour was engraved by an Augsberg goldsmith; both ear pieces are decorated with rosettes of flowers.

Historians have challenged whether such a grotesque object was an appropriate gift to be presented from one monarch to another, but this is an example of a piece of armour given to Henry VIII as a diplomatic gesture. The facial design may have been modelled on a king's fool. During the seventeenth century, this helmet was displayed at the Tower of London as part of the armour of Will Somers, who was Henry VIII's jester, but he did not enter court until 1525, a decade after this helmet was created. Its primary use was for court pageants and may have been treated by Henry VIII and his courtiers as a novelty for amusement. Henry may have worn this piece of armour in jest. The remainder of the armour no longer exists, but the helmet is displayed at the Royal Armouries Museum, Leeds, where it is adopted as the symbol for the Leeds site.

The helmet on display at the Royal Armouries Museum, Leeds. (Alamy)

17

Cardinal Thomas Wolsey Statue, Ipswich

Wolsey, Lord Chancellor to Henry VIII

Cardinal Thomas Wolsey was appointed Lord Chancellor by Henry VIII on Christmas Eve, 1515. A statue commemorates Wolsey in St Peter's Street, Ipswich, close to the site of the house where he was born between 1470 and 1473.

Wolsey was the son of a wool merchant who rose to prominence from humble origins to become a reliable political advisor to Henry VIII. He excelled as a scholar at Oxford University and after graduation he took holy orders. Rising through the Church, he became Chaplain to Henry VII in 1507 and later the King's Almoner, responsible for distributing food and money to the poor on behalf of the king. Henry VIII became aware of Wolsey's abilities and potential in 1511, when he was appointed to the Privy Council, performing the role of Royal Secretary. Wolsey was conscientious, charismatic, witty and intelligent which enamoured him to the king, but he was also ambitious, avaricious and was enthusiastic to advance further. Once Henry VIII recognised his value, Wolsey's rise within the court was the most expedient of any subject during his reign, for during 1514 he was appointed Bishop of Lincoln and Tournai, as well as Archbishop of York. In 1515, Pope Leo X made Wolsey a Cardinal and Henry VIII appointed him as Lord Chancellor. Wolsey continued to work hard for his king. Wolsey's biographer, George Cavendish, who had served as a Gentleman usher to Wolsey from 1522 until Wolsey's fall from grace in 1530, wrote about why Wolsey made an impression upon the king and his meteoric rise in his court:

His sentences and witty persuasions in the council chamber were always so pithy that they always, as occasion moved them, assigned him, for his filed tongue and ornate eloquence, to be their expositor unto the king's majesty in all their proceedings. In whom the King conceived such a loving fantasy, especially for that he was most earnest and readiest among all the council to advance the king's only will and pleasure, without any respect to the case. The King, therefore, perceived him to be a meet instrument for the accomplishment of his devised will and pleasure, called him more near unto him, and esteemed him so highly that his estimation and favour put all other ancient counsellors out of their accustomed favour, that they were in before; insomuch as the King committed all his will and pleasure unto his disposition and order. Who wrought so all his matters, that all his endeavour was only to satisfy the King's mind, knowing right well, that it was the very vein and right course to bring him to high promotion. The King was young and lusty, disposed all to mirth and pleasure, and to follow his desire and appetite, nothing minding to travail in the busy affairs of this realm. The which the almoner perceived very well, and took upon him therefore to disburden the King of so weighty a charge and troublesome business, putting the King

CARDINAL THOMAS WOLSEY STATUE, IPSWICH

The statue of Cardinal Wolsey in St Peter's Street, Ipswich, close to the site of his birth, was sculptured by David Annaund and unveiled on 29 June 2011. The inscription on the base of the statue states: 'Thomas Wolsey, born Ipswich 1470 or 1471. Died Leicester 1530. Cardinal, Archbishop, Lord Chancellor and teacher. Who believed that pleasure should mingle with study so that the child may think learning an amusement rather than a toil'. (Author's Collection)

in comfort that he shall not need to spare any time of his pleasure for any business that should necessarily happen in the council, as long as he, being there and having the King's authority and commandment, doubted not to see all things sufficiently furnished and perfected; the which would first make the King privy of all such matters as should pass through their hands before he would proceed to the finishing or determining of the same, whose mind and pleasure he would fulfil and follow to the uttermost, wherewith the King was wonderly pleased. And whereas the other ancient counsellors would, according to the office of good counsellors, divers times persuade the King to have sometime an intercourse in to the council, there to hear what was done in weighty matters, the which pleased the King nothing at all, for he loved nothing worse than to be constrained to do anything contrary to his royal will and pleasure; and that knew the almoner very well, having a secret intelligence of the King's natural inclination, and so fast as the other counsellors advised the King to leave his pleasure, and to attend to the affairs of his realm, so busily did the almoner persuade him to the contrary; which delighted him much, and caused him to have the greater affection and love to the almoner. Thus, the almoner ruled all them that before ruled him; such did his policy and wit bring to pass.[33]

Wolsey's power and influence over the king and court was strong and he served Henry loyally for fifteen years, remaining in favour for longer than any other courtier. During that time, he was supreme in state and Church, and was empowered to dictate and steer foreign and domestic policy on behalf of the king. Wolsey's ability to manage the administration of the realm allowed Henry to pursue his interests of hunting, jousting and sport. However, Henry supervised his Chancellor and made the ultimate decisions regarding matters of state. Both Henry and Wolsey were intelligent and shared similar opinions on political issues.

However, there were members of the court, from noble birth, who resented Wolsey's rapid rise. The king was promoting a person of humble origins to play a role in state decisions and the governing of the country.

Wolsey brought peace between England, France, the Holy Roman Empire, Spain and the Vatican through the Treaty of London, in October 1518. He worked tirelessly on this agreement in a bid to resolve disputes among these factions within Europe. In order to improve Anglo-French relations Wolsey was responsible for arranging the betrothal of Princess Mary to the Dauphin Francis, the French heir. It was during the celebrations for this peace treaty that Wolsey began the arrangements for the meeting of Henry with King Francis I of France near Calais at the Field of the Cloth of Gold. He believed that the differences between France and England could not be settled until both kings met in person, in the spirit of harmony. Wolsey was also involved in the failed attempt to get Henry elected as Holy Roman Emperor in 1519.

Wolsey enjoyed a life of affluence that surpassed that of the king. He acquired a ninety-nine-year lease from the Knights Hospitallers on the manor house at Hampton during the spring of 1515, which was demolished and rebuilt into the large double-courtyard house now known as Hampton Court Palace. It was here that Wolsey established a household that would rival the king's. Wolsey's coat of arms above the gateway into Clock Court is one of few remnants that indicate that this palace, which contained a thousand rooms, was once owned by him. Wolsey received unprecedented power over the Church of England, exceeding the stature of the

CARDINAL THOMAS WOLSEY STATUE, IPSWICH

ABOVE and RIGHT: Directly behind the statue on the corner of St Peter's Street and Silent Street stands a house built in the fifteenth century at about the time of Wolsey's birth. A plaque commemorates the birth of Wolsey on the opposite side of the road. (Author's Collection)

CURSON LODGE

THIS EARLY-TUDOR BUILDING IS A RARE SURVIVAL OF A MEDIAEVAL INN. THE SURVIVING RANGE ALONG SILENT STREET WAS ALWAYS INTENDED FOR THIS PURPOSE. THE CORNER PROPERTY OF ST NICHOLAS STREET MAY HAVE BEEN USED AS A MERCHANTS HOUSE AND SHOP. THIS WAS LATER ABSORBED BY THE INN. AN IMPRESSIVE GROUND-FLOOR HALL AND A SUITE OF LODGING CHAMBERS ON THE FIRST FLOOR WERE ACCESSED FROM A GALLERY AT THE BACK.

THE BUILDING WAS RESTORED IN 2007 BY
THE IPSWICH BUILDING PRESERVATION TRUST

NEAR THIS 15TH. CENTURY HOUSE
ON THE OPPOSITE SIDE OF THE WAY
STOOD IN 1472 THE HOME OF
ROBERT AND JOAN WOLSEY,
WHERE THE GREAT CHILD OF HONOUR
THOMAS WOLSEY,
CARDINAL, ARCHBISHOP, CHANCELLOR,
PASSED HIS BOYHOOD.
IN HIS POWER AND PRIDE
HE RANKED HIMSELF WITH PRINCES
AND TROD THE WAYS OF GLORY.
IN HIS FALL
HE DIED A HUMBLE MAN
AT LEICESTER ABBEY
ABOUT THE HOUR OF EIGHT
ON THE MORNING OF NOVEMBER 29TH 1530
AND WAS THERE BURIED AT DEAD OF NIGHT

Archbishop of Canterbury on his appointment as papal legate by Pope Leo X in May 1518. It also heightened his ambition that one day he would become Pope, but that would be dependent upon support from the Holy Roman Emperor and the King of France.

Elizabeth Blount, mistress of Henry VIII, bore the king an illegitimate son in June 1519. Wolsey was designated godfather to the newborn baby, whom was named Henry Fitzroy, and arranged for Elizabeth to be married to Gilbert Tailboys. Henry Fitzroy remained with his mother, but Wolsey was responsible for his welfare.

During 1520, Wolsey was preoccupied with the preparations for the meeting of Henry VIII and Francis I at the Field of the Cloth of Gold, which took place in June 1520 at Val d'Or (Golden Vale), south from Calais.

In December 1521, Wolsey's wealth expanded when he was appointed Abbot of St Albans and acquired the associated properties, The More and Tittenhanger. However, his aspirations of becoming Pope were dashed on the death of Pope Leo X when Emperor Charles V renegaded on his promise to support Wolsey, and instead put forward his tutor, who was elected as Pope Adrian VI in 1522.

As the king grew older, his maturity broadened his mind and he became aware of Wolsey's wealth. As work on Hampton Court Palace was completed, Henry realised that it was more magnificent than his own palaces and, after hints, Wolsey presented it to the King in June 1525. During that same year, Wolsey founded Cardinal College in Oxford, financed from income generated from dissolved monasteries. He also established a college in his hometown at Ipswich.

By 1527, Henry was resigned to the fact that he could never conceive a son, a male heir, with Katherine. Exploring ways of breaking his marriage with his first wife, he therefore confided in Wolsey about his manifest doubts regarding the validity of his marriage to Katherine. He believed that by marrying his brother's widow he had committed a sin and that his inability to produce a male heir was evidence of God's disapproval. Wolsey played a prominent role in this matter. Seeking an annulment from the Pope would prove futile for the timebeing at least, as he was being held a prisoner by Emperor Charles V and would not grant Henry an annulment because the Emperor was Katherine's nephew. Wolsey ventured to France to seek support from King Francis for

This portrait of Cardinal Thomas Wolsey, by Sampson Strong, can be seen at Christ Church, Oxford. (Christ Church, Oxford)

The ruins of the dissolved Blackfriars Monastery in Ipswich, close to where Cardinal Thomas Wolsey was born. Blackfriars was founded in 1263, following the gift of the land from Henry III and work started on building the monastery two years later. Dominican friars resided here until the monastery was closed by Henry VIII in 1538. (Author's Collection)

Henry's annulment. George Cavendish recalled the cardinal's diligence during this diplomatic mission:

> The next morning . . . he rose early, about four of the clock, sitting down to write letters into England unto the King, commanding one of his chaplains to prepare him to mass, insomuch that his said chaplain stood revested until four o'clock at afternoon; all of which season my lord never rose once to piss, nor yet to eat any meat, but continually wrote his letters, with his own hands, having all that time his nightcap and keverchief on his head. And about four of the clock, at afternoon, he made an end of writing, commanding one Christopher Gunner, the king's servant, to prepare him without delay to ride empost to England with his letters.[34]

Wolsey also explored the possibility of a French marriage for Henry, oblivious to the deepening

On 26 May 1528, Henry VIII empowered Cardinal Wolsey to 'supress the priory of St Peter', which was positioned in the street where Wolsey was born, and to convert the priory into a college. The gate and the worn symbol of the Wolsey coat of arms is all that remains of Wolsey's College in College Street, Ipswich. It was known as the Water Gate and was built to serve as an entrance for visitors arriving at the college from the River Orwell, which in Tudor times was much wider and passed close to the college and the adjacent St Peter-by-the-Waterfront Church. Construction of the school ceased when Wolsey fell from the king's favour. In 1532, unused building material, including lead, masonry and timber, was relocated to London where it was used to expand Wolsey's London residence, York House, which would later be known as Whitehall when Henry VIII took possession of it. (Author's Collection)

relationship between the king and Anne Boleyn, believing that she was only his mistress. While he was in France, Anne's affair with the king had become widely known among the court and she was becoming a powerful and influential force, being in a position to promote her family and friends within that court, which would threaten Wolsey's standing and authority. Opposing elements of Henry's Privy Council were also plotting against Wolsey. Supporters of Queen Katherine and members of Anne Boleyn's family were determined to usurp Wolsey's power and influence at court. Wolsey's attempts to obtain an annulment were undermined when the Pope sent Cardinal Lorenzo Campeggio to England to encourage a reconciliation between Henry and Katherine in October 1528. Wolsey's failure to resolve Henry's 'Great matter' and make the path clear to divorce Katherine and remarry Anne Boleyn signalled his downfall. In October 1529, Chapuys reported to Charles V: 'The downfall of the Cardinal is complete. He is dismissed from the Council, deprived of the Chancellorship, and constrained to make an inventory of his goods in his own hand, that nothing may be forgotten. It is said that he has acknowledged his faults and presented all his effects to the King.'[35]

Wolsey was not welcomed at court and went to Cawood Castle where, in November 1530, he was arrested for high treason, accused of enlisting support from foreign powers to further his own personal advantage and of engaging in secret correspondence with the Vatican. As he was being escorted to London for his eventual execution, the desperately unwell Wolsey died at Leicester Abbey on 29 November 1530. Charles Wriothesley wrote that 'some reckon he killed himself with purgations',[36] while it was widely believed that he died from dysentery. Wolsey was buried in Leicester Abbey without ceremony at midnight on the day that he died. It was only after his death that Henry realised that Wolsey had carried the burdens of state, and appreciated his abilities as an administrator and organiser. Chapuys reported to Charles V: 'A gentleman told me that a short time ago the King was complaining to his Council of something that was not done according to his liking and said in a rage that the Cardinal was a better man than any of them for managing matters; and repeating this twice, he left them'.[37]

The 'Silvered and Engraved' Armour of Henry VIII, 1515

Armour Crafted to Celebrate the Marriage of Henry VIII to Katherine

Henry VIII established the royal workshop at Greenwich in 1511 and this complete piece of armour is believed to have beeen among the first produced in this workshop. Completed in 1515, it was made for combat and jousting. This armour is an exquisite piece of art, its decoration commemorating the marriage of Henry VIII to Katherine of Aragon.

Henry sought craftsmen who had worked for Maximilian I in Flanders to build his armour. Peter Fevers was paid £15 (valued at £10,000 in 2019) for the construction of the 'Silvered and Engraved Armour' in August 1515. The armour, covered completely with silver and with a gilt skirt around the base, was engraved by a Belgian craftsman. An indenture written on 16 February 1514 stated that: 'Paul van Vrelant, of Bruxelles, harness gilder, . . . witnessing that Vrelant undertakes within three months to grave and gild certain harness for the king's body for 40l'.[38] This indenture confirmed that the original estimate for this work was £40 (valued at £27,000 in 2019), *l* denoting £ during the Tudor period. However, the cost of the work was grossly underestimated because when Vrelant completed the work, he presented a bill amounting to 121*l*. 6*s*. 8*d*. on 15 June 1514, for which Henry issued a warrant at Eltham to pay. Vrelant would work for the English monarch for the next five years.

Vrelant's work on the 'Silvered and Engraved Armour' is ornately detailed. It expresses Henry's love for his first wife, Katherine of Aragon, their initials H and K intertwined by true lovers' knots in gilt around the skirt. Their union is celebrated among the foliage pattern all over the armour with the engraved blossoming Tudor roses and ripe pomegranates of Aragon. On the toe caps on each sabaton, the plate defence for the foot, there is engraved the castle emblem of Castile and on the other foot a Tudor portcullis, which symbolises the union of England and Spain. On the rear of each greave a female figure emerges from the calyx of a flower and on the neck-band of the figure on the left greave are inscribed the letters 'GLVCK', which means 'good fortune'. St George is emboldened on the breast plate and St Barbara features on the back plate. The lives of these saints are also depicted on the horse armour.

THE 'SILVERED AND ENGRAVED' ARMOUR OF HENRY VIII, 1515

The 'Silvered and Engraved Armour' of Henry VIII. (Alamy)

19
The Longbow

Henry's Law on Archery

In 1515 Henry VIII instituted a law stating that archery was the predominant sport in the kingdom. The law decreed it was mandatory for all males between the ages of 7 and 60 to practise archery using a longbow, with the exception of judges and clergymen. The parents and guardians of boys were ordered to possess a longbow in their homes and to provide each boy with a longbow and two arrows in order to teach them the skill of archery. Those who did not comply were punished with a fine.

A longbow was a precision weapon which could be used to shoot an arrow accurately across a long distance of 200m towards a target. Skilled archers were capable of shooting twelve arrows per minute in succession. Shot in unison in volleys, it was difficult for anyone to escape such a fusillade on the medieval battlefield and it was not equalled until the arrival of semi-automatic weapons during the nineteenth century. The longbow was regarded as a formidable weapon, decisive in the English victory at Agincourt in 1415.

A depiction of Longbows in use. (Author's collection)

Henry wanted to divert the nation's attention away from playing football and bowls to improving and maintaining their use of the longbow in preparation for war. The use of the longbow at the Battle of Flodden Field, against the Scottish, was attributed to Henry's initiative to encourage archery.

Henry also ordered that instruction in archery should take place on holy days and that buttes be set up in towns to provide training spaces. Approximately 200 buttes were established in Shoreditch and Finsbury, north of the city of London, where men could practise archery. Henry VIII would sometimes practise at a butte situated in Tothill Fields, Westminster and could shoot an arrow with accurate precision. John Taylor, Clerk of the Parliaments, mentioned in his diary that he competed with the Yeoman of the Guard when in Calais on 8 July 1513. The king 'was practising archery in a garden with the archers of his guard. He cleft the mark in the middle, and surpassed them all, as he surpasses them in stature and personal graces.'[39]

Letter from Henry VIII to Cardinal Thomas Wolsey, 1518

A Daughter is Born

Henry VIII conveyed his dissatisfaction that his wife did not give birth to a son during June 1516. Henry was conscious that without a male heir, England would likely descend into a bloody civil war on a scale fought during the latter part of the previous century. A daughter as heir to the throne would make the Tudor dynasty weak and vulnerable to members of the aristocracy who had a direct and legitimate claim to the throne.

At 4am on 18 February 1516, Queen Katherine gave birth to Princess Mary at Greenwich Palace. Henry VIII was disappointed at the sex of his newborn child. His dissatisfaction that a son and heir to the throne had not been born was expressed in conversation to Sebastian Giustinian, a Venetian diplomat. Giustinian reported:

> On the 21st the Princess was christened. The sponsors were Wolsey and the Duchess of Norfolk. Congratulated the King today, and said that the Signory would have been more satisfied if it had been a son. His majesty then made me draw nearer, having, however, in the first place, returned many thanks to your highness for this compliment, saying. 'We are both young; if it was a daughter this time, by the grace of God the sons will follow'.[40]

In the letter written to Thomas Wolsey in June 1518, Henry expresses his anxiety for Katherine to conceive another child and the personal content demonstrates the close, intimate nature of his relationship with his Lord Chancellor. He confided:

> My lord cardinal, I recommend unto you as heartily as I can, and I am right glad to hear of your good health, which I pray God may long continue. So, it is that I have received your letters, to the which (because they ask long writing) I have made answer by my secretary. Two things there be which be so secret that they cause me at this time to write to you myself; the one is that I trust the queen my wife be with child; the other is chief cause why I am sloth to repair to London ward, because about this time is partly of her dangerous times, and by cause of that, I would remove her as little as I may now. My lord, I write thus unto you, not as an ensured thing, but as a thing wherein I have great hope and likelihood, and by cause, I do well know that this thing will be comfortable to you to understand; therefore, I do write it unto you at this time. No more to you at this time, *nisi quod deus velit inceptum opus bene finire*. Written with the hand of your loving prince, Henry R.[41]

The letter shows that Henry is convinced that the queen was pregnant and his reference to 'dangerous times' relates to previous miscarriages. Henry acknowledged Mary as his heir, but he wanted a son, a male heir to prevent anyone contesting the throne. He was concerned that if a female monarch succeeded him, then various

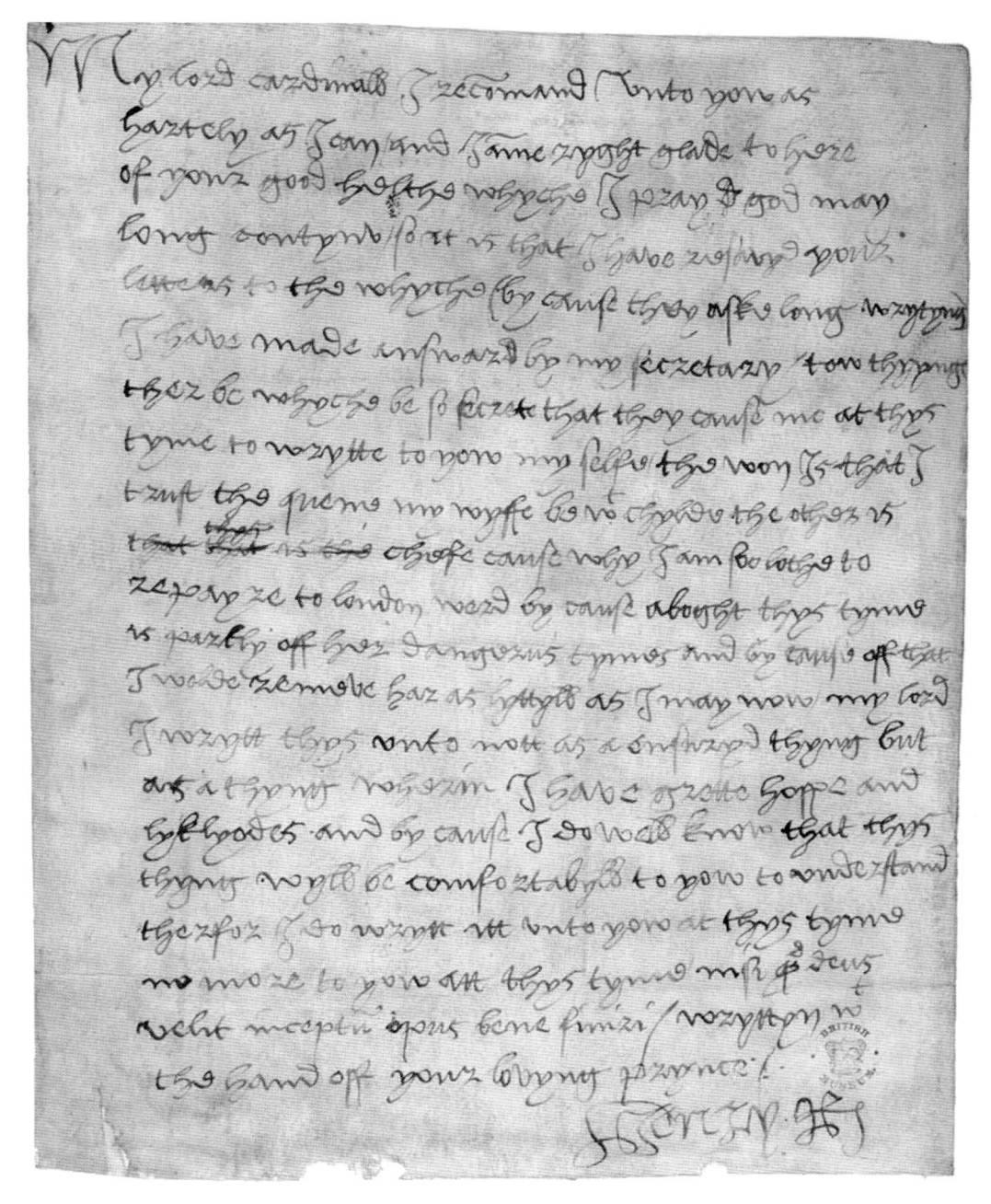

LETTER FROM HENRY VIII TO CARDINAL THOMAS WOLSEY, 1518

Letter written by Henry VIII to Thomas Wolsey expressing his hopes for the birth of a male heir. (Alamy)

factions would challenge her legitimacy to reign over England. James V of Scotland was a likely contender, as was the Duke of Buckingham, who was a direct descendant of Edward III and possessed a stronger legitimate claim to the throne of England than Henry VIII. Henry's optimism for a legitimate male heir to safeguard the Tudor dynasty expressed in this letter was again suppressed when Katherine gave birth to a still-born daughter later that year.

21

Greenwich Tiltyard

The Tiltyard – More than a Jousting Courtyard

The tiltyard was the scene of many lavish pageants. Foreign ambassadors were invited to spectate at these events and these were intended to demonstrate the physical and political strength of the king. Diplomats would write accounts of what they had seen and send them back to their respective countries. The tiltyard was not merely a place to enjoy the sport of jousting.

In 1516, Henry ordered the construction of a permanent tiltyard at Greenwich Palace. It was built south-east of the palace and ran northwards from where Queen's House stands, across the lawn and the Romney Road to the Royal Naval College. It measured 650ft in length and 250ft wide. A 6ft-high wooden wall, known as the tilt, prevented the jousters from colliding. A firm surface was required so that horses could gallop along the tiltyard, but it had to be soft enough to cushion the fall of an unhorsed knight or a horse. This was achieved by laying sand over layers of lime plaster and gravel. Two towers, built using bricks, stood adjacent to viewing platforms east of the tiltyard. The foundations of these towers were excavated beneath the lawns of the Queen's House.

After the ratification by Henry of a treaty of amity and confederation between himself, Maximilian and Charles of Castile, an alliance that was aimed at the King of France, a tournament was held for the Spanish envoys on 7 July 1517 at Greenwich. Henry jousted six times and it is recorded that he ran against his friend, Charles Brandon, the Duke of Suffolk.

Sebastian Giastinian, Venetian ambassador, reported to the Doge that 'on the 7th was a stately joust with new and costly decorations. The king jousted with Suffolk like Hector and Achilles'.[42] Edward Hall recorded that:

[The] King and the Duke ran fiercely together, and broke many spears, and so did all the other, that it was hard to say who did best: but when the courses were run, they ran violent one at another, so that both by the report of Sir Edward Guilford, Master of the Armoury, and also of the Judges and Heralds at these Jousts were broken five hundred and six spears.[43]

Niccolo Sagudino, secretary to Giastinian, provided more detail in his report of the jousting tournament on 7 July 1517:

To do honour to the Flemish envoys, the ambassadors were invited to a joust on the 7th. The King entered the lists about two. First came the marshal in a surcoat of cloth of gold, surrounded by thirty footmen in yellow and blue livery; then came the drummers and trumpeters in white damask, followed by forty knights in cloth of gold; 'and after them twenty young knights on very fine horses, all dressed in white, with doublets of cloth of silver and white velvet, and chains of unusual size, and their horses were barbed with silver chainwork, and a number of pendant bells, many of which rang. Next followed thirteen pages, singly, on extremely handsome horses, whose trappings were half of gold embroidery and the other half of purple velvet embroidered with gold stars. Then came fifteen jousters armed, their horse armour and surcoats being most costly; and alongside of each was one on horseback, sumptuously dressed, carrying his lance, with their footmen.' Then appeared the King in silver bawdkin, with thirty gentlemen on foot, dressed in velvet and white satin. Among the jousters were the Duke of Suffolk, the Marquis of Dorset, and my Lord Admiral. The King jousted with Suffolk, and tilted eight courses, both shivering their lances at every time, to the great applause of the spectators. The jousts lasted four hours, but the honour of the day was awarded to the King and the Duke. Between the courses the King and other cavaliers made their horses jump and execute acts of horsemanship, to the delight of everybody. Under the windows were the Queens of England and France. The adjoining chamber was occupied by the Cardinal and his attendants.[44]

A jousting tournament took place on 7 October 1518 to celebrate the betrothal of the young Princess Mary to the French Dauphin at Greenwich. An imitation castle, made from timber, named the 'castle of loyalty' was built adjacent to the tiltyard measuring 20ft square and 50ft high to celebrate Christmas in 1524. Knights were given the challenge to assault the castle and to take part in a jousting tournament. Constructed to specifications ordered by Henry VIII, the carpenters building this castle did not understand the king's plans and the structure was not sufficiently strong to support the knights, wearing heavy suits of armour, mounting it. This lavish affair had to be abandoned, although the jousting went ahead. Henry took part in the tournament which was observed by Scottish ambassadors and impressed his guests by his strength and performance on the tiltyard. Edward Hall recorded:

> Then the knights threw away their robes, and then it was known that it was the King, and the Duke of Suffolk whose bardes and bases were gold, embroidered with purple, silver, and black, very curiously. After them followed the Earl of Devonshire, the Lord Montacute, the Lord Roos, Sir Nicholas Carew, Sir Frances Brian, Henry Norris, Anthony Knevet, and five others. Every man ran eight courses, in which courses the King brake seven spears. Every man that day did well, so that Scots much praised the men of arms of England, but most of all them praised and marvelled at the King's strength, for they saw his spears were broken with more force, then the other spears were.[45]

Model of the tiltyard at Greenwich Palace on display at the Old Royal Naval College Visitor Centre. (Author's Collection)

HENRY VIII IN 100 OBJECTS

GREENWICH TILTYARD

The tiltyard at Greenwich Palace ran northwards from where the east wing of the Queen's House stands (on the right of this view), across the lawn and across the Romney Road to the Royal Naval College (on the left). (Author's Collection)

Henry VIII continued to joust throughout his reign and it was at Greenwich while jousting on 24 January 1536 that he was knocked from his horse wearing full armour. The horse that he rode was wearing armour and rolled over him, crushing him on the ground. Henry was badly wounded by the fall and according to a third-hand account written by Dr Pedro Oritz, Charles V's ambassador in Rome, the king could not speak for 2 hours, intimating that he was unconscious. The Imperial Ambassador to England, Eustace Chapuys, reported the severity of this fall: 'On the eve of the Conversion of St. Paul, the King being mounted on a great horse to run at the lists, both fell so heavily that everyone thought it a miracle he was not killed, but he sustained no injury'.[46] This incident highlighted the dangers of the joust and the precariousness of the monarch without a male heir taking part in such tournaments. It is believed that the anxiety Anne Boleyn suffered following the accident caused her to miscarry, and during the months that followed her relationship with the king broke down. The injury would have a lasting effect upon Henry VIII, who suffered an ulcerated leg throughout the remainder of his life, which made him immobile and unable to participate in further jousting tournaments.

22
The Medieval St Paul's Cathedral

The Treaty of London in 1518

Work started on constructing the original St Paul's Cathedral in 1087 during the last year of the reign of William the Conqueror, and its steeple, which dominated the London skyline, was one of the tallest steeples in Europe. The cathedral stood for six centuries until it was destroyed during the Great Fire of London in 1666.

Henry VIII would have been familiar with the great cathedral of St Paul's and it was there on 3 October 1518 that he and French ambassadors took an oath relating to the Treaty of London. When Pope Leo X started proceedings to bring peace among Catholic European powers, encouraging them to devote their energies to confronting the Ottoman Empire,

The Treaty of London continued to help forge Anglo-French relations 500 years later when former Secretary of State for Digital, Culture, Media and Sport, the Right Honourable Matt Hancock MP, presented the Treaty of London to French Cultural Minister Françoise Nyssen at a UK-France Summit held on 18 January 2018. (Courtesy of the Department of Digital, Culture, Media and Sport)

prevent future wars and encourage diplomacy when negotiating trade deals. It was a non-aggression pact, but also committed these nations to defend each other if attacked. Wolsey negotiated this, for 'the King himself scarcely knows in what state matters are'. The treaty stated:

(1.) Peace is declared between the confederated Kings. (2.) Mutual aid in case of invasion is guaranteed by land, (3.) and by sea. (4.) Power of passing through the confederates' territory guaranteed. (5.) No confederate to allow his subjects to serve any one confederate against any other. (6.) No confederate to afford protection to the vassal of any other without consent of that other. (7.) No confederate to do or allow to be done anything to the injury of any other, or of his heirs or successors or of his or their possession. (8.) No confederate to receive any rebels against another. (9.) The undermentioned to be comprehended: Spain, Scotland, Denmark, Hungary and Portugal, Margaret Archduchess of Austria, Ferdinand brother of the King of Spain, Venice, the Duke of Urbino, the Dukes of Cleves and Juliers the house of the Medici, the Florentines, the Duke of Ferrara, the Hanseatic League, the Swiss. On the part of France: the Venetians, Florentines, . . . the Dukes of Savoy, . . . Gueldres, the Marquises of Mantua, Mont[ferrat,] . . . and Saluzzo. (10.) The Pope to accept the league, and name his confederates within four months after notice given. (11.) 2 Oct. 1518.[47]

A plan of the layout of the medieval St Paul's Cathedral is marked out on the ground outside the south-western corner of the building today. It was in the original cathedral that Henry VIII and French ambassadors took an oath ratifying the Treaty of London in 1518. Some four years later, on 7 June 1522, Henry VIII and Charles V heard Mass at the cathedral. (Author's Collection)

in March 1517, Cardinal Wolsey used this papal enterprise as an opportunity to launch his own initiative. This was called the Treaty of London, also known as the Treaty of Universal and Perpetual Peace. His aim was to settle past disputes among European nations, to

The English and French nations would initiate this treaty before it was ratified by the Pope

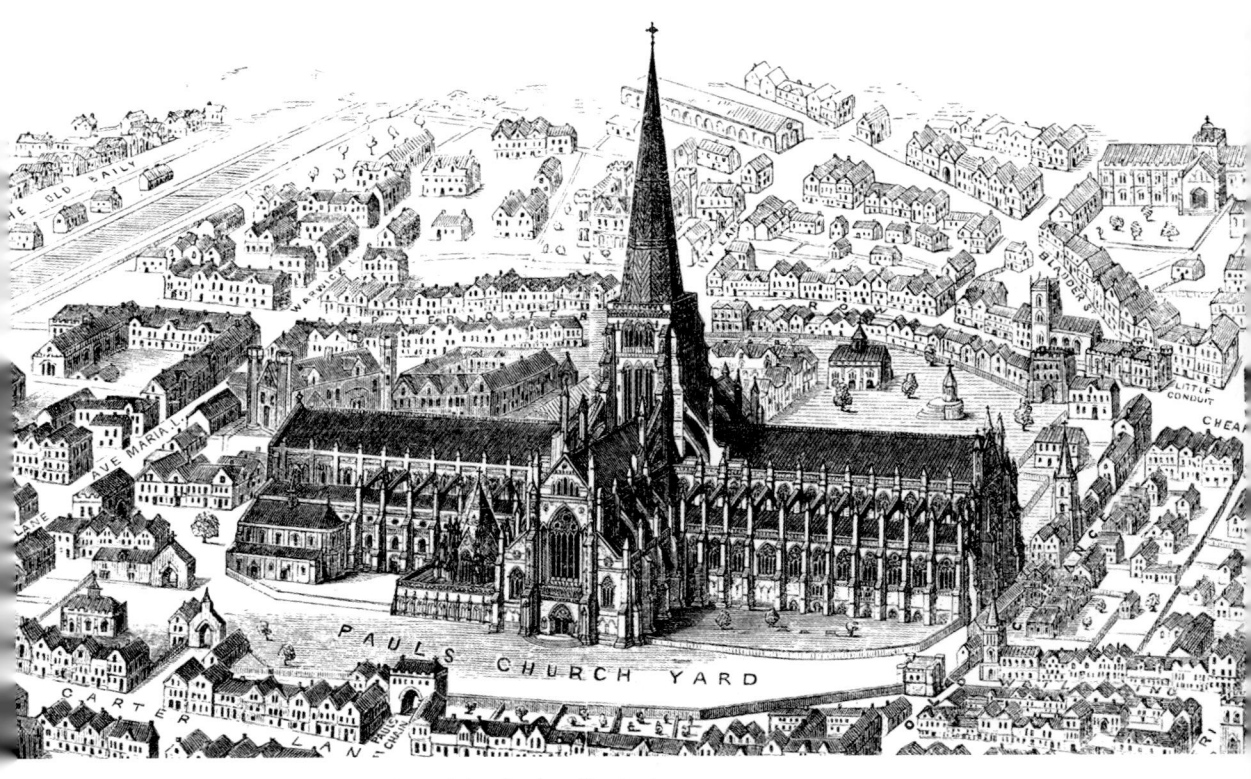

A drawing of the old St Paul's Cathedral. (Author's Collection)

and other nations. In addition to this treaty, England and France would unify their countries with the betrothal of the young Princess Mary, aged 2, to Francis, the French Dauphin, Tournai would be conceded to the French and the two kings would commit to meet in person the following year.

At the High Altar of St Paul's Cathedral, Henry VIII, together with foreign ambassadors, signed the treaty and swore to uphold its terms. The Venetian diplomat Sebastian Giustinian reported to the Doge the details of the ceremony that took place in the cathedral:

> On the 3rd the general peace was proclaimed at St. Paul's. That day the King, the two legates, all the ambassadors, the Lords and Bishops were present at a solemn mass, celebrated by Wolsey with unusual splendour. After a grave oration by Pace, the King, the Cardinal and the French ambassadors proceeded to the high altar, where the peace was read and sworn to, in a tone audible only to the parties concerned.[48]

Cardinal Wolsey celebrated his achievement of securing the Treaty of London with a banquet at his London home, York Place. Henry and his sister, Mary, danced before the guests in disguise.

The treaty succeeded in enhancing Henry VIII's reputation on the international stage and promoting England as a major power. Though Henry did meet Francis I on the Field of the Cloth of Gold in 1520, the treaty failed to bring permanent peace in Europe for England and Spain would unite against France within the next decade.

23

Portrait of King Henry VIII, c. 1520

A Portrait for Power

This image of Henry VIII was painted by an unknown Anglo-Dutch artist in 1520, the year that he met Emperor Charles V in Dover and King Francis I on the Field of the Cloth of Gold near English-occupied Calais in France.

On learning that the French king was bearded, Henry decided to grow his own beard. The Venetian ambassador, Sebastian Giustinian, described Henry during the previous year in 1519 as 'twenty-nine years old, and much handsomer than any sovereign in Christendom, a good deal handsomer than the King of France; very fair, and well proportioned. On hearing that Francis I. wore a beard, Henry allowed his own to grow. His beard was of a bright gold colour.'[49]

Katherine was not happy that Henry grew his beard in homage to the French king and was concerned that England was becoming too closely associated with France, whose relations with Spain in the past had been acrimonious. The Pope, Emperor Charles V of the Holy Roman Empire and King of Spain and King Francis I of France were highly regarded, strong leaders who held the balance of power in Europe. Henry VIII was in the process of establishing himself and England as a major power. However, during that period, England was not held in the same esteem as other nations. It is probable that the painting aimed to show the youthful Henry to be strong, serious and contemplative, a man who was politically astute with sufficient gravitas to deal with other European leaders. Henry was well educated, cultured and a well-rounded individual, as Giustinian testified:

> He is very accomplished, a good musician; composes well; is a most capital horseman; a fine jouster; speaks French, Latin and Spanish; hears three masses a day when he hunts, and sometimes five on other days. Attends the daily office in the Queen's chamber, consisting of vespers and compline. He is very fond indeed of hunting, and never takes this diversion without tiring eight or ten horses, which are stationed beforehand along the line of country he means to take. Before he gets home they are all exhausted. He is extremely fond of tennis, at which game it is the prettiest thing in the world to see him play, his fair skin glowing through a shirt of the finest texture.'[50]

The portrait also portrays a youthful, dashing, physically attractive monarch in the prime of his life. During this period, Henry proved that he could conceive a son, albeit not with his current wife. Katherine's final pregnancy in 1518 had resulted in the birth of a stillborn daughter on 9 November 1518. Henry embarked upon an affair with Elizabeth Blount, the queen's maid of honour, resulting in the birth of an illegitimate son, Henry Fitzroy, in June 1519.

PORTRAIT OF KING HENRY VIII, C. 1520

Henry VIII, painted *c.* 1520. (Alamy)

24

Leeds Castle

Henry VIII's Visit to Leeds Castle

Henry VIII and Katherine stayed at Leeds Castle for one night on 22 May 1520 on their journey from Greenwich Palace to Dover. They were heading for France to meet King Francis I of France on the Field of the Cloth of Gold during the following month. The king and queen were accompanied by an entourage of 5,000 courtiers and attendants as they arrived at Leeds Castle. As they continued their journey towards the coast, the royal party took venison and dairy butter from the Leeds estate to be consumed in France.

Leeds Castle had belonged to royalty since King Edward I bought it in 1278. Built on two connected islands near Maidstone, Kent, Henry VIII took an interest in this castle during his reign. Between the years 1517 and 1523, he transformed the fortress into a royal palace, ordering the refurbishment of Queen Katherine's apartments on the upper floor of the Gloriette Tower. Bay windows were also installed and Henry commissioned the construction of the Maiden's Tower, to accommodate the queen's ladies-in-waiting, and the 75ft-long banqueting hall with a carved oak ceiling.

An aerial view of Leeds Castle. One part of the castle, the Gloriette (on the far left in this image), was built for Eleanor of Castile in the late thirteenth century and is connected to the main castle by a bridge. The Banqueting Hall where Henry VIII ate on 22 May 1520, is on the ground floor of the Gloriette. (Mykhailo Brodskyi/Shutterstock)

During 1532, after returning from France, Henry VIII and Anne Boleyn stayed at Leeds Castle on their journey to London. In early October 1544, Henry was reunited with Katherine Parr at Leeds Castle after his return from the Boulogne campaign. The castle remained in Henry's ownership throughout his reign, but after his death, Edward VI gave the estate to Anthony St Leger as a reward for supressing the rebellion in Ireland.

The Gloriette at Leeds Castle. (Author's Collection)

25

Dover Castle

Henry VIII and Emperor Charles V Meet at Dover Castle

The Great Tower within Dover Castle, originally built during the 1180s by Henry II, was used as an occasional royal residence and a place to welcome distinguished guests. Henry VIII received Emperor Charles V on 26 May 1520 at Dover Castle. After spending the night at Leeds Castle, Henry and Katherine headed for Canterbury, where they intended to celebrate Pentecost at the cathedral before continuing their journey to Dover and proceeding to France to meet Francis I. When news was received that the emperor had made an unscheduled stop off at Dover while sailing to Flanders, Henry dashed from Canterbury to Dover to meet him.

The emperor, who had sailed from Barcelona, Spain, arrived at Hythe, approximately 14 miles west of Dover, at about noon on 26 May 1520. Here contact was established with six English ships, commanded by Vice Admiral Sir William Fitzwilliam. The flotilla proceeded during the early evening to the harbour of Dover, where Cardinal Wolsey received Emperor Charles V and his entourage. The emperor and Cardinal Wolsey rode together in a torchlight procession from the harbour, through the town to Dover Castle where they were lodged. Following centuries of hostility, the people of England regarded France with disdain, so the inhabitants of Dover were pleased to welcome Emperor Charles V, who was also the Spanish king and whose country had similarly endured poor relations with the French. Edward Hall recorded the rapturous reception the emperor received from the locals: 'Then when the Emperor thus had taken land, the reverent father lord Cardinal was as conduit to the same noble Emperor from the shore of Dover unto the castle there: then were all persons cheered the best that there in the town might be.'[51]

Henry VIII had arrived at Canterbury from Leeds Castle that same evening and on hearing that the Emperor had landed at Dover, immediately rode through the night to meet him. The King met the Emperor on the stairs leading into the Great Tower at Dover Castle during the early hours of the morning. Edward Hall wrote:

> The Emperor being thus in the castle of Dover. With haste tidings came to the King, where as he was at Canterbury, who hasted him towards the noble Emperor. And so came riding early in the morning to the castle of Dover, within which castle, the King alighted. The Emperor hearing the King to be come, came out of his chamber to meet with the King, and so meet with him on the stairs or he could come up, where each embraced right lovingly; then the King brought the Emperor to his chamber, where as their communing was of gladness.[52]

It is surprising that such a powerful man as Emperor Charles V should have made an extraordinary effort to visit King Henry VIII, who was regarded as the junior, less powerful monarch. Protocol dictated that if a meeting was to take place, then Henry would have been expected to have met the superior leader in his own country. However, Henry VIII was a lot older than Charles V and had reigned for eleven years which made him more experienced. The fact that Henry was married to Katherine, his aunt, together with the opportunity to forge closer ties with England, might have persuaded Charles to make a brief stop in England, after sailing such a long distance from the Mediterranean on his journey to Flanders. Also, Charles was aware of Henry's impending meeting with King Francis I in France and did not want to be excluded from diplomatic decisions agreed prior to that meeting. Henry and the emperor stayed one night at Dover Castle.

During the following morning, they rode to Canterbury to spend the next four days with Katherine, who was lodging at Archbishop Warham's Palace. Despite pledging a marriage between Princess Mary with the French Dauphin two years previously in London, Henry agreed to the betrothal of Princess Mary to Charles V. Henry probably changed his mind because the 20-year-old Charles V had reigned as King of Spain since 1516 and in 1519 he was elected Emperor of the Holy Roman Empire, which made him ruler of Germany, the Netherlands, Hapsburg territories and Italy. The emperor was an influential, affluent, powerful man, who controlled most of Europe and Henry may have considered it politically and economically beneficial to betroth Princess Mary to Charles V instead of the French Dauphin. Despite the signing of the Treaty of London in 1518, which promoted peace, Francis I of France was concerned that Henry would engage independently with the emperor. He was also uneasy because the emperor was the nephew of Katherine of Aragon, which bonded England more closely to Spain and the Holy Roman Empire.

On 31 May 1520, the emperor sailed from Sandwich for Flanders, while Henry returned to Dover to embark on the diplomatic visit to France to meet Francis I. Considering that Henry was about to renege on the betrothal of his daughter to the French Dauphin, the costly visit to cement peaceful relations between the

Panoramic aerial view of Dover Castle. (Courtesy of Chensiyuan)

two nations became a futile farce prior to setting sail for France. Before the emperor departed for Flanders, Henry had agreed to meet him again on 4 July 1520, near Gravelines, close to Calais after he had met Francis. The emperor and Henry agreed the following at Gravelines, which would undermine England's relations with France:

> In consequence of the new position of Charles as Emperor elect, and the meeting of the two sovereigns, it has been resolved that there shall be this renewal of their treaties, which is to take the place of all others. 1. All former treaties renewed, especially that of 1516, in which prince Ferdinand is to be included. The same to extend not only to the actual possessions of the King of England and to those which were then due to him, but to those which may accrue to him hereafter. 2. Both Powers to have the same enemies and the same friends. Offence or injury to the one to be repelled by the other as done to himself. 3. In case of invasion, neither party to desist until the aggrieved has recovered his rights. 4. If a captain or lieutenant of another state employed by the one do injury to the other contrahent, the one who employs him shall make satisfaction on demand within a month's time. 5. Neither party to enter into treaty with any prince without the consent of the other; and if any treaties exist or hereafter be made contrary to the effect of this, they shall be invalid without the consent of both. 6. Intercourse between the two states to be in conformity with the arrangements made on the 11th April.[53]

The Great Tower was used as residence for the monarch when passing through Dover. It was also used to host foreign dignitaries on state visits to England. (Shutterstock)

26

The Field of the Cloth of Gold, *1520*

Henry VIII Meets Francis I in the Val d'Or

Conscious that the alliance between the Holy Roman Empire and England was becoming stronger, King Francis I was keen to foster closer ties between England and France in order to discourage this alliance, which could potentially have an adverse impact upon French interests and tip the balance of European power negatively against France. Henry was also eager to meet Francis in person. Sir Richard Wingfield was instructed to convey to the French sovereign Henry's overall motivation to establish harmonious relations and 'make such impression of entire love in their hearts that the same shall be always permanent, and never be dissolved'. Henry VIII and Francis I met in the valley called the Val d'Or (translated as golden vale) and this painting depicts the various moments of that meeting on the Field of the Cloth of Gold.

The painting entitled *The Field of the Cloth of Gold* depicts various aspects of the political summit, which lasted approximately three weeks. Henry and Katherine stayed in the town of Guisnes, south of Calais, which is pictured in the upper left corner of the painting. Francis and his retinue were based at Ardres. The painting shows Henry bejewelled and riding majestically to meet Francis I. Edward Hall described his appearance on that day: 'His grace was apparelled in a garment of cloth and silver of Damaske, ribbed with Cloth of Gold, so thick as might be, the garment was large, and plated very thick, and canteled of very good entail, of such shape and making, that it was marvellous to behold.'[54]

Cardinal Wolsey and Sir Thomas Wriothesley, Garter King of Arms are seen riding alongside the king as Thomas Grey, Marquess of Dorset carries the Sword of State further ahead. Katherine is believed to be pictured dining in the tent on the far right and being transferred in a litter behind that tent.

Henry was accompanied by his entire court and in order to accommodate them constructed a large temporary palace formed of tents, pavilions and expensive furnishings, including sumptuous tapestries. The site of this marvel derived its subsequent name 'The Field of the Cloth of Gold' from the materials used to build these structures. It was a demonstration of political strength, wealth and opulence, and Henry's aim was to promote England as a powerful nation and augment his stature on the international stage.

The towns of Calais and Ardres are seen in the distance. In the centre foreground on the right is a palace which was constructed upon a brick foundation, with glass windows, but canvas walls and roof supported by a timber framework gave the false impression that the entire building was solid. The interior was furnished and expensive Arras cloth of gold and silk hung in each chamber within the palace. Two red and white Tudor roses adorn the entrance to this palace. The building was much larger than depicted in this painting and Henry sent carpenters and builders, along with materials, to France to build what was a dubbed a 'palace of illusion'. Gioan Joachino, a Venetian diplomat at the French court, wrote:

> This palace has a round tower at each corner, and a lofty portal, wide and magnificent,

The Field of the Cloth of Gold was painted by several unknown British artists, *c.* 1545. It is displayed in the Wolsey Room at Hampton Court Palace. (Google Art Project/Royal Collection)

in the direction of Ardres, placed in the centre of the façade between two handsome round towers, like a fortress, as high as the palace; they are built entirely of bricks, with loopholes (*finestrate*) and battlements defended by statues of armed men, in the act of discharging stones from the '*scapetti*', and iron balls from the cannons and culverins. At a distance of some twelve paces from these two towers are two beautiful painted fountains representing images of Bacchus, with very large and handsome basins, into which wine is to flow constantly, in abundance.[55]

Red and white wine flowed from the two fountains situated in the temporary palace for everyone to freely consume, which resulted in unruly behaviour as individuals who drank in excess are pictured either vomiting or brawling close to these fountains.

The initial meeting of Henry VIII and Francis I is depicted inside the golden tent in the rear. The interior of the tent is decorated with blue velvet, embroidered with French fleurs-de-lys, which indicates that it is a French tent. Hall recorded that the meeting of the two sovereigns took place outside in a valley, a neutral place. It was a tense moment before the meeting because both sides were on alert and fearful that they would be attacked. Henry was accompanied by his bodyguard comprising sixty archers on horseback armed with longbows and arrows, but their concerns were unfounded. Edward Hall described the meeting of the two sovereigns:

> Then up blew the trumpets, clarions, and all other minstrels on both sides, and the Kings descended down toward the bottom of the valley of Ardern, in sight of both nations and on horseback met and embraced the two Kings each other: then the two Kings alighted, and after embraced with being and courteous manner each to other, with sweet and goodly words of greeting: and after few

Thomas Grey, Marquess of Dorset, carries the Sword of State as he leads Henry VIII, Cardinal Wolsey and Sir Thomas Wriothesley, Garter King of Arms, into Guisnes. (Google Art Project/Royal Collection)

The red and white wine that flowed from the two fountains situated outside the palace was free for everyone to consume. As a consequence, it caused raucous, anti-social behaviour as those individuals who indulged to excess became drunk, as depicted in the painting, and engaged in drunken brawls or vomiting. (Google Art Project/Royal Collection)

words, these two noble Kings went together into the rich tent of clothe of gold, that there was set on the ground for such purpose, thus arm in arm went the French King Francis the first of France, and Henry the Eighth King of England and of France.[56]

The Venetian diplomat Gioan Joachino also described the initial meeting between Henry VIII and Francis I:

On the opposite hill the English company was ranged in like order, and had arrived first on the ground, on reaching which the French music ceased. After a short pause the English instruments struck up, and the French responded. When they had been silent for a few moments, the two Kings, who were opposite to each other, moved forward on horseback, each accompanied by two mounted attendants. With the English King were Cardinal Wolsey and the Constable [Thomas Grey, Marquis of Dorset]. With the King of France, the Admiral and the Constable. Both the Constables bore the swords of state aloft unsheathed. As the

A replica of one of the wine fountains used at the Field of the Cloth of Gold is on display within Base Court at Hampton Court Palace. The Great Hall can be seen left in the image. (Author's Collection)

space had been well divided, the two Kings arrived simultaneously in the centre of the valley, where a spear had been planted, distant some 100 paces from the tent. Before arriving at the spot, when at a distance of 30 paces from their respective companies, which had remained behind at the barriers, the two Kings at one and the same time uncovered, saluting each other bareheaded, and then, hastening forward, they embraced thrice on horseback, always cap in hand; after which they both dismounted in such haste that it could scarcely be distinguished which was the first, but the King of England was the first.

Accompanied each by two running footmen (*staffieri*), they then again embraced so lovingly, that but few on our side could avoid shedding tears of joy or gladness. Such were the embraces that I know not whether closer could be imagined, and they were upwards of twenty in number. They then walked slowly towards the tent, the King of England placing the King of France on his right hand, and with their heads bare they remained a good while under so scorching a sun, that it could not have been hotter in St. Peter's at Home. Their Majesties were accompanied into the tent by the Cardinal and the Admiral, the two Constables remaining outside walking up and down and the running footmen of the two Kings and of their four attendants, being mounted on horseback and a long way off, rode to and fro, first in the direction of the English company and then of ours, but kept their ranks.[57]

The initial meeting between the two sovereigns, which lasted for 2 hours, was friendly and cordial, as was confirmed by Gioan Joachino who saw them leave the tent:

Whilst outside the tent, the two Kings embraced each other repeatedly, as if they had then met for the first time, addressing each other in such language as to leave it doubtful whether they were more brothers than friends, or friends rather than brothers. The one said to the ministers and noblemen of the other, 'there is now no farther need of trouble for my brother and I will see to our own interests'. And then, when the Cardinal being already on horseback said, 'Sire, it is too late, most especially as the King *your* brother is the farthest off from his lodging; may it please your Majesty to take to horse': the King of England replied, with a hearty laugh, 'You may

THE FIELD OF THE CLOTH OF GOLD, 1520

Henry VIII meets Francis I in the golden tent at the Field of the Cloth of Gold. (Google Art Project/Royal Collection)

In the top right-hand corner of the painting can be seen a tiltyard where jousts and combat on foot tournaments took place during the conference. The tree of honour stands on the corner of the tiltyard which was an imitation tree which displayed the heraldic shields of the noble participants. The two kings and their queens are seen watching at the side of the tiltyard. This tiltyard was converted into a chapel on 23 June 1520 where Cardinal Wolsey conducted Mass. (Google Art Project/Royal Collection)

go yourself, but I choose to remain with the King my brother'; and again did they embrace. At length, after a great struggle, they both mounted on horseback, taking leave first in the act of mounting, and again when mounted. But it would be long to repeat the loving words uttered by the King of England to the French nobility, to whom he said that he would devote his money, realm, and person to the service of the King his brother.[58]

The tiltyard where jousting and combat on foot tournaments took place during the conference is pictured in the top right-hand corner, the two kings and their queens observing the tournament from the side. The tree of honour stands on the corner of the tiltyard and it was an imitation tree on which the shields of participating knights were displayed. Henry VIII and Francis I took part in the jousting tournament. Soardino, Mantuan Ambassador at the French court, wrote to the Marquis of Mantua:

> Few spears were shivered, and no notable strokes were made, save in one encounter, when the King of England's spear was splintered, but his hand received no injury. The lists were without counter-lists, so that the horses often swerved, and strokes were made but rarely. The tilting commenced at 4 or 5 pm, and lasted until after 7 pm.[59]

On 23 June, the tiltyard was utilised as a chapel where Cardinal Wolsey, aided by five other cardinals, performed Mass attended by the two kings. A firework in the shape of a salamander was fired into the sky during Mass and it is pictured in the upper left corner of the painting. It was reported that:

> A great artificial salamander or dragon, four fathoms long, and full of fire, appeared in the air, from Ardre. Many were frightened, thinking it a comet, or some monster, as they could see nothing that it was attached. It passed right over the chapel at Guisnes, as fast as a footman can go, and as high as a bolt shot from a cross-bow.[60]

This major diplomatic spectacle proved to be an expensive exercise that stretched England's exchequer costing Henry one-seventh of his annual income.[61] Intending to be a political convention to reinforce positive relations between England and France, this three-week conference transformed into an extravagant party where both monarchs postured in an attempt to impress each other with expensive gifts, lavish banquets and jousting tournaments. Instead of forming a bond, they built tension when Henry challenged Francis to a wrestling match and was humiliated when he lost.

The conference, which ended on 24 June, proved to be a futile waste of money and time. French ships were being prepared to sail prior to Henry leaving England, and when Henry learnt of this mobilisation of French sea power, he refused to meet Francis until the French king guaranteed that no French ship would leave port until Henry had returned home.

It was destined to fail because Henry met the emperor before the meeting at Dover Castle and after the meeting on the Field of the Cloth of Gold at Gravelines on 25 June, in less extravagant, but sincere circumstances; and Francis began the fortification of Ardres. Henry had already decided that England would form an alliance with the Holy Roman Empire, because he had agreed to betroth Mary to Charles V when she came of age.

Peace would not last because hostilities between France and the English–Holy Roman Empire alliance would resume two years later in 1522. Venetian diplomat Antonio Giustinian summarised the relationship between the European monarchs, Henry VIII, Francis I and Charles V: 'These sovereigns are not at peace, they adapt themselves to circumstances, but hate each other cordially.'[62]

27
Henry VIII's Tonlet Armour, 1520

Armour for the Field of the Cloth of Gold

In early 1520 a suit of armour was being prepared for Henry to compete in foot combat as part of his meeting with King Francis I at the Field of the Cloth of Gold. However, in March different specifications for the event were received and the armour under construction was abandoned, unfinished and undecorated. The articles for this combat specified that the armour had to be similar to that worn by Francis I as Henry was meant to be competing on the same team, to feature 'a tonnelett and bacinet'. A tonlet was a skirt and a bacinet was a large helmet and this new suit of armour, known as Henry VIII's Tonlet Armour, is displayed at the Royal Armouries, Leeds.

The Tonlet Armour, was hastily assembled using newly built parts and those from existing suits of armour in the stores. There are spur slots on the leg harnesses which would have been used when mounting a horse. This would have been superfluous for combat on foot. The rear of the bacinet is marked with the insignia of the Italian Missaglia family, the 'm' and 'y' beneath a crown, together with an 'm' positioned under a split cross and was made in Milan specifically for this type of tournament. Some of engravings on the tonlet were left incomplete, which suggests that the armourers were unable to finish the inscriptions before the deadline.

Henry wore this Tonlet Armour during the last days of the Field of the Cloth of Gold tournaments on 22 and 23 June when fighting on foot took place. It was reported that on these dates 'the combats at the barriers were performed on foot, with thrusting and casting lances, and short and two-handed swords.'

The contest involved two opponents wearing suits of armour fighting on foot across a barrier on the tiltyard. They were armed with spears, swords, daggers and axes. Edward Hall wrote about the foot combat that Henry and Francis participated in on 22 June:

> Now was the noble Kings ready to do Battle on foot at the Barriers, the Queens on their stages: then entered bend after bend on foot and pressed to the Barriers, every one in his hand a Puncheon spear, wherewith without any abode feyned and lashed always one at another, two for two as the lotte fell. When the spears were spent, then swords to them were given. Then pressed to the Barriers the two valiant Kings, and other, then was no tarrying but fought with such force that the fire sprang out of their armure. Thus, bend they were all delivered by the two noble Kings and their aides of retain.
>
> Then in came a bend with two hand swords and casting darts to answer that challenge xii. Men well-armed, which pressed to the barriers and mightily threw their spears the one to the other, ready or not ready, none favoured other more than

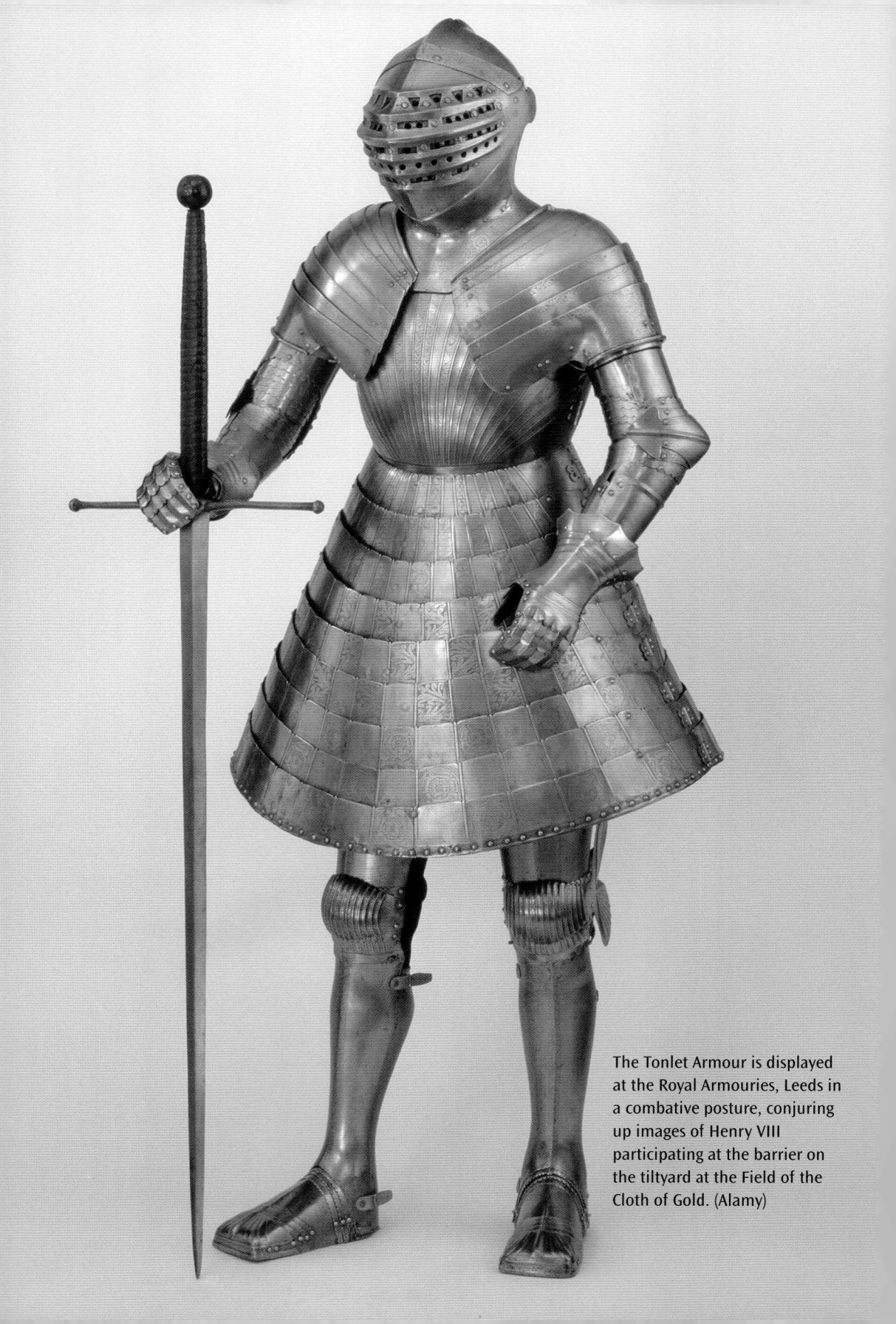

The Tonlet Armour is displayed at the Royal Armouries, Leeds in a combative posture, conjuring up images of Henry VIII participating at the barrier on the tiltyard at the Field of the Cloth of Gold. (Alamy)

two enemies or at utterance, and ever still two for two, till all were delivered concerning the challenge, so this two same Kings safe in body and limes ended the battle for the day at the barriers with great honour.[63]

King Henry, wearing the Tonlet Armour, and King Francis returned to the tiltyard the following day. It was reported that Henry disarmed his opponent with a few strokes on the final day of the tournament. This would have only added to the discord between the two monarchs.

28

Thornbury Castle

Henry VIII Seizes the Duke of Buckingham's Property

Thornbury Castle in Gloucestershire was owned by Edward Stafford, Third Duke of Buckingham. Construction began in 1511 and the castle is a fine example of a Tudor country home. Buckingham served as Lord High Steward at Henry VIII's coronation and bearer of the crown. He was appointed to the Privy Council when Henry ascended the throne and later served as a captain, commanding 500 soldiers during the siege of Thérouanne in 1513 and also became Lord High Constable of England. Buckingham resented Henry because he believed he had a stronger claim to the throne and that he should have been king.

Belonging to the old aristocracy, Buckingham was a direct descendant of Thomas of Woodstock, the youngest son of Edward III. Buckingham's ancestry made him a strong contender to the throne, more so than the Tudors. Henry surrounded himself with councillors and friends at court, who were from humble origins, had no titles or pedigree and were not of aristocratic birth, which gave Buckingham further reason to dislike the king and the culture of his court. Despite being summoned to challenge the king and his friends as an answerer at the tilt in a joust on May Day 1517, he declined because he preferred to run with the king as a challenger than against him. Buckingham was affluent, owning land across the country, and an extremely powerful man. Henry VIII regarded him as a threat throughout his early reign, but kept him close at court. Buckingham made efforts to keep in favour, entertaining Henry at Penshurst Place, his residence in Kent, for several days hunting during August 1519. Richard Pace reported to Wolsey on 11 August that 'this night the King goes to Otford. The Duke of Buckingham makes him excellent cheer. Penshurst.'

Buckingham accompanied the king to France at the Field of the Cloth of Gold in 1520. During the following year, rumours circulated that Buckingham was about to commit treasonous acts against the king, which prompted Henry to authorise Wolsey to investigate. A case was brought against Buckingham and he was arrested on a barge on the River Thames close to Westminster and incarcerated in the Tower of London in April 1521. Buckingham was tried by a commission led by Thomas Howard, Duke of Norfolk on 13 May during which many of his servants testified against him. There was sufficient evidence to condemn Buckingham against his alleged treason. He had sent his chancellor from Thornbury to London 'to buy cloth of gold and silver and silks, each time to the value of 300 marks, intending to give them to the knights and gentlemen of the King's guard to procure adherents'. Some of the gold, silver and silk purchased was brought to Buckingham at Thornbury and it was reported that he 'distributed to various subjects of the King to fulfil his treasonable purpose'. He was accused of assembling his own soldiers who were 'to carry arms and habiliments of war at his pleasure into Wales, with a view of fortifying himself against the King'.[64]

Buckingham was heard threatening the life of the king in a conversation with Charles Knyvett. The court heard that:

He [Buckingham] would have done what his father intended to do to Richard III at Salisbury, when he made suit to come to the King's presence, having upon him secretly a knife, so that when kneeling before the King he would have risen suddenly and stabbed him. In saying this, the Duke put his hand treasonably upon his dagger, and said that if he were so ill treated he would do his best to execute his purpose. This he swore by the blood of our Lord.[65]

Although Henry did not have tangible evidence of Buckingham's treason, he felt insecure and would act swiftly, irrespective of any evidence being available and would execute anyone who challenged his right to the throne. Buckingham's indiscretions sealed his fate and he was found guilty of intending to kill the king and was beheaded on Tower Hill at 11am on 17 May 1521.

Buckingham's execution for treason meant that his land, including Thornbury Castle, was forfeited to the Crown. Construction of the north part of the estate ceased after the duke's death. A detailed description of the property featured in a survey of the duke's lands conducted on behalf of Henry VIII by Thomas Magnus and William Walweyn:

> The lordship of Thornbury, adjoining the King's great lordship of Barkelay [Berkeley], is of the value of 238*l*. 11*s*. 5¾*d*. A wood called Filmour contains 100 acres. The manor or castle stands to the north of the parish church, and has an inner and an outer ward, foursquare. The entrance into the inner ward is on the west. 'The south side is fully finished with curious works and stately lodgings. The said west side and north side be but builded to one chamber height; all these works being of a fair ashlar, and so covered with a false roof of elm, and the same covered with light slate. The east side, containing the hall and other houses of offices, is all of the old building, and of a homely fashion. The outer ward was intended to have been large, with many lodgings, whereof the foundation on the north and west side is taken and brought up nigh to laying on a floor. The windows, jawmes and cewnes are wrought of freestone, the rest of rough stone cast with lime and sand. On the south of the inner ward is a garden, and about (around) the same a goodly gallery, conveying (leading) above and beneath from the principal lodgings both to the chapel and parish church, the outer part of the said gallery being of stone, enbattled, and the inner part of timber, covered with slate.' On the east of the castle is a goodly garden to walk in, enclosed with high walls, enbattled; the 'conveyance' thither is by the gallery and other privy ways. There is also a large orchard, in which are many alleys to walk in openly, and round about the orchard are other alleys 'on a good height', with 'roosting' places, covered with white thorn and hazel. The orchard communicates, by several posterns, with the New Park, which contains about four miles; within it are 700 deer.[66]

Henry owned Thornbury Castle for the remainder of his reign. It was recorded that he spent seven days at the estate during 1535. On the death of Henry's daughter, Mary I, in 1558, the property was returned to the Duke of Buckingham's descendants. Half a century after its construction, Thornbury Castle stands intact and is now a hotel and restaurant.

Thornbury Castle, home of Edward Stafford, Third Duke of Buckingham. (Yulia Bogomolova/Shutterstock)

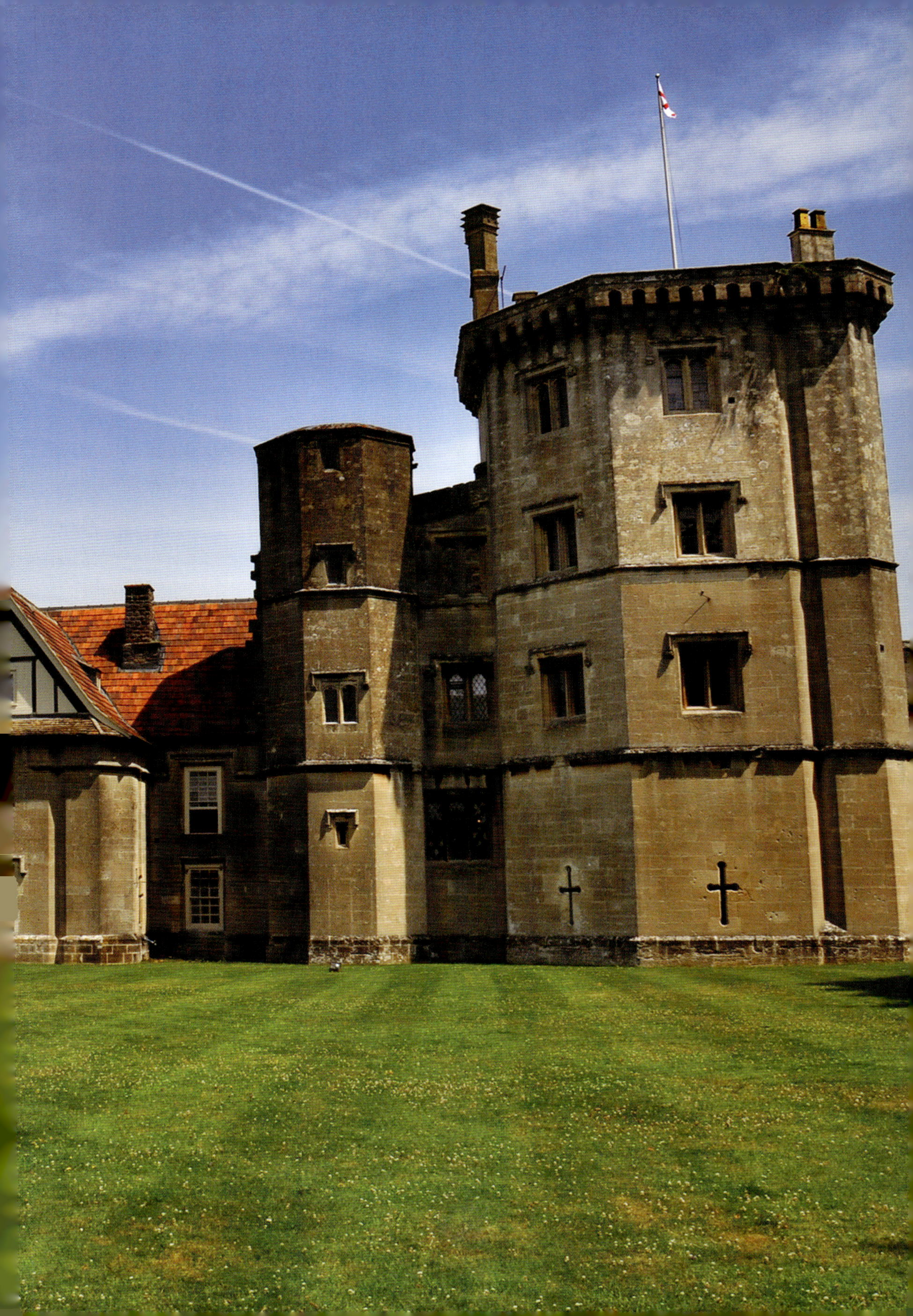

Henry VIII's Portable Lock, Hever Castle

Maintaining the Monarch's Safety

An original and a replica portable lock are on display on the two doors that lead to the dining room at Hever Castle. Henry ruled through terror and fear, disposing of anyone who opposed him, usually resulting in their execution. With no male heir, Henry's dynasty was vulnerable to challenges from noblemen, like Edward Stafford, Duke of Buckingham who thought that they had a legitimate claim to the throne. This original portable lock demonstrates how Henry's reign was constantly under threat from usurpation revealing his own insecurities and concerns about being assassinated. It was skilfully crafted using iron, wrought, carved and gilded by the king's locksmith, Henry Romaynes (alternatively spelt as Romains). He was responsible for fitting locks on all doors in the king's chambers within his royal residences. Romaynes lived and worked close to St Martin-in-the-Fields in London.

Each year Henry would embark on a royal progress during the summer months when he would tour the country and visit the houses of noblemen. Henry used these events to assert his power across the realm and give the people an opporunity of seeing their king. The safety and security of the king while travelling across the county was paramount and at every place he stayed, these portable locks were personally fitted to the door of the king's bedchamber by Romaynes. Sturdy and robust, they would form an adequate barrier against anyone intent on harming or killing the king. Two keyholes are concealed behind a central sliding plate, decorated with the arms of Henry VIII positioned above two Tudor roses. Henry appointed an officer of the king's guard to retain the master key that opened the door that this lock was attached to. A similar lock, which was made for Beddington House in Surrey, is on display at the Victoria & Albert Museum, London. There are other similar locks made during Henry's reign at the entrance to St George's Chapel, Windsor Castle and on display at the Walters Art Museum, Baltimore, USA.

Portable lock belonging to Henry VIII. (Courtesy of Hever Castle; www.hevercastle.co.uk)

Assertio Septem Sacramentorum Adversus Martinum Lutherum *by* Henry VIII

Henry's Challenge to Martin Luther's Ideology and Defence of the Catholic Church

Martin Luther was a German theologian and Augustinian friar who criticised the corrupt practices within the Roman Catholic Church. In 1517, he wrote the '95 Theses' which denounced papal abuses and the sale of indulgences, a practice whereby people who believed that they had personally or that a deceased relative had sinned paid money to be absolved and escape punishment in purgatory. Luther challenged the authority of the Catholic Church through highlighting the fact that the Pope was not mentioned in the Bible. In 1521, encouraged by Cardinal Wolsey, Henry VIII wrote a response to challenge Martin Luther's ideology in a book entitled Assertio Septum Sacramentorum adversus Martinum Lutherum, *translated as* Defence of the Seven Sacraments against Martin Luther.

Luther wrote a series of pamphlets attacking the Catholic Church and these were read across Europe and instigated the reformation known as Lutherism, which would later evolve into a new religion that from 1529 would be referred to as Protestantism. He promoted a faith where an individual would pray directly to God and explore his or her beliefs without the need for priests or the church. Luther's books were being read by scholars at universities in Oxford and Cambridge. In 1521, Pope Leo X excommunicated Luther from the Catholic Church. European monarchs were concerned that this new religion would not only undermine the Church, but also cause derision, discord and division across their lands.

In the title *Assertio Septum Sacramentorum adversus Martinum Lutherum* Henry directly contested Luther's assertion that there were only two sacraments, solemn rites introduced by Jesus Christ to confer grace. Writing this treatise became Henry's primary focus to the extent that he temporarily neglected his passion for hunting. Thomas More read drafts and and consultated and advised the king, but it was Henry's work.

Henry dedicated the book to Pope Leo X, and twenty-seven copies were sent to Rome. Henry signed one book covered with cloth of gold and highly illuminated title page and this was presented to the Pope by John Clerk, the King's Ambassador at Rome. Inside Henry wrote the following dedication, 'Henry, King of the English, sends Leo the Tenth, this work, as witness of his faith and friendship.'

Pope Leo X and the College of Cardinals were very impressed with Henry's eloquent defence of the Catholic Church and his opposition to heresy. On 11 October 1521, Henry's support was rewarded when Pope Leo X, with the unanimous assent of the cardinals, proclaimed him 'Defender of the Faith' and ordered a bull to be sent.

Henry's book was a resounding success, with twenty editions published, but Henry would eventually regret writing the work. He declared in the book that 'We are so much bounden to the See of Rome that we cannot do too much honour to it.' The book would prove to be an embarrassment for Henry when England broke away from the Catholic Church in Rome in the following decade and he would distance himself as its author by claiming that he was coerced into writing it by bishops. In particular, Henry's view of the sanctity of marriage conveyed in the book would place him in an awkward position when he sought legitimate reasons to end his marriage with Katherine, his first wife. The following paragraph written by Henry VIII in 1521 would prove a complete contradiction in 1530:

> When Christ, God and man, conversing amongst men, not only honoured marriage with his own presence, but also adorned it with his first miracle, has he had not taught, that marriage is to be honoured? ... I see the miracle that he wrought, admonishes us that insipid water of carnal concupiscence, by the secret grace of God, is changed to wine of the best taste. But why search we so many proofs in so clear a thing? especially, when that only text is sufficient for all, where Christ says, 'Whom God has joined together, let no man put asunder.' O the admirable word that was made flesh! Who thinks it not to have been abundantly sufficient, that God has joined the first of mankind, and that the bounty of so great a God is to be admired by all men? But now we are taught from the truth itself, that those who are lawfully married, are not rashly joined together; but by the ceremonies of men, but by the invisible co-operation of God himself: and therefore, it is forbidden, that any should spate those whom God has joined together.[67]

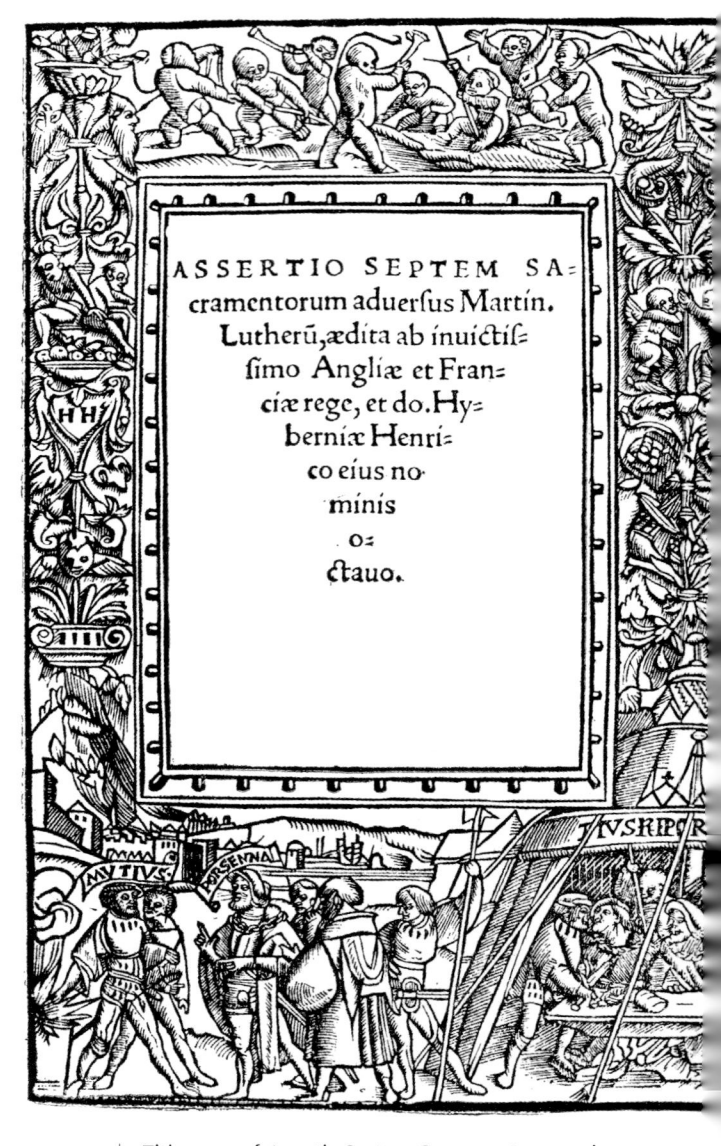

Title page of *Assertio Septum Sacramentorum adversus Martinum Lutherum* written by Henry VIII. (Alamy)

31

King Henry VIII Gatehouse, Windsor Castle

A Palace to Impress

Henry VIII ordered the construction of the Lower Ward Gate in 1511. Situated at the entrance to Windsor Castle, it bears the arms of Henry VIII and the pomegranate, the emblem of Queen Katherine of Aragon. It is now known as the Henry VIII Gatehouse. Over the centuries Windsor Castle has been used by sovereigns to entertain dignitaries. Henry VIII brought Holy Roman Emperor Charles V to the splendour and magnificence of the castle to discuss and agree the Treaty of Alliance in 1522. It is most probable that both monarchs passed through this gate.

During 1522 diplomatic relations between the Holy Roman Empire and France deteriorated. Henry authorised Wolsey to mediate between the rival powers in an initiative to preserve the Treaty of London, but his efforts failed. England held the balance of power in Europe and as the situation between France and the Holy Roman Empire worsened, Henry decided to align the interests of England with the Holy Roman Empire and join forces against France. King Francis I had deployed French troops around English-occupied Calais, imprisoned English merchants in France and refused to pay Henry a pension, all factors that influenced the king's decision. Henry also took into consideration that Charles V governed Spain, Hapsburg territories, the Netherlands and most of Italy, and regarded him as a powerful ally, as well as being the nephew of his wife, Katherine. Towards the end of May Henry VIII declared war upon France.

In order to forge a new alliance a state visit was arranged for Charles V to meet Henry during his journey from Flanders to Spain. Charles arrived at Dover on 26 May 1522 and after being entertained with banquets, jousts and pageants in London, Henry received the emperor at Windsor Castle, where they discussed the details of the new Anglo-Imperial alliance against France. Martin De Salinas, Ambassador of the Archduke and Infante Ferdinand at the Imperial Court, reported:

> The Emperor has left London, and has been going from one country seat of the King of England to another, on his way to Windsor, which 'is the capital of the Order of the Garter'. At Windsor all his time has been occupied in hunting and in despatching business concerning the French war. . . . God alone knows how long the Emperor will stay in England. But as the country is cheap, the living easy, and the King gives many feasts to the Emperor, he [Salinas] and his servants spend little money.[68]

The emperor's entourage was too large and could not be accommodated in its entirety within Windsor Castle, so some of his courtiers were sent back to London.

It was in the upper chambers at Windsor Castle that Henry and Charles agreed the terms for the Treaty of Alliance, which was signed on 16 June 1522. Henry renounced his friendship with King Francis I and reversed previous agreements

The King Henry VIII Gatehouse which was built to gain access to the Lower Ward at Windsor Castle. The construction of Windsor Castle began during the reign of William the Conqueror in 1080. (Daniela Migliorisi/Shutterstock)

KING HENRY VIII GATEHOUSE, WINDSOR CASTLE

between England and France. They vowed to support each other in defending their dominions which they possessed and lands which were retaken by France, for which they planned to regain. One of the clauses stated that 'if one of the contracting princes conquers towns, castles, from the King of France which by right belong to the other contracting party, such towns, castles, are to be restored to their rightful proprietor within one month after their conquest'.[69] They also pledged military support if either country was attacked by another state. Regarding themselves as defenders of the Catholic Church, they offered Pope Adrian VI the opportunity of being the figurehead of their alliance, the treaty stating that 'he [Pope Adrian] has always been honoured by the contracting princes and is now more revered by them than ever. The contracting parties, therefore, bind themselves to ask the Pope, through their ambassadors, to become the head of their league.'[70]

On 16 June, Henry hosted a banquet in St George's Hall at Windsor Castle at which a play was performed. Written by William Cornish, it was full of anti-French sentiment. According to Martin De Salinas, 'after supper, however, a French play was performed by young gentlemen. It was a farce, and in it the King of France and his alliances were ridiculed.'[71]

A further secret treaty was signed by the emperor and Henry VIII at Windsor Castle on 19 June 1522. This alliance was cemented with the betrothal of the young Princess Mary to Charles V when she came of age. But four years later the emperor could not wait any longer for Mary to become a woman and therefore broke the terms of the agreement and went on to marry Isabella of Portugal in 1526.

The Round Table, Great Hall, Winchester

The Adaptation of the Round Table

Built in 1290 during the reign of Edward I, the table symbolises King Arthur's Round Table. This round table was redecorated under the orders of Henry VIII in 1522; painted in white and green, it displays the Tudor rose at its centre. Surmounted upon the Tudor rose, the seated and bearded figure of King Arthur resembles Henry's image.

The Great Hall is all that remains of Winchester Castle, which was a favoured residence of Henry VIII's father and the birthplace of his brother, Arthur. The Round Table hangs majestically in the Great Hall. Henry's act of self-indulgence in redecorating the table represents his right to the throne of England and demonstrates his confidence as monarch. He had reigned for thirteen years and repulsed challenges to his crown from the likes of Edmund de la Pole in 1513 and Edward Stafford, Duke of Buckingham in 1521. By incorporating the symbol of the Tudor dynasty upon the Round Table, Henry not only reaffirmed his legitimate right to the throne but connected his reign with the chivalric sovereignty of King Arthur and his

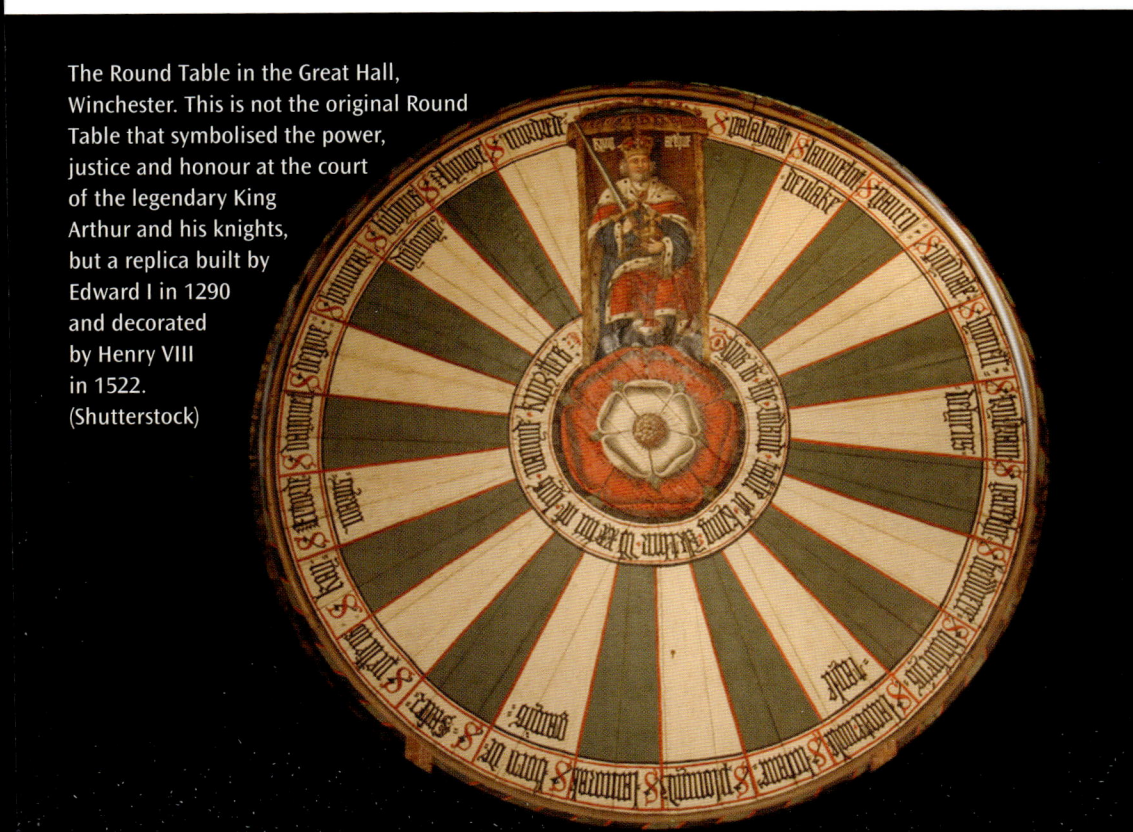

The Round Table in the Great Hall, Winchester. This is not the original Round Table that symbolised the power, justice and honour at the court of the legendary King Arthur and his knights, but a replica built by Edward I in 1290 and decorated by Henry VIII in 1522. (Shutterstock)

knights, along with the values of courage, honour and justice which Henry aspired to. More importantly, Henry wanted to encourage the perception that he was directly linked to Arthur and to the emperors of Ancient Rome. This would have resonated with Emperor Charles V, who was the Holy Roman Emperor, during his second state visit to England on 22 June 1522. On this occasion Henry entertained him at Winchester Castle and would have shown him this Round Table when they dined in the Great Hall. Charles V could not claim that he was directly linked to the Roman emperors, but Henry was willing to make that assertion, although it was false.

After leaving Winchester, Charles V headed to Hampton, now known as Southampton, where he boarded a ship. The fleet immediately implemented one of the terms of the treaty signed at Windsor, which was that 'until a great war with France can be begun, both contracting princes bind themselves to infest the coasts and frontiers of France, and to do her as much harm as they can'.[72]

33

Charles Brandon, Duke of Suffolk and Friend of Henry VIII

Henry's Near Miss With a Lance

Henry VIII and the Duke of Suffolk enjoyed playing sport together and they would frequently joust on the tiltyard. In 1524 Charles Brandon almost killed Henry VIII by accident on the tiltyard at Greenwich.

The Duke of Suffolk's father, Sir William, was standard bearer for Henry VII at Bosworth, where he was killed in 1485. Charles's mother died in childbirth and when his guardian and grandfather passed away in 1491, Henry VII brought the orphaned Charles to court to act as a companion to Prince Arthur. When Arthur married Katherine of Aragon, Brandon remained in London and attended upon Henry. Brandon was seven years older than Henry and would become the prince's closest confidant. Brandon distinguished himself at Tournai during 1513 and Henry rewarded him with the title of Duke of Suffolk. Brandon became the king's brother-in-law when he married Mary Tudor in secret in 1515. Mary had married the older Louis XII, thirty years her senior, as part of a peace treaty with France in 1514. The marriage was a political union and Mary, who was aged 18 at the time, was not physically attracted to the older French king and agreed to the union out of a sense of duty. She was relieved and freed from this marriage when the French monarch died on 1 January 1515. She was reluctant to be forced into another arranged marriage for political purposes and married Brandon in secret as he escorted her back home. Mary was passionately in love with Brandon and was willing to risk her brother's fury for marrying without his permission. Despite Henry's initial reservations, he supported the couple. Brandon was the king's favourite courtier and their friendship would last until Brandon died in 1545.

On 10 March 1524, Brandon nearly killed Henry during a tournament. The king had forgotten to close and secure the visor of his helmet. Brandon was short-sighted and could not see that the king's visor was not closed. As he rode along the tiltyard during the run his lance struck the side of the king's helmet, which knocked it off his head. Had the lance hit the king's face, he would have certainly been killed but fortunately was unharmed. Edward Hall wrote about the accident:

> The x day of Marche the King having a new harness made of his own devise and fashion, such as no armorer before that time had seen, thought to assay the same at the tilt, and appointed a Justes to serve him. On foot were appointed the Lord Marques Dorset and the Earl of Surrey, the King came to the one end of the tilt, and the Duke of Suffolk to the other: then a gentleman said to the Duke, sir the King is come to the tilts end. I see him not said the Duke on my faith, for my head piece taketh from me my sight: with these words God knoweth by what chance, the King had his spear delivered him by the Lord Marques, the visor of his head piece being up and not down nor fastened, so that

Princess Mary Tudor and Charles Brandon, Duke of Suffolk, *c.* 1516. There are a number of versions of this double portrait celebrating the marriage of Mary Tudor to her brother's closest friend. (Courtesy of Woburn Abbey)

his face was clean naked. The gentleman said to the duke, sir the King cometh then the duke set forward and charged his spear, and the King likewise unadvisedly set toward the duke: the people perceiving the kings face bare, cried hold, hold, the duke neither saw nor heard, and whether the King remembered that his visor was up or no few could tell: Alas what sorrow was it to the people when they saw the splinters of the dukes spear strike on the Kings head piece. For of a surity the duke struck the King on the brow right under the defence of the head piece on the very coyffe scull or bassenet piece where unto the barbet for power and defence is charnel, to which coyffe or bassenet never armour taketh head, for it is evermore covered, with the visor, barbet and volant piece, and so that piece is so defended that it forseth of no charge: But when the spear on that place lighted. It was of great jeopardy of death insomuche that the face was bare, for the Dukes spear broke all to shavers, and bare the King's visor or barbet so far back by the countre buffe that all the King's headpiece was full of splinters. The Armorers for this matter were much blamed and so was the lord Marques for the delivering of the spear when his face was open, but the king said that none was to blame but himself, for he intended to have said himself and his sight. The duke incontinently unarmed him and came to the King, shewing him the closeness of his sight and swear that he would never run against the King more. But if the King had been a little hurt, the King's servants would have put the Duke in jeopardy. Then the King called his Armorers and put all his pieces together and then took a spear and ran six courses very well, by the which was great joy and comfort to all his subjects there present.[73]

34

Eltham Ordinances

Court Austerity Measures

Anxious to reduce spending within the royal household, during 1526 Henry VIII and Wolsey produced the Eltham Ordinances. This was an attempt to minimise waste and to reorganise, regulate and reform the court. It was named after the palace where they produced the document.

Approximately a thousand people attended to Henry VIII at his royal palaces. Some servants and even Yeoman of the Guard brought their friends into the court, individuals who had no direct role in the service of the king but enjoyed the comforts of the royal palaces at the King's expense. They may have eaten food and lived in the lodgings that was not meant for them, which was a considerable drain upon the king's finances. The first page of the Eltham Ordinances explained the overall purpose of the document, which was a series of articles dictating budgets and behaviour at court:

> Articles devised by the King's Highness with the advice of his council for the establishment of good order, and reformation of sundry errors and misuses in his most honourable household and chamber; which his grace chargeth his head officers and others to whom it shall appertain, to see duly to be observed, obeyed, and executed, as they will avoid his highness displeasure.[74]

These terms of reference suggest a legacy of negligence in terms of managing royal household budgets and possibly even corruption, and Henry VIII wanted to stop these practices.

The articles within the Eltham Ordinances demonstrate how Henry wanted to control and regulate all aspects of court life including the kitchens, the serving of dinner and supper, the components of the Privy Council, the role of the servants and courtiers and standards of behaviour.

The articles of the Eltham Ordinances also impacted upon the structure of the Yeoman of the Guard, the king's bodyguard. Henry VII installed the Yeoman of the Guard as his personal body guard in 1485 and this continued to protect the monarch throughout Henry VIII's reign. Strong, alert, tall men were recruited into the ranks and would stand outside the royal apartments 24 hours a day. Attired in scarlet livery coats, they would accompany the king on his journeys across the country and abroad. They would remain close to the king at all times in order to protect him. When Henry VIII ascended the throne, he raised the number of the Yeoman of the Guard from 120 to 600 and they accompanied him during the 1513 French campaign and formed part of the garrison of the captured town of Tournai between 1514 and 1519. During the meeting with Francis I at the Field of the Cloth of Gold, 200 Yeoman of the Guard armed with gilt halberds lined a path for the king through the crowds. However, in 1526, the cost-cutting exercise initiated by the King and Wolsey reduced their ranks to 100.

Wolsey used the Eltham Ordinances as a mechanism to maintain his position of influence with the king, who was maturing and able to make his own decisions as he got older. He also used the ordinances to consolidate his own power within the court, eliminating the roles of those within the court who threatened him, were intimate with the king or had too much influence. At the same time, he strengthened his own power. His aim to remove certain courtiers, such as Sir William Compton, Sir Francis Bryan, Sir Nicholas Carew and Thomas and George Boleyn, succeeded when he downsized the size of the Privy Council from twelve to six members.

However, Wolsey's own downfall in 1527 meant that he was unable to fully implement the Eltham Ordinances. The initiative failed to deliver in its bid to stop extravagance and wastage in the court of Henry VIII. In 1539, Cromwell drafted the Greenwich Ordinances which also aimed to administer the royal court more economically and efficiently. Cromwell's measures proved far more effective to the extent that they were used up until to the nineteenth century.

The largest surviving sixteenth-century kitchens are at Hampton Court Palace. Each time Henry VIII visited the palace he would bring an entourage of 800 courtiers. When Henry took ownership of Hampton Court Palace, his visits became more frequent, which meant that the kitchens needed to be expanded. This work was conducted during 1529–30 and the kitchens comprised fifty rooms and in addition three cellars. One kitchen specifically cooked for the household, another was devoted primarily to preparing meals for officers of the household and the king and queen's privy kitchen cooked solely for them. The Eltham Ordinances detailed where food was procured and provided guidance on how the kitchens were managed and kept clean. They reveal that the Officer of the Greencloth was accountable for all aspects of the Royal Household, including supplying the kitchen with good quality food that had been purchased at a fair price. The Eltham Ordinances included measures that prevented pilfering from the kitchens and that those consuming the food received the appropriate portions according to status. It also detailed the responsibilities of the 350-strong workforce employed in the royal kitchens. (Benjamin B/Shutterstock)

35

Hever Castle

The Family Home of Anne Boleyn

Anne spent her childhood years at Hever Castle before being sent abroad. It was there that Henry VIII fell in love with her during 1526, visiting her on numerous occasions. After Anne's death Henry eventually passed Hever Castle on to Anne of Cleves, his fourth wife.

Hever Castle in Kent is renowned as the childhood home of Anne Boleyn, the ill-fated second wife of Henry VIII. The building of Hever Castle began in 1270 and consisted of a walled bailey and gatehouse surrounded by a moat. Geoffrey Bullen, Lord Mayor of London, bought the castle in 1462. His grandson, Thomas Bullen (the name was latter known as Boleyn during Henry's reign), transformed the property when he built a house within the walls. Having grown up at Hever, Anne was sent to the Netherlands, where she became lady-in-waiting to Archduchess Margaret. Her father was an ambassador serving in the court of Emperor Maximilian. In 1514, Anne's father secured a position for her at the French court attending upon Mary Tudor, wife of King Louis XII and sister to Henry VIII.

When Anne's father's four-year tenure as ambassador in France came to an end, Thomas Bullen was appointed Treasurer of the Household in King Henry's court and brought Anne back to England in 1522. The tedious, mundane life in the secluded confines of Hever Castle did not stimulate Anne, who had enjoyed life at the European courts, where she had become a cultivated, cultured, well-mannered young lady. She was appointed lady-in-waiting to Queen Katherine, however, in 1523, her intellect and charm attracted the attentions of various admirers including the poet Thomas Wyatt. Her heart was captivated by Lord Henry Percy, but King Henry VIII, who might have had plans for Anne to marry another nobleman for political purposes, did not approve of this union and expelled Anne from court. To her annoyance she spent her banishment at Hever Castle locked in her bedroom and prevented from communicating with her chosen love before being sent once again to Europe.

While Anne was away, Mary, her elder sister, became the king's mistress, which brought advancement and favours to the family. In 1523 her father was created Knight of the Garter and in 1525 he received the peerage as Viscount Rochford. Her brother George was appointed as a member of the Royal Privy Council. When Anne returned to court in 1525, Henry's interest in Mary had waned and it is believed that he became interested in Anne during 1526. Her father encouraged the situation. His moral compass and sense of ethics were overcome by his own ambitions and he was prepared to use his daughter as a pawn in order to secure and maintain his own position within Henry's court. Further titles came his way and he was elevated to Earl of Wiltshire and Earl of Ormonde.

Henry fell in love with Anne Boleyn during 1526 and he visited her at Hever Castle on numerous occasions. These visits caused logistical problems for the household as they were frequent and mostly unscheduled and spontaneous.

Hever Castle. (Philip Bird LRPS CPAGB/Shutterstock)

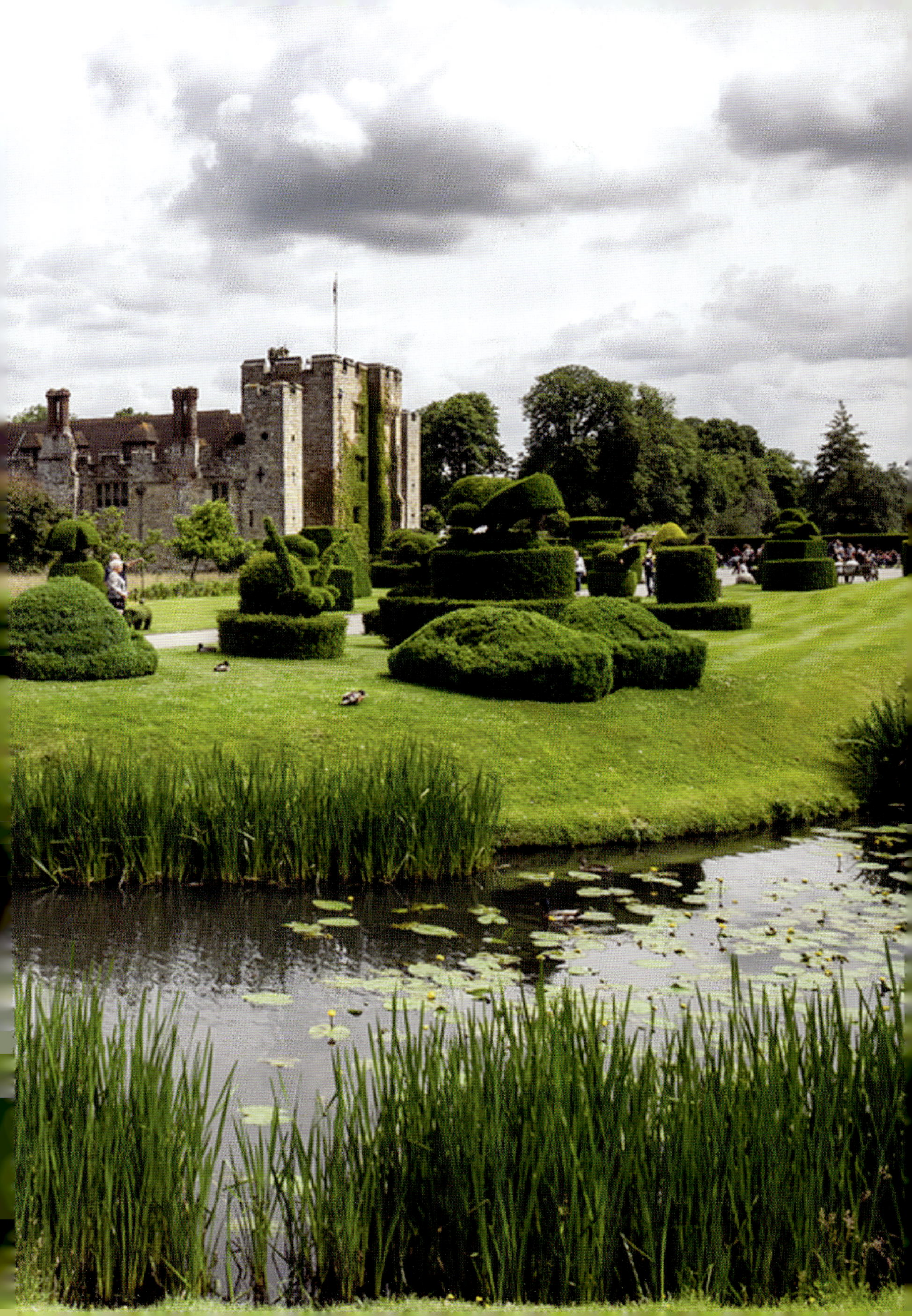

The room occupied by Anne Boleyn as a young girl at Hever Castle. (Courtesy of Hever Castle; www.hevercastle.co.uk)

Located in her bedroom at Hever Castle, this wooden cabinet carries Anne Boleyn's name. (Courtesy of Hever Castle; www.hevercastle.co.uk)

Henry's carnal relations with his wife Katherine had ceased, together with the prospect of her producing a male heir. It is thought that he first proposed marriage to Anne in 1527, when he was still married to Katherine and he made the proposal because Anne refused to become his mistress. She resisted with assertiveness, proclaiming, 'Your wife I cannot be in respect of my own unworthiness and also because you have a Queen already. Your mistress I will not be.' Anne's firm stance would have serious implications for the future of England because it would later incite Henry to divorce Katherine and establish a new religious order for him to facilitate that action, in order to marry Anne Boleyn. In order to satisfy his heart's intentions and sexual desire, Henry revealed his doubts about the validity of his marriage to Katherine during the spring of 1527.

During the summer of 1528, the sweating sickness was rife within the court in London. Early symptoms were cold, violent shivers together with headaches and feelings of fatigue, culminating in hot sweats and delirium. Many sufferers died within hours of the first appearance of symptoms. On 16 June 1528, the court was disbanded and Henry retired to Waltham to avoid infection. Anne and her father, suffering symptoms of this condition, returned to Hever Castle. Henry sent his physician to Hever to tend to them. In a letter to Anne, he wrote:

> There came to me in the night the most afflicting news possible. I have to grieve for

The Long Gallery at Hever Castle measures 100ft and was built above the Great Hall by Anne Boleyn's father in 1506. It was used as a place to exercise inside, to display the family's expensive pieces of art and to host guests – both Henry VIII and Anne Boleyn would have walked along this passage. (Courtesy of Hever Castle; www.hevercastle.co.uk)

three causes: first, to hear of my mistress's sickness, whose health I desire as my own, and would willingly bear the half of yours to cure you. Secondly, because I fear to suffer yet longer that absence which has already given me so much pain. God deliver me from such an importunate rebel! Thirdly, because the physician [Dr Chambers] I trust most is at present absent, when he could do me the greatest pleasure. However, in his absence I send you the second [Dr Butts], praying God he may soon make you well, and I shall love him the better. I beseech you to be governed by his advice, and then I shall hope soon to see you again.[75]

In July 1528, Henry wrote of his longing to be with Anne at Hever: 'As touching your abode at Hever, do therein as best shall like you, for you know best what air doth best with you; but I would it were come thereto, if it pleased God, that nother of us need care for that, for I ensure you I think it long'.[76]

Anne and her father both recovered from the sweating sickness, and she would eventually marry Henry in 1533 when she changed her surname from Bullen to Boleyn. At that time, Henry was a loyal Catholic and believed that he was on the throne and the Tudor dynasty reigned as a result of God's favour. Anne, a Protestant Reformer, possessed heretical books and championed the new religion in France at court;

At the end of the Long Gallery at Hever Castle there is an alcove where Henry VIII sat and wooed Anne Boleyn during their courtship. This alcove is known as the 'Lovers' Window', and Henry would also hold court here and receive local noblemen and magistrates from Kent. Today the alcove contains a mannequin of Anne Boleyn reading one of Henry's love letters. Anne remained at Hever while Henry made efforts to secure permission from Pope Clement VII to divorce Katherine. Henry kept Anne informed of progress through letters. (Author's Collection)

Henry's reconciliation with Anne Boleyn, depicted, in this etching by George Cruickshank, in an alcove similar to the one at Hever Castle. (Library of Congress)

she was not a loyal Catholic, but an evangelist. She realised that these new religious ideas could be used to overcome the Pope's refusal to accept her intended marriage to Henry, and she would influence the king and sway him away from his Catholic faith.

The marriage between the king and Anne had fatal consequences for her and her brother, George, and this is examined later. Henry VIII acquired Hever Castle after the death of Thomas Boleyn in 1539 and he gave it to Anne of Cleves as part of his divorce settlement the following year.

36
Henry VIII's Room

A Bedroom Fit For a King

Whenever Henry VIII toured the country on a royal progress or to visit the homes noblemen, a large burden was placed upon the household to accommodate his large entourage. Thomas Bullen would have wanted to impress his royal guest when he visited Hever Castle. This is the largest bedroom in Hever Castle and although there are no records of where Henry VIII slept during his frequent visits, it is thought likely it was in this room. The ceiling originates from 1462 and the tester *bed, made from carved oak, dates from 1540 and would be the type of bed that Henry would have used. Tester beds consisted of a carved wooden canopy, which was either suspended from the ceiling by cords or, in this case, supported by two posts and a headpiece at the back. The word tester is derived from the Latin word* testa *meaning head. An inventory of the possessions of John Fisher, Bishop of Rochester, on 27 April 1534, compiled in preparation for Henry's visit to Rochester, mentions 'In his own bed chamber: A bedstead with a mattrass, a counterpoint of red cloth lined with canvas. A celer and tester of old red velvet nothing worth.'*

King Henry VIII's bedchamber at Hever Castle. (Shutterstock)

37

Henry VIII's Writing Desk

A Highly Decorated Piece of Furniture

This writing box was produced before Henry initiated divorce proceedings against Katherine in 1527. Boxes like this were recorded in inventories in 1547 after Henry's demise. Its history is uncertain but Henry may have used it to write letters, possibly to Anne Boleyn, during this period. The box may subsequently have been presented to an ambassador or foreign dignitary as a royal gift.

This writing box was made in about 1525 in the court workshops of Henry VIII. Fashioned out of walnut and oak, the outer lid displays the insignia of Henry and Katherine, the Tudor rose, a portcullis, an impaled rose and pomegranate, the fleur-de-lys, the castle, accompanied by the cypher H.R., and the sheaf of arrows. Their initials form part of the decoration. The interior is lined with gilded leather, which is painted with the royal coat of arms and heraldic emblems relating to Henry and Katherine of Aragon. Ink and writing equipment, together with important documents, would have been stored in the interior of the box which is adorned with religious symbols. The images of Mars, the Roman god of war, Venus, the goddess of love and fertility, and her son, Cupid, flank Henry's coat of arms. The head of Jesus Christ and the figures of St George and the Dragon are featured on the lid of the interior. The front of the box shows a male and female head while the falling panel displays the heads of Paris, Prince of Troy, and Helen, the Spartan queen from Greek mythology. The edge of the outer lid is covered in parchment bearing the inscription: 'DEUS REGNORUM EC[CLESIAE] CHRISTIAN[A]E MAXIMUS PROTECTOR IMPERII DA SERVO TUO HENRICO OCT[AVO] REGI ANGLIAE DE HOSTE TRIUMPHUM M[AGNUM]'. Quills for writing would have been stored in the long drawer at the rear of the writing box.

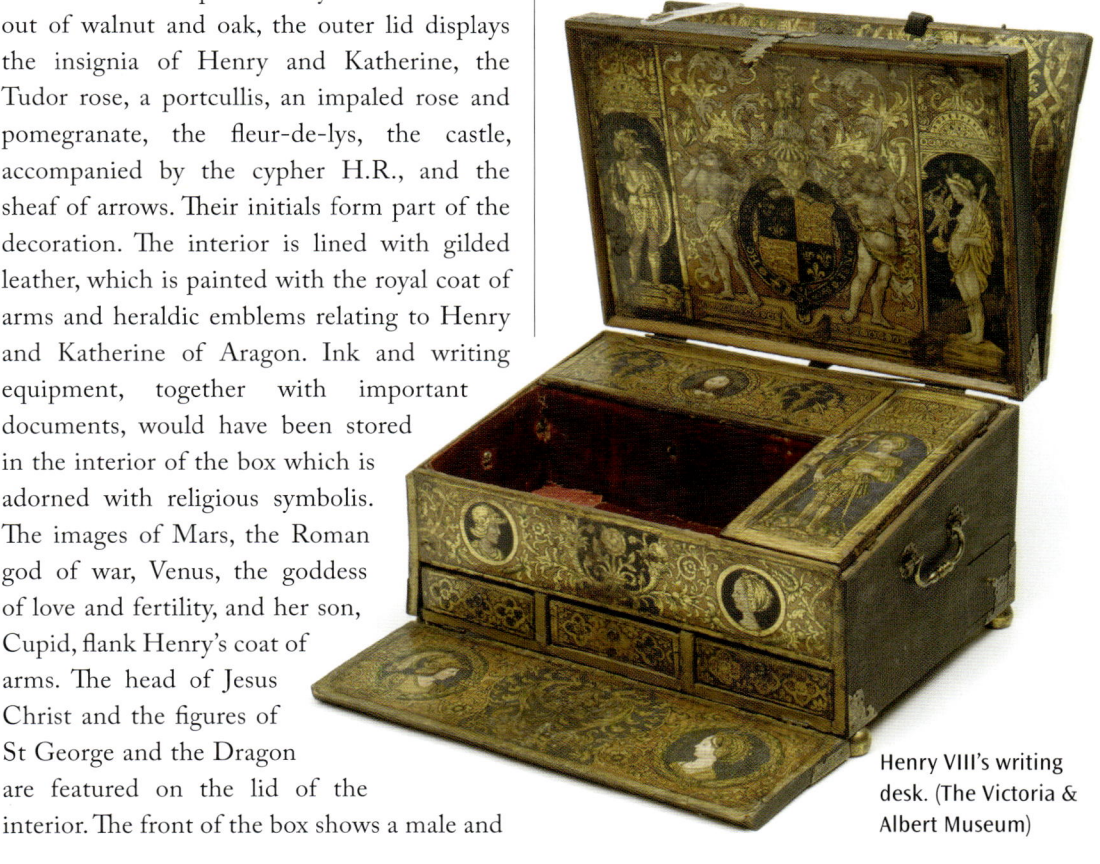

Henry VIII's writing desk. (The Victoria & Albert Museum)

38

Love Letter Written by Henry VIII to Anne Boleyn

The King Courts His Queen

Seventeen love letters written to Anne Boleyn by the hand of Henry VIII, in French and English, have survived to the present day. They reveal the extent of his desire and passion. These letters are held in the archives of the Vatican.

It is unknown how the Vatican obtained possession of these letters, but it is believed that they were used to build a case against Henry's pursuit of a divorce from Katherine. All these letters are undated, but this particular letter, written in English, is thought to have been penned towards the end of the summer of 1528. Henry wrote:

Mine own sweetheart, this shall be to advertise you of the great elengeness [sic, loneliness] that I find here since your departing; for, I ensure

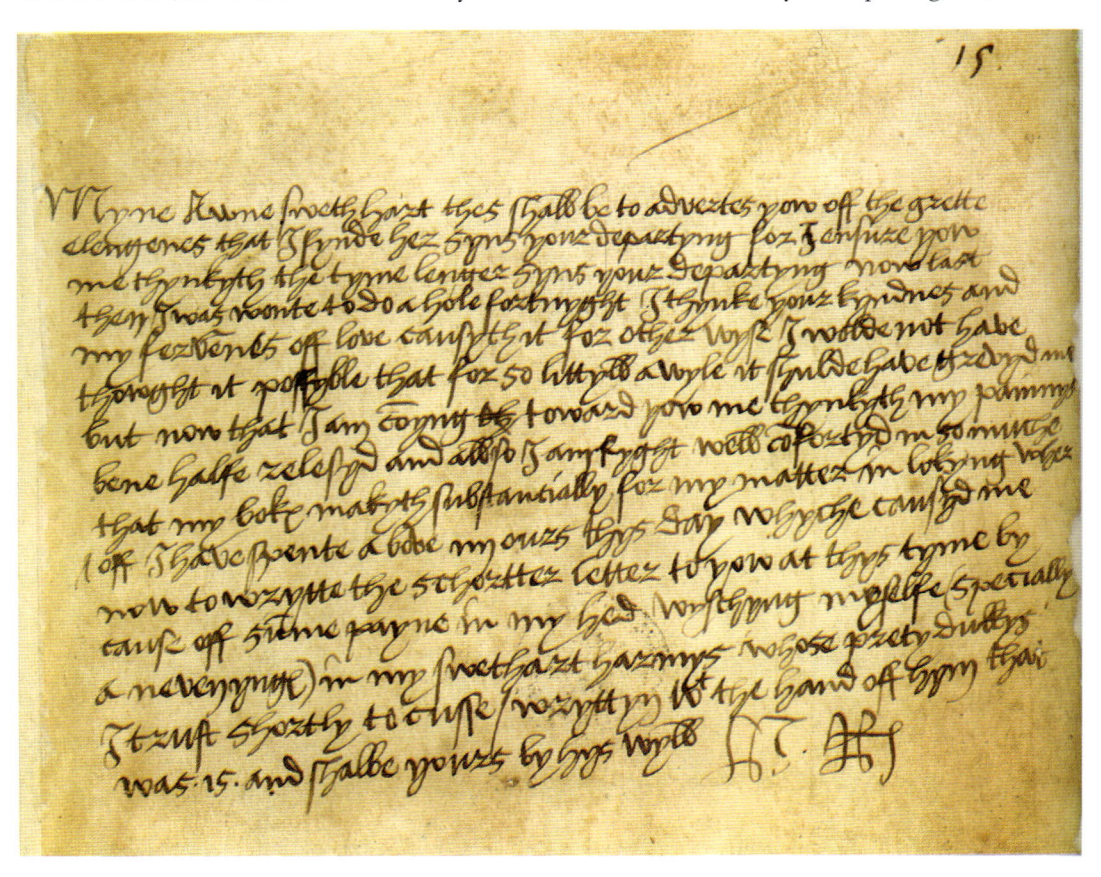

The surviving letter. (Alamy)

LOVE LETTER WRITTEN BY HENRY VIII TO ANNE BOLEYN

you methinketh the time longer since your departing now last, than I was wont to do a whole fortnight. I think your kindness and my fervency of love causeth it; for, otherwise, I would not have thought it possible that for so little a while it should have grieved me. But now that I am coming towards you, methinketh my pains be half released; and also I am right well comforted in so much that my book maketh substantially for my matter; in looking whereof I have spent above four hours this day, which caused me now to write the shorter letter to you at this time, because of some pain in my head; wishing myself (especially an evening) in my sweetheart's arms, whose pretty dukkys [breasts] I trust shortly to kiss.

Written by the hand of him that was, is, and shall be yours by his own will, H.R.[77]

The book which Henry refers to in this letter was the treatise that defended his divorce from Queen Katherine, which he was composing at the time and occupied his evenings during this period. He had been married for Katherine for nineteen years when this letter was written.

Treaty of Amiens, 1527

Peace at Last?

After his victory over the French at the Battle of Pavia and the capture of King Francis I on 24 February 1527, Emperor Charles V was willing to make peace with the French king later that year. Charles also gave the impression that he was unhappy with Henry and abandoned the agreement that betrothed him to Princess Mary, which left Henry feeling humiliated. Henry then endeavoured to make peace with France too. The Treaty of the More, signed at the royal residence of More in Hertfordshire, was signed by Henry and French ambassadors acting on behalf of the French Regent, Louis, which initiated peace between England and France on 6 September 1525. Henry also agreed to petition Pope Clement VII to exert pressure upon Charles V to release Francis. When Francis was released in 1526, Henry promised not to agree a peace deal with Charles V.

French ambassadors arrived in London during February 1527 to negotiate a peace treaty. After being entertained with banquets and tournaments, an agreement was made between the two nations culminating in the Treaty of Westminster, which was signed on 30 April 1527.

On 18 August 1527, Henry VIII and Francis I signed the Treaty of Amiens which ratified agreements that had been made during April 1527. It was the concluding agreement which strengthened the ties and guaranteed peace between England and France. The treaty protected the privileges of English merchants trading in France. It withheld consent to a General Council to be summoned by Charles V until the Pope was released from captivity by the emperor. The treaty was confirmed by Francis as a treaty of perpetual peace. Another term of the treaty intended to unify both countries through Princess Mary being contracted to marry Francis' second son, the Duke of Orleans. The treaty ensured peace with France until 1535.

Seen below is the final document confirming the agreed terms of the Treaty of Amiens, which was delivered to Henry by French ambassadors in October 1527. The illuminated front page is printed on gold leaf which demonstrates the importance of the treaty. A portrait of King Francis I is seen in the top left corner. His fleur-de-lys shield is surrounded by the collar of the Order of St Michael and ensconced by a crown held by two angels alongside his motto, 'Nutrisco et extinguo'. The king's emblems of the salamander among flames spurting water are also featured.

A treaty of perpetual peace between England and France signed between Francis I and Henry VIII, in 1527. This is the French ratification of the treaty, signed at Amiens. The strands at the bottom were attached to Francis' unusual gold seal. The peace lasted fewer than twenty years. (The National Archives)

40

Bridewell Palace

Henry VIII's Residence at Blackfriars

A plaque on a wall of the building at 14 New Bridge Street, London, together with several streets named after Tudor connections, is the only physical evidence of the existence of Bridewell Palace during the reign of Henry VIII. It was a place of great siginficance for him, particularly in the early years of his reign.

According to Cavendish, Wolsey's biographer, the king gave the cardinal a house at Bridewell in Fleet Street, from where he could attend the king in court. The construction of Bridewell Palace, between Fleet Street and the River Thames, began in 1515 under Cardinal Wolsey's orders. It was built on the west bank of the River Fleet which flowed from two streams from Hampstead Heath. Wolsey intended to use it as a home as it was close to the Dominican priory at Blackfriars, located east of the River Fleet. Wolsey planned to oversee the work carried out at Bridewell but became distracted by the building of Hampton Court Palace, eventually passing the land to Henry VIII who continued the construction of the palace. The complex was completed in 1522 and the king used it as his primary London residence for eight years.

The red-brick palace contained two courtyards with royal apartments, a riverside garden terrace containing a tennis court and a bridge connecting to the Dominican priory at Black Friars, which provided further accommodation space for the king. During the state visit in 1522, Emperor Charles V's 2,000 attendants and 1,000 horses were lodged at the priory for three days, while the emperor's noblemen were accommodated in Bridewell Palace. The emperor wrote that on 6 June 1522 he entered London in great triumph, not only like brothers of one mind, but in the same attire'.

Acknowledging that his wife Katherine would never be able to bear him a son, Henry had already installed his 6-year-old illegitimate son, Henry Fitzroy, as a Knight of the Garter on 23 April 1525. It was at Bridewell Palace on 7 June 1525, that Henry VIII further strengthened Fitzroy's position by proclaiming him as First Earl of Nottingham, Duke of Richmond and Somerset. He had conceived Fitzroy with his mistress, Elizabeth Blount, and clearly desired to promote him over all other dukes as part of a plan to install him as a potential heir to the throne in the absence of a legitimate son. State papers recorded the ceremony at Bridewell Palace:

> Henry Fitzroy was first created earl of Nottingham, as follows: First, he was clad in the habit and state of an earl, and so led between the earl of Arundel on the right and the earl of Oxford on the left. Before them went the earl of Northumberland, bearing the sword in the scabbard by the point, garnished with the girdle. The said earls were in their robes of estate. Before them went Garter, carrying the patent, and his company, and before them lords, knights, and esquires. He was thus conducted from the long gallery into the King's chamber, where the King stood under the cloth of estate, well accompanied by lords spiritual and temporal, my lord Cardinal, &c. The young lord then kneeled to the King, who commanded him to stand up.

BRIDEWELL PALACE

The plaque in New Bridge Street, Blackfriars, London, which marks the site of Henry VIII's Bridewell Palace. (Author's Collection)

> HERE STOOD THE PALACE OF BRIDEWELL
> BUILT BY HENRY VIII IN 1523
> AND GRANTED BY EDWARD VI IN 1553
> TO THE CITY OF LONDON TO HOUSE
> BRIDEWELL ROYAL HOSPITAL FOUNDED BY
> ROYAL CHARTER IN THE SAME YEAR.
> THE PRESENT BUILDING WAS ERECTED IN 1802
> AND IN 1862 THE COURT ROOM OF BRIDEWELL
> ROYAL HOSPITAL WAS INCORPORATED THEREIN

The King then received the patent from Garter, as the lord Chamberlain was absent, and 'took it' to Sir Thos. Moore, who read it aloud. On coming to the words *gladii cincturam*, the young lord kneeled down, and the King put the girdle about his neck, the sword hanging bendwise over his breast. When the patent was read, the King gave it to the young earl, who returned, as he came, into the gallery, and was led out again in the habit of a duke, between the dukes of Norfolk and Suffolk. Before him went the earl of Arundel, carrying the 'cape' of estate with the circlet on it; the earl of Oxford, carrying the rod of gold; the marquis of Dorset, bearing the sword by the point; and the earl of Northumberland, carrying a duke's robes of estate. Garter and his company led the way as before. The patent was read, the robe, sword, cape, and circlet were put on, and the gold rod and patent handed to him.[78]

By 1527, Henry was determined that he was going to marry Anne Boleyn and applied for a dispensation from Rome to allow him to do so. The process was not simple for in 1528, Pope Clement VII commissioned two legates, Cardinal Lorenzo Campeggio and Cardinal Thomas Wolsey, to hear the case for this marriage. The two legates held preliminary meetings at Bridewell Palace before holding an inquiry in Blackfriars to listen to the arguments before considering whether to advise the Pope to grant Henry VIII permission to divorce Katherine of Aragon. George Cavendish recorded:

> It was by the council determined, that the King, and the Queen his wife, should be lodged at Bridewell. And that in the Black Friars a certain place should be appointed whereas the King and the Queen might most conveniently repair to the court, there to be erected and kept for the disputation and determination of the King's case, whereas these two legates sat in judgment as notable judges; before whom the King and the Queen were duly cited and summoned to appear. Which was the strangest and newest sight and devise that ever was read or heard in any history or chronicle in any region; that a King and a Queen to be convened and constrained by process compilatory to appear in any court as common persons, within their own realm or dominion, to abide the judgement and decrees of their own subjects.[79]

Katherine had the support of the people. As she walked from Bridewell Palace across the River Fleet to Blackfriars priory she was cheered by Londoners. The Spanish Ambassador to the English court, Don Iñigo de Mendoza, reported to Charles V the discord among the people regarding Henry VIII's poor treatment of Queen Katherine:

> The King has resided here in London for 20 days. It is very seldom that he makes so long a stay. Whilst passing from their Royal residence to the Dominicans through a gallery communicating with that convent, the Queen was so warmly greeted by immense crowds of people, who publicly wished her victory over her enemies, so that this kingdom may be saved from utter ruin, that the King ordered that nobody should be again be admitted to the place.[80]

Henry became anxious that his actions in seeking a divorce from his queen might have a negative impact upon his popularity among his subjects. He therefore convened a meeting on 8 November 1528 with noblemen, judges and councillors from the City of London at Bridewell Palace to explain his reasons for his actions and his scruples of conscience that he had not broken canon law. Mendoza continued his report to Charles V:

> Perceiving, moreover, that his subjects are discontented with what he is aiming at, he resolved to send for the mayor and aldermen of this city and told them in public that the French King had asked his daughter, the Princess Mary, in marriage for his son, the Duke of Orleans, but wished to know, before the marriage took place, whether she was legitimate or not. For this reason, and also because most of the prelates and other theologians (*doctos hombres*) of his kingdom had assured him that he had sinned mortally in his marriage with the Queen, he was desirous of ascertaining the truth of the case, that his conscience might be quieted, and this kingdom have a legitimate heir when his days should be over. He trusted in God that the arrival of this new Legate [Cardinal Campeggio] from Rome would be the means of having the question settled, so that all his subjects might live in a state of greater peace and happiness than they had ever enjoyed before.[81]

Henry also used the verse from Leviticus which forbade a man to marry his brother's widow and

Bridewell Palace, 1666. The palace was built on the western bank of the River Fleet, which flows from two streams on Hampstead Heath. (Author's Collection)

that it would result in the union being childless as an argument for annulling his marriage to Katherine. The chronicler Edward Hall recorded what Henry said to these leading dignitaries:

> And although it hath pleased almighty God to send us a fair daughter of a noble woman and me begotten to our great comfort and joy, yet it hath been told us by diverse great clerks, that neither she is our lawful daughter nor her mother our lawful wife, but that we live together abominably and detestably in open adultery, in so much that when our ambassador was last in France and motion was made that the Duke of Orleans should marry our said daughter, one of the said chief counsellors to the French King said, it were well done to know whether she be the King of England his lawful daughter or not, for well known it is that he begat her on his brother's wife which is directly against gods law and his precept. Think you my lords that these words touch not by body and soul, think you that these doings do not daily and hourly trouble my conscience and vex my spirits, yes we doubt not but that if it were your own cause every man would seek remedy, when the peril of your soul and the loss of your inheritance is openly laid to you. For this only cause, I protest before God and in the word of a prince, I have asked counsel of the greatest clerks in Christendom, and for this cause, I have sent for this legate as a man indifferent only to know the truth and so to settle my conscience, and for none other cause as God can judge. And as touching the queen, if it be adjudged by the law of God that she is my lawful wife, there was never thing more pleasant nor more acceptable to me in my life both for the discharge and clearing of my conscience and also for the good qualities and conditions the which I know to be in her. For I assure you all, that beside her noble parentage of the which she is descended (as you well know) she is a woman of most gentleness, of most humility and buxomness, yea and of all good qualities appertaining to nobility, she is without comparison, as I this twenty years almost have had the true experiment, so that if I were to marry again if the marriage might be good I would surely chose her above all other women.[82]

These noblemen were unaware that Henry had been embroiled in a clandestine relationship with Anne Boleyn since 1526. During December 1528, he began to conceal Anne in lodgings at Greenwich Palace and his focus was set on preparing an argument to divorce Katherine.

From 1530 Henry VIII used Bridewell Palace as a royal residence less frequently because it was small, too close to the River Fleet, which emitted foul smells, and he preferred properties that would provide more privacy. The king therefore leased Bridewell Palace to French ambassadors at the English court making the palace the earliest recorded embassy in England. It was here in 1533 that the artist Hans Holbein painted *The Ambassadors*, which features diplomats Jean de Dinneville and Georges de Selve, Bishop of Lavaur. When Thomas Cromwell became aware of Holbein's artistic abilities he commissioned him to paint his portrait. Holbein established a good reputation within Henry VIII's court and was deluged with work from other important courtiers requiring portraits of themselves.

French diplomats used Bridewell Palace as an embassy until 1553, when Edward VI transformed the palace into a house of correction for vagrants, known as a Bridewell. The royal apartments were destroyed during the fire of London in 1666, although some of Tudor buildings remained until they were demolished in 1864.

41

The Black Friar

Blackfriars Priory, Site of the Divorce Hearing of Henry VIII and Queen Katherine

Blackfriars Priory was built in 1276 between Ludgate Hill and the River Thames on the eastern bank of the River Fleet from the northern bank of the Thames. In 1529, the Great Hall of the Dominican priory was used as a court to prove that the marriage of Henry VIII and Katherine of Aragon was unlawful and warranted annulment. Nothing remains of the priory, but a statue of a black friar stands above the entrance to the Black Friar public house, which was built on the site of the priory at Blackfriars at the junction of Queen Victoria Street and New Bridge Street.

Henry was becoming increasingly anxious that Katherine had not borne him a male heir. He was in a relationship with Anne Boleyn and looking for a reason to leave Katherine and marry Anne with the sanction of the Catholic Church. Anne and Henry approached Cardinal Wolsey for help in getting approval from Rome to grant an annulment to his marriage to Katherine so that they could proceed. Pope Clement VII was a prisoner of Charles V, who had sacked Rome in 1527, and it was unlikely that the Pope would permit Henry to divorce Katherine, who was Charles' aunt. However, when Pope Clement VII escaped from the Castel Sant'Angelo in Rome disguised as a gardener, he permitted a hearing to take place in London to hear the case for Henry to divorce Katherine. The Pope sent Cardinal Lorenzo Campeggio, who together with Wolsey, listened to Henry's case at Blackfriars to ascertain whether there were legitimate grounds for him to divorce Katherine. The Pope gave secret instructions to encourage a reconciliation between Henry and Katherine, or induce Katherine to live in a convent, 'should profess in some religious community, and take vows of perpetual chastity' which would allow Henry to remarry. Campeggio, who was in ill health and suffering from gout, arrived in London in October 1528. He was unable to convince Katherine to move to a convent, as it became apparent to him that a reconciliation was impossible. Campeggio reported to the Pope, 'he sees nothing, he thinks of nothing but Anne, and he is constantly kissing her and treating her as if she were his wife'.

The Bishop of Winchester, Stephen Gardiner, represented the king. Henry suggested that Archbishop William Warham represent counsel for Katherine but being Archbishop of Canterbury and a subject of the king, she did not consider him suitable because he would be biased in favour of her husband. Instead she appointed John Fisher, Bishop of Rochester, as her counsel.

Wolsey was confident that there was a strong case for Henry to receive his annulment. However, before the legatine court began its work, Katherine produced a copy of a document written by Pope Julius II and sent to her mother in Spain at the time of her marriage to Arthur which undermined Henry's claim that the papal dispensation was erroneous. The original copy was held by Charles V in the Royal Archives in Spain. Henry declared it to be a forgery. He forced Katherine to write a letter to Charles V to request that he hand over the document to two English ambassadors who he sent to Spain

A pub named The Blackfriar is a visual reminder that a friary once stood here during the reign of Henry VIII. It was there that the case for Henry VIII to divorce Katherine was heard. (Ron Ellis/Shutterstock)

A depiction of the Black Friar above the pub's entrance. (Author's Collection)

to collect the original and bring it to him in England so he could analyse it. Henry was aware that it could jeopardise his case for annulment and probably intended to destroy the document. Katherine sent Thomas Abel, her chaplain, who could speak fluent Spanish to her nephew's court to explain that the letter and request was written under duress and instructed him not to hand over the document. In January 1529, Abel reached Charles V before Henry's representatives and subsequently the emperor became uncooperative and refused to hand over the document.

The legatine court began proceedings on 31 May 1529, with the bishops of England and Campeggio appointed judges. Attracting public interest, the case was unprecedented because it was the first time that an English king and queen had been summoned to appear before a court. King Harry of England was called and he answered the court and sat in his allocated chair.

When Katherine was called, she rose from her chair, ignored the court and knelt before the king. In broken English, she asked, 'Alas! Sir, how have I offended you? What offence have I given you, intending to abridge me of life in this manner?' before declaring that during their twenty-year marriage, 'I take God to witness I have been to you a true and loyal wife.'[83] Katherine was subjected to talking about her intimate sexual relations in front of the cardinals and the public, and she affirmed 'when ye had me at the first, I take God to be my judge, I was a true maid without touch of man'. Katherine then pleaded with Henry 'to spare the extremity of this new court' until she could obtain advice from her family in Spain. Withdrawing with dignity, Katherine made a low curtsey to the king and departed from the chamber. Ignoring repeated calls to return to the commission, she played no further role. The court continued with proceedings in her absence and Bishop John Fisher would defend her marriage to Henry.

On 1 July 1529, Henry VIII's 'scruple of conscience' was presented at the legatine court at Blackfriars. The document stated that Henry had referred his concerns relating to the validity of his marriage with Katherine to the following prelates, Archbishop Warham, Bishops Clerk, Fisher, Kite, Longland, Standish, Turnstall, Voysey and West and that they had concurred that he had grounds for concern and that the matter should be forwarded to Rome for the Pope's consideration and judgement. This document caused much controversy when Bishop Fisher claimed that he had not signed this document and that his signature had been forged.

On 23 July Campeggio adjourned and referred the case to be judged by Pope Clement VII in Rome in October later that year. The Pope was more concerned with problems in Italy because Emperor Charles V had captured Rome during May 1527. Given that the case for Henry VIII

A depiction of Catherine of Aragon pleading her case against divorce from Henry VIII. (Public Domain)

to divorce Katherine was weak, the Pope hoped that if the decision to grant permission for Henry VIII to marry Anne Boleyn was delayed, he may lose interest in Anne and the problem would no longer exist.

Henry was unconvinced that he would receive a fair hearing in Rome and the situation was now in a state of flux. Wolsey had failed to get Henry an annulment from the Pope and he was unable to divorce Katherine or marry Anne Boleyn. Henry stormed out of the Blackfriars Priory as Charles Brandon, Duke of Suffolk declared, 'it was never merry in England, whilst we had cardinals amongst us'. Wolsey from that moment knew that his future looked bleak, and reminded Brandon of the time when he defended him when he was banished from court after marrying Henry's sister without permission, 'Sir, of all men within this realm, ye have least cause to dispraise or be offended with cardinals, for if I, a simple cardinal, had not been, you should have had at this present no head upon your shoulders.'

The events at Blackfriars left Henry enraged at Wolsey, whose downfall was now certain, and an anxious Katherine feeling isolated and dishonoured. On 30 July 1529, Don Iñigo de Mendoza, Spanish Ambassador in England, reported to Charles V:

> The Queen is much vexed, for she has taken all the medicine prescribed for her, and finds the remedy deferred. Her husband is more irritated than before, 'con estos auctos', but she has firm hope that with your Majesty's aid the Pope will not delay justice longer. The

At 7 Ludgate Broadway there is a plaque marking the site of Blackfriars Priory, which stretched from the River Thames where The Blackfriar pub is situated up to Ludgate Hill. (Author's Collection)

Queen has written to me that she perceives that all the King's anger at his ill success will be visited on Wolsey.[84]

Katherine's predications relating to the cardinal's fate came to fruition when during October 1529 Henry dismissed him as Lord Chancellor, requested him to return the Great Seal and, urged by the Boleyn family, charged him under the decree of praemunire which forbade papal intrusion in English affairs without royal assent and for the receipt of bulls from Rome. Wolsey was indicted on forty-four charges, but Henry decided not to proceed against him. Instead, Henry seized properties belonging to Wolsey including York Place and he took full custody of Hampton Court Palace. Wolsey was an immensely wealthy individual; his estate was valued at 500,000 crowns.

As for the failure to obtain an annulment at Blackfriars, Henry was determined to achieve his objective fully conscious that he would break the heart of Katherine, provoke her nephew Emperor Charles V and risk conflict with Spain and the Holy Roman Empire as well as inciting a confrontation with the Pope and the Catholic Church. The failure to obtain a divorce at Blackfriars would begin the process of England breaking away from the Catholic Church and the establishment of a new religion, the Church of England. Henry was advised to consult with scholars and theologians in European universities to scrutinise the legality of his divorce with Katherine. In order to gain answers favourable to his cause for divorce, he sent financial bribes. In 1531, Henry ordered the publication of the results of this exercise in a book entitled *Determination of the Most Famous Universities*.

42

Hampton Court Palace

Henry Seizes Wolsey's Palace

Cardinal Wolsey rebuilt Hampton Court Palace when he took a ninety-nine-year lease from 1515, and it took ten years to complete. Situated 10 miles south-west of London and connected by the River Thames, the palace was designed to accommodate his large entourage, as well as to welcome and entertain important guests such as monarchs, politicians and foreign dignitaries. Its construction was influenced by European palaces and would match the prestige of Wolsey.

Henry and Katherine were first entertained by Wolsey at Hampton Court Palace in 1517, as renovations were taking place. Construction was completed by 1525 and Henry visited Wolsey at Hampton Court on numerous occasions throughout the 1520s. Wolsey was honoured and humbled when the king visited and in correspondence he would write from 'your majesty's house' at Hampton Court. The magnificent palace was far superior and elaborate than any of the properties owned by Henry VIII and after the king made subtle hints to Wolsey, the cardinal offered his envious master the palace and its entire contents. In exchange, Henry gave Wolsey Richmond Palace, however the cardinal was permitted to use Hampton Court for hosting diplomats.

Wolsey's position at court as the king's closest confidant became precarious when he failed to obtain Henry a divorce from Katherine, which angered Henry and Anne Boleyn. When Wolsey fell from grace in November 1529, Henry VIII took complete possession of Hampton Court Palace. Although Wolsey had leased the property for ninety-nine years, Henry's lawyers were able to secure its freehold. Wolsey's coat of arms was stripped from the palace and Henry ordered

Hampton Court Palace. This is Base Court looking towards the Anne Boleyn Gatehouse and the Great Hall (to the left). In the foreground is a replica fountain that was used at the Field of Cloth of Gold (see Object 26) and which spouted wine in 1520. The King and guests would pass through the entrance to the palace into Base Court. It was there that guests would be allocated a room for their visit, by the Serjeant Porter. Accommodation for the King's household and rooms for forty-five guests were available around Base Court. (Shutterstock)

The ceiling of the Great Hall in Hampton Court Palace. The Great Hall was primarily used as a dining room for the royal household, including courtiers and servants. Henry did feast within this hall during state occasions when there was dancing and merrymaking, but he would usually be served his daily meals within the privacy of his own private chamber. (Plus One/Shutterstock)

further refurbishments, including the construction of the Bayne Tower, which served as his private accommodation until 1533. This tower still survives today but cannot be accessed by visitors.

Hampton Court Palace became the centre of government whenever the king was in residence, and he continued to use it frequently and would host ceremonies of state and and engage with foreign leaders and diplomats within this place of splendour. Henry was also able to indulge his passions for hunting, tennis and bowling at Hampton Court.

Henry often used a state barge to travel between his palaces at Greenwich, Bridewell, Whitehall, Richmond and Hampton Court. He owned several state barges and it was his favoured method of travel, in order to avoid the crowded streets of London. These barges were maintained and operated by Royal Watermen. There was also a private road that linked Whitehall and Hampton Court, known as the King's Road.

It was at Hampton Court Palace, that after enduring three nights and two days of painful labour, Jane Seymour provided Henry with a male heir when Prince Edward was born at 2am on 12 October 1537. The king was overjoyed by the birth of a son, who was christened in the Chapel Royal three days later on 15 October. Within three weeks, joy was eclipsed with sorrow when Jane died of complications following the birth on 24 October 1537 at Hampton Court. It was on 1 November 1541, in the Chapel Royal within the palace that Archbishop Thomas Cranmer left a letter on Henry VIII's seat in his pew detailing that his fifth wife, Katherine Howard, had sexual relations before her marriage to the king and during the royal progress to the north of England with Thomas Culpepper.

43

Remains of Whitehall Palace

Henry Takes Possession of Whitehall Palace

Henry VIII's Whitehall Palace contained 1,500 rooms and was considered the largest palace in Europe during the Tudor period. It stretched along the embankment of the River Thames towards Downing Street to the west and northwards towards Charing Cross. Henry's wine cellar still exists beneath the Ministry of Defence building and on the Victoria Embankment side there are the remains of a 280ft-long terrace that projected 70ft into the River Thames. This terrace enabled members of the royal

The river wall and steps at Henry VIII's Tudor palace at Whitehall, now in the grounds of the Ministry of Defence building at Victoria Embankment, London. (Author's Collection)

family to disembark from state barges and access the state apartments of the palace. There were two curved flights of steps at each end of the terrace, the northern stairwell being excavated in 1939, together with a section of the Tudor palace river wall.

The original building was known as York Place, which was built in the thirteenth century. When Wolsey was appointed Archbishop of York in 1515, he established his London residence at York Place. He immediately set about expanding the property.

After Wolsey's downfall, Henry brought Anne Boleyn to York Place to view the cardinal's home on 2 November 1529. They disembarked from their barge alongside the steps seen here. Eustace Chapuys reported to Charles V that 'the King came from Grennis [Greenwich] by water and landed at the house which once belonged to the Cardinal, where he has found handsome and well-furnished apartments provided with everything that could be wished'.

Henry, with the aid of lawyers, seized York Place in February 1530 and presented it to

Anne Boleyn as a gift. He ordered refurbishments to the palace, including the construction of five indoor tennis courts and two bowling alleys. A tiltyard was also built on the west side of the palace where Horse Guards Parade is now sited. Stones were brought from the demolished Kennington Palace, south of the River Thames, to be used in the modification of York Place. White stone was used in the reconstruction of the Great Hall within the palace and from 1532 it was referred to as Whitehall.

Henry secretly married Anne Boleyn at Whitehall Palace sometime between November 1532 and January 1533. His marriage to Katherine had not been annulled and he therefore committed bigamy when he married Anne. Three years later, on 20 May 1536, the day after Anne Boleyn's execution, Henry married Jane Seymour at Whitehall Palace, the service conducted by Bishop Stephen Gardiner. Whitehall Palace became the Henry's primary London residence and was renamed the King's Palace of Westminster.

Henry died at Whitehall Palace on 28 January 1547. After Henry's death, Whitehall Palace continued to be used as a royal residence and would become one of the largest palaces in Europe rivalling the Vatican. William Shakespeare is reputed to have been part of the first performance of *King Lear* in the Great Hall in the presence of King James I. The Banqueting House, built by Inigo Jones in 1622, formed part of Whitehall Palace and it was here on 30 January 1649 that Charles I was executed. The palace suffered a fire in 1691, but a second fire completely destroyed it in 1698. The stairs seen here and Henry's wine cellar are all that remain of this significant royal palace.

44

A Surviving Tudor Cauldron

Richard Roose Boiled to Death for Treason on the Orders of Henry VIII

This cauldron was found beneath debris and mud aboard the Mary Rose *when she was recovered from the Solent in 1982. It was used to boil broth for the crew to consume. Similar cauldrons were, however, used for the purpose of execution during the reign of Henry VIII.*

On 18 February 1531, Richard Roose allegedly poisoned pottage, a type of thick soup or stew, that he had cooked for his employer, John Fisher, Bishop of Rochester at his London residence. Fisher refused to eat the stew. He would frequently fast, however on this occasion he was already unwell due to anxiety about Henry VIII's coercion of the bishops of England to accept his decision to divorce Katherine of Aragon. The remainder of Fisher's household did eat the food cooked by Roose and felt the effects of the poison, including two individuals who died as a consequence.[85]

Chapuys reported to Charles V:

> The matter of the bishop of Rochester's cook, a very extraordinary case. There was in the Bishop's house about ten days ago some pottage, of which all who tasted, that is nearly all the servants, were brought to the point of death, though only two of them died, and some poor people to whom they had given it. The good Bishop, happily, did not taste it. The cook was immediately seized, at the instance of the Bishop's brother, and, it is said, confessed he had thrown in a powder, which he had been given to understand would only hocus (*tromper*) the servants without doing them any harm. I do not yet know whom he has accused of giving him this powder, nor the issue of the affair. The King has done well to show dissatisfaction at this; nevertheless, he cannot wholly avoid some suspicion, if not against himself, whom I think too good to do such a thing,

This cauldron was found aboard the *Mary Rose* and used to cook food for the crew. A similar cauldron was also used to boil to death Richard Roose for his attempt to poison Bishop John Fisher and the murder of two individuals who ate the food. (Author's Collection)

at least against the lady and her father. The said bishop of Rochester is very ill and has been so ever since the acknowledgment made by the clergy, of which I wrote.[86]

Chapuys suspected that the king was involved in the attempt to kill Fisher. Henry had a motive and would benefit from Fisher's demise, because he represented Queen Katherine at Blackfriars in 1529 and had vehemently opposed Henry's attempts to get an annulment so that he could be free to marry Anne Boleyn. Chapuys would later speculate that the Boleyns might have also been involved, but there was no direct evidence that implicated the king or the Boleyns in this assassination attempt. Henry went to the House of Lords to look into this incident and as a result the Poisoning Act 1531 was introduced, criminalising poisoning as an act of treason. The Act stated:

> In the time of this parliament . . . one Richard Roose, of Rochester, Cook . . ., of his most wicked and damnable disposition did cast a certain venom or poison into a vessel, replenished with yeast or barm, standing in the kitchen of the Bishop of Rochester's Palace at Lambeth March, with which yeast or barm and other things convenient porridge or gruel was forthwith made for his family . . . whereby not only the number of 17 persons of his said family which did eat of that porridge were mortally infected or poisoned, and one of them . . . thereof is deceased, but also certain poor people which resorted to the said Bishop's place and were there charitably fed with the remain of the said porridge and other victuals were in the likewise infected, and one poor woman of them . . . is also thereof deceased . . . The said poisoning be adjudged high treason; and that the said Richard Roose, shall be therefore boiled to death, without benefit of clergy. And that from henceforth, every wilful murder . . . by poisoning shall be reputed, deemed and judged in the law to be high treason, and the offender deprived of his clergy and boiled to death.[87]

Richard Roose's actions were not a direct attack upon the king or state, and it is difficult to see how his alleged crime could be categorised as high treason when it was committed within the confines of the Bishop of Rochester's residence and the victims were the servants within that household and those destitute outside the building who were given the food as an act of charity. Henry may have wanted to make an example of Roose to deter anyone within his own kitchens from attemping a similar act in relation to him. On 5 April 1531, Roose was taken to Smithfield where he was lowered into a cauldron and boiled to death in public.

45

Emblems Celebrating the Marriage of Henry VIII and Anne Boleyn, Hampton Court Palace

Henry VIII Marries Anne Boleyn

At Hampton Court Palace, on entering the Great Hall, turn left and you will see a carved cypher of H and A on the wooden panelling. When Anne fell from favour carpenters rushed to remove all traces of her, but they missed this one. There are also still stone cyphers bearing the initials H and A alongside the stone badge of Anne Boleyn adorning the ceiling of the entrance to Anne Boleyn's Gateway at Hampton Court Palace.

Cyphers bearing the entwined initials of Henry VIII and Anne Boleyn, together with her emblem, were incorporated within the decorations at Hampton Court Palace to celebrate their marriage. By 1532, Henry was confident that he was close to marrying Anne Boleyn and she was queen in all but name as they both embarked upon a royal progress during that summer and on a state visit to France. Anne Boleyn had refused to share a bed with Henry for several years, but she relented during December 1532. Henry discovered that Anne was pregnant the following month. Anticipating that Anne would give birth to a male heir and to ensure the legitimacy of that child as heir to the throne, Henry secretly married Anne on 25 January 1533 at York Place (Whitehall Palace); however, Edward Hall claimed that Henry married Anne after they returned from France in November 1532.

On 31 October 1532, a Venetian diplomat reported that:

> Madame Anne is not one of the handsomest women in the world, she is of middling stature, swarthy complexion, long neck, wide mouth, bosom not much raised and in fact has nothing but the King's appetite, and her eyes, which are black and beautiful, and take great effect upon those who served the Queen when she was on the throne.[88]

Henry's marriage to Anne would cause a massive constitutional problem because he was still married to Katherine of Aragon, which meant that this second marriage was bigamous, and England therefore had two queens. Before announcing to the nation that he had married Anne Boleyn, Henry began the process to affirm his position as supreme head of the English Church and asserted that the Pope in Rome had no jurisdiction in England. He ordered Thomas Cromwell, King's Councillor and Master of the King's Jewel House, to build a legal framework that would remove the jurisdiction of the Vatican to ensure that Henry's divorce was authorised by the Church of England. The Act of Restraint of Appeals introduced to Parliament on 3 February 1533, which transferred the powers of the Catholic Church to the King of England, was the result of Cromwell's work. It declared England to be an empire and affirmed

The ceiling of Anne Boleyn's Gateway, Hampton Court Palace. The Tudor rose is emblazoned in stone at the centre and is surrounded by the cyphers and emblems of Henry VIII and Anne Boleyn. (Shutterstock)

Cyphers and heraldic emblems decorated the Great Hall on the wooden panelling and ceiling to celebrate the marriage of Henry VIII and Anne Boleyn, but when he married Jane Seymour, he ordered their removal. This cypher was missed by the carpenters and has survived over the centuries that followed. (Author's Collection)

the independence of the Church within the nation state. The use of the term empire differs here from what is meant by the Roman and British empires, which expanded through conquering of other lands. In the context of Tudor England, empire refers to an isolationist policy, where the nation becomes insular and governs itself in relation to spiritual matters without foreign influence. It gave England autonomy to preside over its religion and made the sovereign its head. It meant that papal law could not be invoked and that matters relating to religion could only be dealt with in England. The Act removed the Pope's legitimacy in deciding over Henry's annulment and prevented Katherine from appealing to the Pope. This Act would ultimately enable Henry to obtain a divorce from Katherine and legitimise his marriage to Anne. It also signified the first direct challenge by Henry upon the Pope's authority and would begin the process that would lead to the Reformation of the Church of England.

On 30 March 1533 Thomas Cranmer, who was previously the King's Chaplain and a friend of the Boleyn family, was appointed Archbishop of Canterbury. He was also a supporter of the annulment and within days of becoming the Archbishop of Canterbury he set about authorising a divorce. On 5 April 1533, he convened the convocation of the clergy at St Paul's Cathedral, which agreed, with the exception of Bishop John Fisher, that Henry's marriage to Katherine was void and recommended that Henry be given the title of Supreme Head of the English Church.

When Henry married Anne Boleyn, he ordered that all traces of his first wife be removed from the royal palaces. To celebrate the king's second marriage, skilled craftsmen decorated the palaces with Henry and Anne's initials. Cyphers were carved into the wooden panelling of the Great Hall and stone cyphers were carved into the stonework around the palaces.

Nineteenth-century copies of the cyphers of the entwined initials of Henry and Anne, alongside her emblem, adorn the vault beneath the Anne Boleyn Gateway at Hampton Court. The stone badge is the heraldic emblem of Queen Anne depicting a white falcon, wearing a crown and holding a sceptre, surmounted on a tree stump, covered with Tudor roses. The cyphers and stone badges carved on the ceiling of this gateway not only serve to celebrate Henry's love for and marriage to Anne Boleyn, but symbolise his determination to reinforce the changing domestic and political circumstances regarding ministers, courtiers and servants. Although Henry wanted his court and country to celebrate his second marriage, there were many people in England and abroad who were appalled at his treatment of Katherine which caused much resentment towards Anne. Chapuys compared the treatment of Katherine to that of someone who had been found guilty of treason in a letter to Charles V:

> That the King and his Council, having made such disorder, ought to forbear to irritate your Majesty by little things, such as the maltreatment of the Queen in changing her name and diminishing her attendance, and taking away her arms from her barge, and those which were engraved in stone in the gate of the great hall of Westminster, ignominies which have not hitherto been used except towards those attainted of treason.[89]

When Anne Boleyn fell from the king's favour and he married Jane Seymour in 1536, Henry treated Anne in a similar way to Katherine by ordering the removal all traces of her in the royal palaces. However, craftsmen omitted to remove the emblems on the ceiling on the Anne Boleyn Gateway and a carved cypher on the wooden panelling in the Great Hall at Hampton Court Palace.

46

Window Bearing Crests of Henry VIII and Anne Boleyn, Greenwich Palace

Henry VIII Proclaims Anne Boleyn as his Wife and Queen

This window was constructed from stone excavated from various windows at Greenwich Palace, on the site of the Old Royal Naval College. The material has been skilfully reassembled to form a typical window from the 1530s that stood in the Tudor palace and is displayed at the Visitor Centre at the Old Royal Naval College, Greenwich. The replica stained glass displays the arms of Henry VIII on the right and the arms of Queen Anne on the left which would have been displayed when the new queen arrived at Greenwich in 1533. All references to Katherine of Aragon were removed from all windows in Greenwich Palace and other residences and were replaced with re-glazed windows displaying the arms and emblems of Anne Boleyn. Examples of similar stone window can be seen at the Great Gatehouse at the entrance to Hampton Court Palace.

The coat of arms of Henry VIII displays the Tudor crown, alternating with the white and red roses of the Houses of York and Lancaster. The rose beneath the crown is half red and half white, signifying the union of the two opposing sides in the War of the Roses. The arms of Anne are more complex, showing the emblems of several English and French noble families. Both windows display the motif of interlocking initials, H and A. As we have seen previously, examples of this motif exist at Hampton Court Palace in wood carved into a wooden panel in the Great Hall and in stone on the ceiling of the Anne Boleyn Gateway.

On 9 April 1533, Henry instructed Katherine to stop using the title queen, and three days later, Anne Boleyn was declared Queen of England at Greenwich Palace. People who thought that Katherine was still queen were astounded when Anne appeared at Mass on the following Easter Sunday as Queen of England. On 21 April 1533, Chapuys reported to Queen Katherine's nephew, Charles V:

> This feast of Easter the prior of the Augustines in his sermon recommended the people expressly to pray for Queen Anne; at which they were astonished and scandalised, and almost every one took his departure with great murmuring and ill looks, without waiting for the rest of the sermon. The King was greatly displeased, and sent word to the Mayor that on dread of his displeasure he should take order that nothing of the kind happened again, and that no one should be so bold as to murmur at his marriage. The Mayor hereupon assembled the trades and their officers of the several halls, and commanded them, on pain of the King's indignation, not to murmur at his marriage, and to prevent their apprentices from so doing, and, what is worse and more difficult, their wives. The King in vain forbids and makes prohibitions, as it only makes the people speak more against it in private, and these prohibitions only serve to envenom the heart of the people. Four days ago, the King sent to the Queen [Katherine] to forbid her and her servants from using the title of

Stained glass windows depicting the coat of arms of Henry VIII (right) and Anne Boleyn (left). The stone which encases these windows is original material excavated from the site of Greenwich Palace. (Author's Collection)

Queen; and, not content with this harshness, he has forbidden the Princess [Mary] either to write or send any message to the Queen.[90]

Although Henry had achieved his will, Chapuys reveals the discontent within England regarding his marriage to Anne and the report highlights that Henry needed to reinforce his position and enforce his subjects to accept his new wife and queen. Stained glass windows bearing the cyphers and emblems were used to emphasise that point in the minds of his subjects. Henry's defiant act would alienate the Pope, but could potentially jeopardise peace in Europe. Henry had mistreated Charles V's aunt and there was a risk that Spain would launch a military attack upon England. Dr Pedro Ortiz wrote to Charles V on 3 May 1533:

The last news from England, and one much to be astonished at, is that the King

The window bearing the coat of arms of Henry VIII. (Author's Collection)

The window bearing the coat of arms of Anne Boleyn. (Author's Collection)

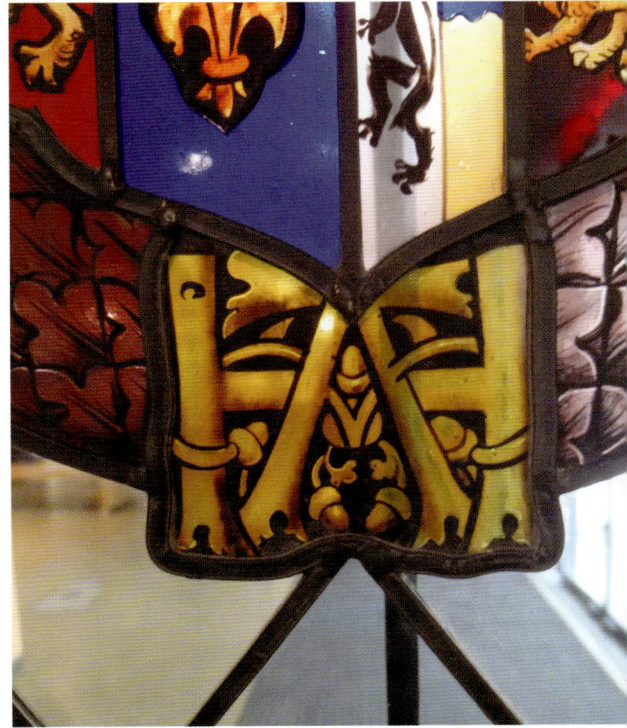

Detail of Anne Boleyn's coat of arms highlighting the interlocking initials of Henry VIII and Anne Boleyn. (Author's Collection)

has *de facto* and publicly married that Anne, disregarding completely all inhibitions from the Holy Apostolic See. If he thinks that his marriage can be lawful, he is very much mistaken, being, as it is, a manifest heresy and evident schism within the Church. This shows what power the Enemy of Mankind has gained over him (the King) and that for the punishment of such offence and mortal sin, and the due execution of the justice of God, it now behoves the Emperor, should the final sentence be anywise delayed, to seize, without waiting for any further declaration from His Holiness, any favourable opportunity that may offer itself of unsheathing the sword which God has placed in his hands for the repression of similar offences and scandalous insults against the Church and its ministers.[91]

The convocation of clergy held on 5 April had agreed that the marriage between Henry and Katherine was invalid. Before Anne could be crowned queen, the English Church still had to annul the marriage. On 23 May 1533, Archbishop Cranmer held an ecclesiastical court at Dunstable Priory that proclaimed that the marriage was annulled. Five days later Cranmer declared the legitimacy of Henry's marriage to Anne which meant that the coronation of Anne Boleyn could proceed.

Three years later in 1536, Anne Boleyn fell from the king's favour and Henry VIII ordered the master glazer at Greenwich Palace to remove all the stained glass windows within the palace and replace them with ones featuring the emblems of Jane Seymour.

47

Queen's Stairs, Tower of London

Anne Boleyn's Arrival at the Tower of London Prior to her Coronation
Important visitors, such as Kings, Queens and high-ranking officials arrived at Queen's Stairs to enter the Tower of London. A flotilla of small boats, decked with rich cloth of gold and silk, carrying noblemen, clergy and representatives from city companies escorted Anne on her journey of pomp and pageantry along the River Thames from Greenwich Palace to the Tower of London on 29 May 1533 prior to her coronation two days later at Westminster Abbey. Anne Boleyn disembarked from her barge at Queen's Stairs.

The Chamberlain to Anne Boleyn had taken Katherine's barge and ordered her coat of arms to be stripped and replaced with Anne's own emblems. Chapuys had warned Thomas Cromwell that this action would antagonise the relationship with Emperor Charles V and in order to prevent Katherine's nephew from getting more irate at the situation, Henry reproached those responsible for desecrating the barge. Chapuys reported a conversation with an English courtier to Charles V:

> He told me afterwards that the King his master had taken in very good part the warnings I had given to Cromwell to avoid occasions of irritating your Majesty; that he had been very much grieved that the arms of the Queen had been not only taken from her barge, but also rather shamefully mutilated; and that he had rather roughly rebuked the Lady's chamberlain, not only for having taken away the said arms, but for having seized the barge, which belonged only to the Queen, especially as there are in the river many others quite as suitable. I praised the King's goodwill touching the arms, and for the rest I said there was no need of excuse, for what belonged to the Queen was the King's still more.[92]

However, despite the open reprimand regarding the fate of his former wife's barge, Henry permitted Anne to use it to transport her along the River Thames, for Chapuys wrote: 'whatever regret the King may have shown at the taking of the Queen's barge, the Lady has made use of it in this triumph and appropriated it to herself'.

The first barge featured a large dragon that bellowed fire from its mouth and was followed by the Mayor of London. Charles Brandon, Duke of Suffolk and Anne's father, the Earl of Wiltshire were in other barges as they were rowed along the River Thames. Edward Hall recorded that another barge 'contained the Queen's device, a mount, with a white falcon crowned standing thereon, upon a "rowte" of gold, environed with red and white roses. Round the mount sat virgins singing and playing.'[93]

Another contemporary report stated:

> The Queen left Greenwich on Thursday, about four o'clock in the afternoon, in a 'barque raze', like a brigantine, which was painted with her colours outside, with many banners. Her ladies attended her. She was accompanied by 100 or 120 similar vessels, also garnished with banners and standards. They were fitted out with small masts, to which was attached a great quantity

QUEEN'S STAIRS, TOWER OF LONDON

Queen's Stairs. Anne Boleyn arrived here on 29 May 1533, two days before her coronation at Westminster Abbey. It is possible that her daughter, Princess Elizabeth, later Queen Elizabeth I and also incarcerated in the Tower on 18 March 1554, used the same steps to enter the prison. (Author's Collection)

of rigging, as on large ships; the rigging being adorned with small flags of taffeta, and, by the writer's advice, with 'or clinquant', as it reflects the sun's rays. There were many drums, trumpets, flutes, and hantbois. They arrived in less than half an hour at the Tower of London, where the cannon fired a salute. It was a very beautiful sight; for, besides the vessels, there were more than 200 small boats, which brought up the rear. The whole river was covered.[94]

Despite the magnificent sight of approximately a hundred vessels accompanying Anne Boleyn on her journey along the River Thames, the spectators on the banks were solemn, for their allegiances and sympathies remained with Queen Katherine. Chapuys reported the mood of the event to Charles V, revealing that the people of England were hoping that he and Holy Roman Empire would intervene: 'The said triumph consisted entirely in the multitude of those who took part in it, but all the people showed themselves as sorry as though it had been a funeral. I am told their indignation increases daily, and that they live in hope your Majesty will interfere.'[95]

Sir William Kingston, Constable of the Tower of London, ensured that the approach to Queen's Stairs was clear to enable Anne Boleyn to disembark from the barge. On arriving at Queen's Stairs, she was welcomed by a salute from guns positioned on the roof of St Thomas's Tower, above Traitor's Gate. During the period 1532–3, work to strengthen the roof with strong timbers took place on the orders of Henry VIII to accommodate the heavy guns that provided the salute. Stonemasons also strengthened Traitor's Gate, for in September 1532 their progress was reported: 'Finished two great pillars of Caen stone under St. Thomas's Tower, and certain hard stone set about the arch and the foundation of the walls about the floodgate under the said tower, "as the pulling down of an old wall, the which wall is almost half finished".'[96] The reason for this redevelopment was not revealed and although rumours indicated that it was in relation to Anne Boleyn, no one knew that it was in preparation for her coronation. Chapuys speculated in September 1532: 'The repair of the Tower of London was begun a month ago. Some think it is for the Queen's lodging during the King's absence; but this is not credible, unless he wishes the people to mutiny.'[97]

Once Anne Boleyn reached the top of Queen's Stairs, she was welcomed by Henry VIII who had already travelled by barge ahead of her. Cranmer commented that 'the King always went before her in a barge secretly'.

Edward Hall described the moment when Anne arrived at these stairs and ascended them onto the wharf:

> There was a marvellous shot out of the Tower as ever was heard there. And at her landing there met with her the Lord Chamberlain with the officers of the armies and brought her to the King, which received her with, loving countenance at the Postern by the water side and kissed her, and then she turned back again and thanked the Mayor and the citizens with many goodly words and so entered into the Tower.[98]

Directly opposite Queen's Stairs is the Byward Tower where it is believed that Henry VIII and Anne Boleyn entered the Tower of London, where they spent the night before proceeding to Westminster. It was reported that 'somewhat within the Tower she was received by the King, who laid his hands on both her sides, kissing her with great reverence and a joyful countenance'. The account of Edward Hall suggests that Henry welcomed Anne at the drawbridge.

QUEEN'S STAIRS, TOWER OF LONDON

An artist's impression of Queen's Stairs and Postern Gate at the Tower of London. Katherine Howard, Henry's fifth wife would also enter the Tower of London from these steps when she was brought to the Tower of London as a prisoner on 10 February 1542. (Information Panel at Queen's Stairs/Author's Collection)

During a banquet that evening Henry created eighteen Knights of the Bath, who would attend upon Anne during the procession from the Tower of London to Westminster the following day.

It is stated that after her arrest on 2 May 1536, Anne Boleyn was brought to the Tower of London and entered via Traitor's Gate. However, it has been argued that Anne was still Queen of England at that point and that members of the royal family would not have been brought through Traitor's Gate and she may therefore have arrived at Queen's Stairs under different circumstances as a queen, arrested for treason and accused of committing adultery among several of her subjects. Wriothesley wrote:

> On the second day of May, Mr Norris and my Lorde Rochford were brought to the Tower of London as prisoners, and the same day, about five o'clock at night [the afternoon], the Queen Ann Boleyn was brought to the Tower of London by my Lord Chancellor [Sir Thomas Audley], the Duke of Norfolk, Mr Secretary [Thomas Cromwell], and Sir William Kingston, Constable of the Tower; and when she came to the court gate, entering in, she fell down on her knees before the said lords, beseeching God to help her as she was not guilty of her accusations, and also desired the King's grace to be good unto her, and so they left her their prisoner.[99]

Given that the Lord Chancellor and the Duke of Norfolk accompanied her on the barge, it is highly probably that they disembarked at Queen's Stairs instead of passing through Traitor's Gate.

48

Westminster Abbey

Anne Boleyn Crowned Queen of England

The coronation of Anne Boleyn was a sombre occasion that took place at Westminster Abbey on 1 June 1533. A mile-long procession followed behind Anne, who was six months pregnant, as she was carried by litter through the streets of London to Westminster.

Despite the pageantry of hundreds of vessels escorting Anne's barge to the Tower of London two days before the coronation, the people of London favoured Queen Katherine and thought that she had been poorly treated, and they showed their ill-feeling and resentment towards Anne, her successor. It was reported:

> Though it was customary to kneel, uncover, and cry 'God save the King, God save the Queen', whenever they appeared in public, no one in London or the suburbs, not even women and children, did so on this occasion. One of the Queen's servants told the mayor to command the people to make the customary shouts and was answered that he could not command people's hearts, and that even the King could not make them do so. Her fool, who has been to Jerusalem and speaks several languages, seeing the little honour they showed to her, cried out, 'I think you have all scurvy heads, and dare not uncover'. Her dress was covered with tongues pierced with nails, to show the treatment which those who spoke against her might expect. Her car was so low that the ears of the last mule appeared to those who stood behind to belong to her. The letters H. A. were painted in several places, for Henry and Anne, but were laughed at by many. The crown became her very ill, and a wart disfigured her very much. She wore a violet velvet mantle, with a high ruff (*goulgiel*) of gold thread and pearls, which concealed a swelling she has, resembling goitre.[100]

Anne Boleyn sat on the Coronation Chair on a scaffold between the high altar and the choir within Westminster Abbey. Charles Brandon, Duke of Suffolk brought the crown, supported by two lords who carried a rod and sceptre. Anne was crowned by Thomas Cranmer, Archbishop of Canterbury with the crown of St Edward, which being too heavy was immediately removed from her head and replaced by a lighter crown specifically made for her to wear. There was such antipathy towards Anne Boleyn that members of her own family refused to attend her coronation, including Anne's aunt, the Duchess of Norfolk, because of 'the love she bore to the previous Queen'.

Guests who were present at the coronation were verbally abused by the public outside Westminster Abbey. 'The French ambassador and his suite were insulted by the people, who called him "Orson queneve, France dogue" [whoreson knave, French dog]'.

Eustace Chapuys reported to Charles V:

> The coronation pageant was all that could be desired, and went off very well, as to the number of the spectators, which was very considerable, but all looked so sad and dismal that the ceremony seemed to be a funeral

Westminster Abbey. Consecrated by Edward the Confessor in 1065, Westminster Abbey was used for the coronations of Henry VIII, Katherine of Aragon and Anne Boleyn. It also houses the tombs of Henry's parents, Henry VII and Elizabeth of York, as well as his daughters, Queen Mary and Queen Elizabeth I. Henry's fourth wife, Anne of Cleves, is also buried within Westminster Abbey. (Shutterstock)

rather than a pageant for I am told that the indignation of the English against their king is daily increasing.[101]

Although Henry had got his way, he had split from his first wife Katherine, married his second wife Anne Boleyn and had her crowned queen, but he did not have the support of the people he governed or some of his senior counsellors. Sir Thomas More, Lord Chancellor declined an invitation to attend the coronation because it compromised his principles and he disagreed with his majesty's marriage to Anne Boleyn. Henry regarded this as a snub and would not forget it. With Anne pregnant, not knowing whether she was carrying a girl or a boy, there was discord and uncertainty throughout the nation. Henry needed to find a way of ensuring that the position of his new queen and child was secure.

49

The Oath of Allegiance to Henry VIII and his Successors, 30 March 1534

Securing the Line of Succession

Three months after she was crowned Queen of England, Anne Boleyn gave birth to Princess Elizabeth on 7 September 1533. Henry was anxious to subdue any opposition to his marriage to Anne and wanted to ensure that Elizabeth was next in the line of succession to the throne. On 30 March 1534, the Act of Succession was ratified by Parliament in the presence of the king. The Act acknowledged Anne as Henry's lawful wife and recognised Elizabeth as his heir apparent. It also relegated Katherine from Queen to Princess Dowager and declared Princess Mary illegitimate and disinherited. The Act meant that it was treason to address Katherine as queen. Ironically this Act was introduced several days after Pope Clement VII had pronounced Henry and Katherine's union lawful and valid on 23 March 1534.

In addition to the Act of Succession, Henry wanted all his subjects to pledge their allegiance to him, as king, and his heirs. This Oath of Allegiance to Henry VIII and his successors lists all the lords and clergymen who assembled with the Commons of the Lower House before the seated king when the Act of Succession was sanctioned as law. It also appointed Thomas Cranmer, Archbishop of Canterbury, Thomas Audley, Lord Chancellor, the Duke of Norfolk and Charles Brandon, Duke of Suffolk as commissioners to take and to receive the Oath of Allegiance from all dukes, earls, barons, bishops, abbots and knights. The statute also commanded them to report to Parliament the names of those that had taken the oath. Chapuys reported to Charles V, who was concerned for his aunt, Katherine, and his cousin, Princess Mary:

> Since the arrival of the new Scotch ambassador the King has had the succession in case of his death discussed in Parliament. It is decided to exclude the Princess, and the succession to go to the King's issue by Anne Boleyn, and in default to the nearest of kin, the naming of whom is suspended so as to give the Scotch ambassadors more heart to conclude peace, so that their King may be named, in accordance with what the King of England has previously said. Parliament has concluded that if the King dies before his lady, she shall be regent and absolute governor of her children and the kingdom, and that applying the title of queen or princess to anyone except the said Anne or her daughter shall be considered high treason. Confiscation of body and goods is also threatened to all who conceal this crime or murmur against the acts of this parliament, even those in favour of the second marriage and against the papal authority, which is strange and tyrannical. For greater security the King wishes to appoint commissioners to take oaths from the people.[102]

The Act of Succession meant that people in England had to swear an oath that they acknowledged the Act. It was regarded treason

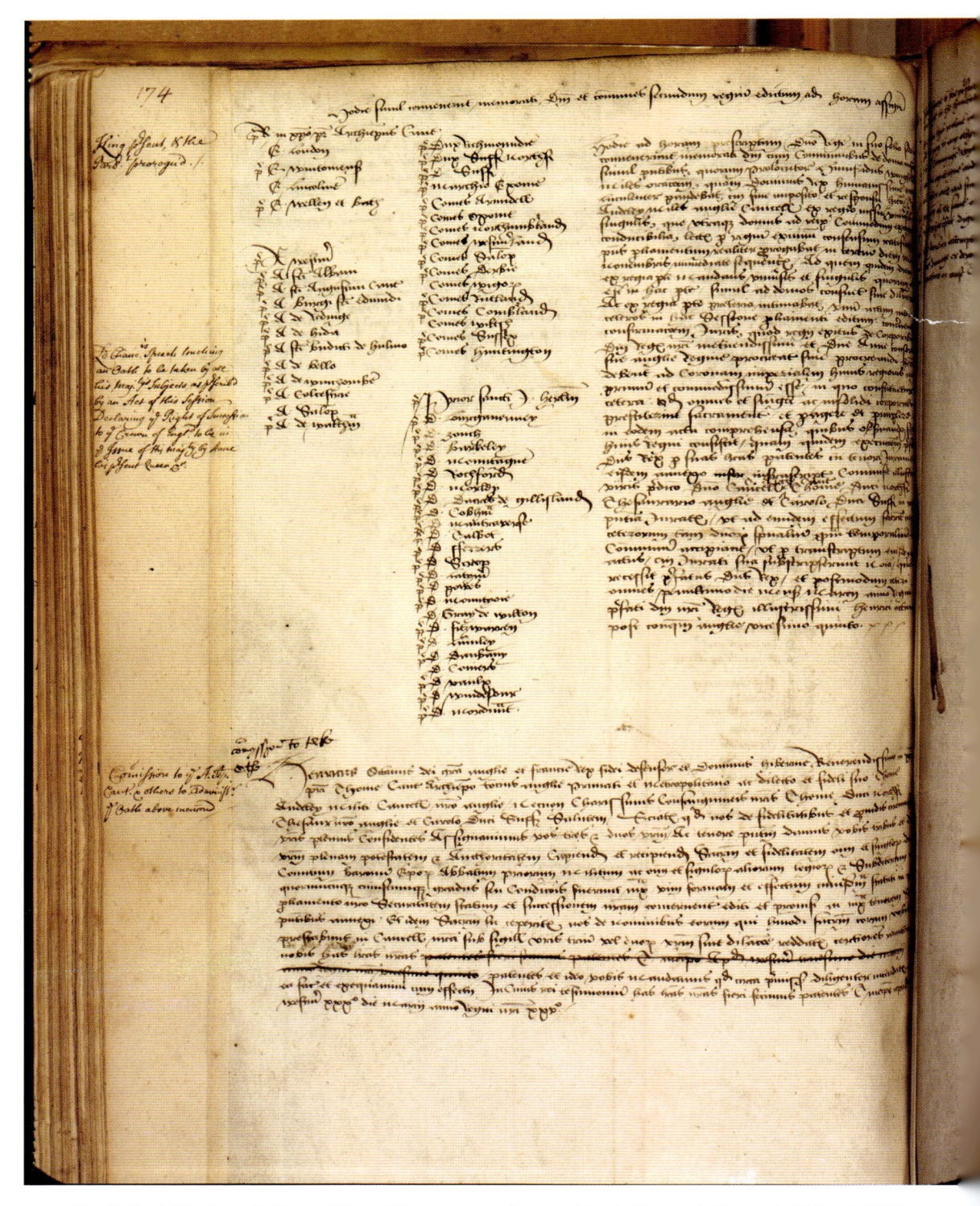

The Oath of Allegiance to Henry VIII and his successors. (House of Lords Manuscript Journal, 30 March 1534, Parliamentary Archives, PIC/T/189)

to refuse to swear to the oath. Henry was transforming into a tyrant as he submitted his subjects to his will.

The wording of the preamble to the oath stated:

> The confirmation of the law that the royal issue begotten now or in the future of the bodies of our fearsome lord the King, and the lady Anne his consort, Queen of England, should be considered first and most fit [for the succession] to the imperial crown of this region of England; whereby it is established that all and singular should swear a corporal oath to undertake and to fulfil all that is in the same Act, on whose observance the good fortune of this realm is founded.[103]

Provisions were put in place for the swearing of an oath by the king's subjects to acknowledge the Act of Succession and accept the supremacy of the sovereign. The wording of the oath was as follows: 'Ye shall swear to bear your Faith, Truth, and Obedience, alonely to the King's Majesty, and to the Heirs of his Body, according to the Limitation and Rehearsal within this Statute of Succession'. Managing the swearing of this oath was a time-consuming and vast exercise as the commissioners journeyed cross the country to enforce the Act of Parliament. Bishop Stephen Gardiner reported on the progress of taking oaths in Winchester to Thomas Cromwell on 5 May 1534:

> Having received on Wednesday last commission to take the oaths on the King's succession, assembled on Monday following, which was yesterday, at Winchester, my lord Chamberlain and others, my lord Audeley, and the abbots, priors, wardens of the Friars, &c., all of whom took the oath very obediently, presenting bills in the names of their parishioners who are above the age of 14. If he desires speed in this matter, wishes others to be put in the commission, for those now named are not more than 12. Taking the oaths requires a long time, especially if those of women are to be included.[104]

The swearing of the oath across the nation was further complicated by the public mood as the people did not support the king's second marriage. Public opinion sympathised with Queen Katherine's plight, believing that she had been mistreated. Henry was forcing the people of his nation to declare their support for the king. Neutrality was not an option and anyone who refused to take the oath was in fact registering their true feelings that they disagreed with the king and were against him. There were people who disagreed with the king but swore the oath in order to avoid punishment. According to Chapuys:

> People swore because they dared not offer opposition, the penalty being forfeiture of life and property, and no one in these times wished to become a martyr; besides which, several reconciled themselves to the idea, by the notion that oaths taken by force, against morality, were not binding, and that even if the oath was a true and legitimate one they could contravene it more honourably than the archbishop of Canterbury there present, who, the day after swearing fidelity and obedience to the Pope, had issued a summons against the Queen, in spite of and against all the advocations, inhibitions, pains, and very grave censures.[105]

Katherine and Princess Mary refused to take the oath. The king's commissioners threatened Katherine with death, but she stubbornly refused. Executing his first wife would incur the wrath of her nephew, Charles V, and Henry had already crossed a line when he divorced Katherine to marry Anne. Katherine's ladies-in-waiting also refused to take the oath were arrested and locked in their rooms. Four members of her household also declined and were sent to gaol.

Katherine was banished to Kimbolton Castle in Cambridgeshire, where she was attended by a small retinue of ladies and lived her remaining years in melancholic isolation as she lamented her husband bringing their marriage of two decades to a conclusion.

Henry ruled by fear and anyone who defied him would be severely punished, especially those subjects who refused to swear the oath to the Act of Succession.

Sir Thomas More Memorial, Chelsea

More Resists Swearing Henry VIII's Oath of Allegiance

Sir Thomas More was among the first individuals to refuse to swear the oath of allegiance during 1534. A bronze statue of More stands on the site of his Chelsea home. He sits on a chair on a plinth bearing his coat of arms at the rear, and the following words 'STATESMAN', 'SAINT' and 'SCHOLAR' are boldly inscribed.

More was born in about 1477/8 in London and his early education began at a school in Threadneedle Street. When he was aged 12, he was placed into the service of Cardinal John Morton, Archbishop of Canterbury, at Lambeth Palace where he was exposed to religion, theology, politics and was able to learn Latin. He continued his education at Canterbury Hall, Oxford from 1492–3 where he studied Latin and Greek, before embarking upon a legal career in 1499 when he entered New Inn, which was one of the Inns of Chancery at Lincoln's Inn. It was during his legal studies that he met the eminent Dutch scholar Erasmus and they both met Prince Henry at Eltham Palace. More contemplated taking holy vows and lived for four years as a Carthusian monk at Charterhouse in London. Here he wore a hair shirt that would cause pain and irritation as an act of atonement and would survive each day with little sleep. His decision not to pursue a life in religion was determined by his desire to marry Jane Colt in 1505. In 1510 he was appointed Under Sherriff of the City of London and in 1515 his book *Utopia* was published in Latin. This was a work of fiction that represented an island nation and created an idealistic religious world that resembled life in a monastery, based on the ideology of humanism, which Henry followed. The book was widely acclaimed in Europe and in 1517 he entered court serving as Henry's unofficial secretary. More was respected by the king and became a confidant. More's guidance with Henry's work *Assertio* was recognised and rewarded with a knighthood in 1521 and he was appointed Under-Treasurer of the Exchequer. More was selected as Speaker of the House of Commons in 1523 where the first plea for freedom of speech within the Chamber was recorded. He was appointed Chancellor of the Duchy of Lancaster in 1523. While serving in this role More was sent as ambassador on two diplomatic missions, to Emperor Charles V in Flanders and King Francis I in France.

As More advanced within the court, he became an affluent man, which enabled him to purchase a house in Chelsea, which at that time was a village outside London. Henry VIII would make unannounced visits to More in Chelsea as he was transported between his royal palaces along the River Thames. More was unaffected by the king's regard for him. More was not naive and knew the sovereign's capacity for unpredictability and ruthlessness a decade before he incurred his wrath. William Roper, who had married More's daughter, Margaret, wrote of the king's visits to More at his Chelsea home:

> And for the pleasure he took in his company would his grace suddenly sometime come home to his house at Chelsea to be merry

The memorial to Sir Thomas More stands on the site of his Chelsea home. The chapel where he worshipped is behind the statue. 'Statesman, Scholar and Saint' are inscribed at the base of the memorial. On 19 May 1935, 400 years after his death, Sir Thomas More was canonised by Pope Pious XI. (Author's Collection)

with him, whither on a time, unlooked for, he came to dinner, and after dinner, in a fair garden of his, walked with him by the space of an hour, holding his arm about his neck. As soon as his grace was gone, I rejoicing thereat, said to Sir Thomas More, how happy he was whom the king had so familiarity entertained, as I had never see him do to any before, except Cardinal Wolsey, whom I saw his grace walk once with arm in arm. 'I thank lord, son', quoth he, 'I find his grace my very good lord indeed, and I believe he doth as singularly favour me, as any subject within this realm: howbeit, son Roper, I may tell thee, I have no cause to be proud thereof, for if my head would win him a castle in France (for then there was war between us), it should not fail to go'.[106]

William Roper also wrote of More's daily routine at his Chelsea home:

As Sir Thomas More's custom was daily (if he were at home), besides his private prayers with his children, to say the Seven Psalms, the Litany, and the suffrages following, so was his guise nightly before he went to bed with his wife, children, and household, to go to his chapel, and there on his knees ordinarily to say certain psalms and collects with them. And because he was so desirous for godly pursuits, sometimes to be solitary and sequester himself from worldly company, a good distance from his mansion-house, builded he a place called the New Building, wherein there was a chapel, a library and a gallery, in which, as his use was on other days to occupy himself in prayer and study there together, so on the Fridays used he continually to be there from morning till evening, spending his time only in devout prayer and spiritual exercises.[107]

Hans Holbein the Younger lodged at Sir Thomas More's home for two years from December 1526. More was impressed with the artist's talent and was able to recommend him as a portrait painter among his social circle.

During October 1529, More was reluctant to accept Henry's offer to become Lord Chancellor. He knew that he would have to deal directly with the annulment of his marriage to Katherine and that could potentially compromise his Catholic faith. William Roper recalled the moment when Henry assured More that he would not be placed in a position where his role as Lord Chancellor would become conflicted with his faith.

> Now shortly upon his entry into the high office of the chancellorship, the King eftsoons again moved him to weigh and consider his great matter. Who falling down on his knees, numbly besought his highness to stand his gracious sovereign, as ever since his entry into his gracious service he had found him, saying, there was nothing in the world had been so grievous to his heart, as to remember that he was not able (as he willingly would with the loss of one of his limbs), for that matter, anything to find whereby he could serve his grace to his contention, as he that always bare in mind the most godly words that his highness spake unto him at his first coming into his noble service, the most virtuous lesson that ever prince taught his servant; willing him first to look unto God, and after God unto him.[108]

After Henry had guaranteed that he would seek advice relating to his great matter from other advisors, More accepted the role and was appointed Lord Chancellor by Henry VIII on 26 October 1529. Chapuys reported to Charles V: 'The Chancellor's seal has remained in the hands of the Duke of Norfolk till this morning, when it was transferred to Sir Thomas More. Everyone is delighted at his promotion, because he is an upright and learned man, and a good servant of the Queen'.[109]

More was of such good character that he did not abuse his position to gain personal benefit or fortune, demonstrated when he refused to accept a payment from bishops who wanted to reward him with £5,000 for safeguarding the interests of the clergy in Parliament after serving as Lord Chancellor. He also refused to be dazzled by the symbols of his position. When at home he would not wear the gold chain of the Lord Chancellor. Instead he focused upon supressing the rise of Lutherean ideology which was sweeping across England. His prosecution of heresy and support of the clergy to judge heretics brought condemnation in some sectors of the court. Thomas Cromwell challenged the jurisdiction of the clergy which sent heretics to execution, with many burnt at the stake, when he introduced a petition in Parliament which criticised this injustice. The matter was discussed in Parliament on 13 May 1532. Chapuys reported:

> Parliament is discussing the revocation of all synodal and other constitutions made by the English clergy, and the prohibition of holding synods without express licence from the King. This is a strange thing. Churchmen will be of less account than shoemakers, who have the

power of assembling and making their own statutes. The King also wishes bishops not to have the power to lay hands on persons accused of heresy, saying that it is not their duty to meddle with bodies (*personnes*), and they are only doctors of the soul. The Chancellor and the bishops oppose him. He is very angry, especially with the Chancellor and the bishop of Winchester, and is determined to carry the matter.[110]

Two days later after the debate in Parliament ecclesiastical jurisdiction was surrendered to the sovereign on 13 May 1532. The Church was no longer independent and all ecclesiastical laws had to be sanctioned by the king. More's faith was compromised and placed in direct conflict with the king. Two days later, More resigned from his position as Lord Chancellor and departed from court life because he was not prepared to alter his principles, faith and integrity. Chapuys reported: 'The Chancellor has resigned, seeing that affairs were going on badly, and likely to be worse, and that if he retained his office he would be obliged to act against his conscience or incur the King's displeasure, as he had already begun to do, for refusing to take his part against the clergy'.

More's defiance and dedication to his faith would have fatal consequences. When Henry invoked the Act of Succession in 1534 and forced his subjects to swear an oath of allegiance to the king and heirs, More refused to take the oath. When he was summoned on 13 April 1534 to appear before commissioners headed by the Archbishop of Canterbury at Lambeth Palace, More knew that he would be leaving his Chelsea home for the last time. More's son-in-law, William Roper, recalled the moment when he embarked on a barge that would transport him to Lambeth Palace:

Then Sir Thomas More, as his accustomed manner was always ere he entered into any matter of importance – as when he was first chosen of the King's privy council, when he was sent ambassador, appointed Speaker of Parliament, made Lord Chancellor, or when he took any weight matter upon him – to go to church and be confessed, to hear mass, and be houseled, so did he likewise in the morning early the selfsame day that he was summoned to appear before the lords at Lambeth. And whereas he evermore used before, at his departure from his wife and children, whom he tenderly loved, to have them bring him to his boat, and there to kiss them, and bid them all farewell, then would he suffer none of them forth of the gate to follow him, but pulled the wicket after him, and shut them all from him, and with a heavy heart, as by his countenance it appeared with me and our four servants there took boat towards Lambeth. Wherein sitting sadly for a while, at the last he rounded me in the ear and said: 'Son Roper, I thank our Lord the field is won.' . . . I conjected afterwards, it was for that the love he had to God wrought in him so effectually, that it conquered all his carnal affections utterly.[111]

Lambeth Palace

Sir Thomas More Refuses to Swear Henry VIII's Oath to the Succession

Within a month of the introduction of the statute for the Act of Succession and the accompanying oath of allegiance to the king and his successors, Sir Thomas More and all the priests from London were summoned to Lambeth Palace. They were to appear before the Archbishop of Canterbury, Thomas Cranmer, the Lord Chancellor, Thomas Audley and secretary Thomas Cromwell, who would act as commissioners appointed to receive the oath from them.

On 13 April 1534 More was brought by barge from Chelsea along the River Thames to Lambeth where he passed through Morton's Tower, the main gatehouse, which is the entrance to Lambeth Palace, the London residence of the Archbishop of Canterbury. More recalled the proceedings in a letter to his daughter Meg, written on 17 April:

> When I was before the Lords at Lambeth, I was the first that they called in. . . . after the cause of my sending for, declared unto me . . . I desired the sight of the oath, which they showed me under the great seal. Then desired I the sight of the act of the succession, which was delivered me in a printed roll. After which read secretly by myself, and the oath considered with the act, I showed unto them, that my purpose was not to any fault either in the act or any man that made it, or in the oath or any man that swear it, not to condemn the conscience of any other man. But to as for myself in good faith my conscience so moved me in the matter, that though I would not deny to swear to the succession, yet unto that oath that there was offered me, I could not swear without the jeopardising of my soul to perpetual damnation. And that if they doubted whether I did refuse the oath only for the grudge of my conscience, or for any other fantasy, I was ready therein to satisfy them by mine oath. Which if they not trusted, what should they be the better to give me any oath. And if they trusted that I would therein swear true, then trusted I that of their goodness they would not move me to swear the oath that they offered me, perceiving that for to swear it was against my conscience.[112]

More acknowledged the Act of Succession and recognised Princess Elizabeth as heir to the throne, but he refused to take the oath. Thomas Audley responded on behalf of the commissioners, said that they were sorry that More declined to take the oath and confirmed that he was the first person to refuse to take the oath. More was ordered to adjourn to another chamber, while the commission took the oaths of the other priests. The commission then gave More another opportunity to take the oath for which he repeatedly refused. Frustrated by More's stubbornness, Cromwell said 'that he had sooner that his own only son had lost his head than that I should thus refused the oath'.

Declining to provide a satisfactory reason for his refusal, More remained silent. He was taken into the custody of the Abbot of Westminster for four days while the king consulted with his

Morton's Tower, Lambeth Palace. The main entrance was built in 1490 during Archbishop John Morton's tenure and was named after him. It is a fine example of a Tudor gatehouse. On 13 April 1534, Sir Thomas More arrived by barge from Chelsea and entered through the gates of Morton's Tower. Inside the palace, Archbishop Cranmer, Thomas Cromwell and Thomas Audley failed to convince More to dismiss his conscience, to reject the Pope's authority and swear oath of allegiance to the king. (Author's Collection)

council to decide how to deal with his refusal to take the oath. Henry was initially prepared to accept More's acknowledgment of the Act and, despite not taking the oath, he was prepared to discharge him. However, Anne Boleyn was not content with the king's decision and influenced him to try to force More to take the oath.

William Roper recalled: 'Yet did Queen Anne by her importunate clamour so sore exasperate the king against him [More], that, contrary to his former resolution, he caused the said Oath of Supremacy to be ministered unto him. Who albeit he made a discrete qualified answer, nevertheless was committed to the Tower'.[113]

52

Traitors' Gate

Sir Thomas More Enters the Tower of London

Traitors' Gate is situated beneath St Thomas's Tower, which was built in the 1270s during the reign of Edward I. It was used as an access point from the river and as a royal residence. During the Tudor period, this gateway became known as Traitors' Gate and symbolises Henry VIII's reign of terror where political prisoners accused of treason entered the Tower of London for incarceration. Sir Thomas More, Bishop John Fisher and several priests who had refused to swear the oath of succession in April 1534 were among those unfortunate souls that arrived at these gates by barge on the River Thames. The majority of prisoners of the state, including Thomas Cromwell, passed through Traitors' Gate on their arrival at the Tower of London and back and forth for their trials at Westminster.

On 16 April 1534, Sir Thomas More and Bishop John Fisher were sent to the Tower because they would not swear the oath of allegiance to the king and his heirs. Henry was punishing them in order to set an example to others who did not acknowledge the Act and hoped that the experience of being incarcerated in the Tower of London would encourage them to change their minds. William Roper recalled the moment when More arrived at Traitors' Gate:

At whose landing Master Lieutenant was ready at the Tower gate to receive him, where the porter demanded of him his upper garment. 'Master porter', quoth he, 'here it is,' and took off his cap and delivered it to him, saying 'I am very sorry it is no better for thee'.

'No Sir' quoth the porter, 'I must have your gown.' And so was he by Master Lieutenant conveyed to his lodging.[114]

More was permitted to bring along his servant, John Wood, to attend upon him while imprisoned in the Tower. Although Wood was illiterate, he was made to swear to report to the lieutenant if he should see or hear More at any time speak or wrote anything against the king or the realm.

The news of More and Fisher's imprisonment in the Tower of London caused fear across the nation and alarm in the royal courts of Europe. Chapuys wrote to the Charles V: 'I am told this morning that the bishop of Rochester [Fisher], the late Chancellor [More] and several other good men have been sent to the Tower because they have refused to swear to the statutes lately made, and in this fear the mayor and governors of this city have today been compelled to swear'.[115]

On 17 April 1534, Henry wanted to eradicate the influence of the Pope's authority within England. He did not want anyone to undermine him as head of the Church of England, although this title had not been ratified by Parliament at that stage. Henry therefore authorised the Earl of Sussex to issue the 'Warrant to cause to be arrested and committed to ward, without bail or mainprise, seditious persons who spread, teach, preach or otherwise set forth pernicious opinions and doctrines, to the exaltation of the power of the bishop of Rome [the Pope]'.[116]

When on 17 April 1534, Archbishop Cranmer suggested to Cromwell that it was acceptable for More and Fisher to accept the Act of Succession

Traitors' Gate. St Thomas's Tower was built by King Edward I between 1275 and 1279. He was able to berth his royal barge within this watergate, inside the Tower of London. (Author's Collection)

Traitors' Gate, as seen from outside the walls of the Tower of London. (Author's Collection)

but not to swear the oath, Cromwell replied with the response of the king.

> Have shown your letters to the King, who does not agree with you that the bp. of Rochester and Mr. More should be sworn to the Act of Succession and not to the preamble, as it would give occasion to all men to refuse the whole, for if they were sworn to the succession and not to the preamble, it might be taken as a confirmation of the bishop of Rome's authority, and a reprobation of the King's second marriage. He thinks, therefore, that they should be sworn to both the Act and the preamble [and trusts to your wisdom to bring it to effect].[117]

Henry needed all prominent men in the Church and at court to conform to the Act of Succession and take the oath in order for the entire nation to follow suit. If More and Fisher were allowed to openly defy the king as head of the Church of England, the stance of More and Fisher would influence and motivate other dissenters whose allegiances were with the Pope. Both More and Fisher had been sent to the Tower of London, at the king's pleasure, for misprision and their property confiscated by the king. More lost everything that was given to him by the king and his Chelsea home. Henry would use the Tower of London as a symbol to enforce his subjects to accept the oath of succession and him as the Supreme Head of the Church of England.

53

Bell Tower

Sir Thomas More Imprisoned in the Bell Tower Within the Tower of London

The Bell Tower is the second oldest tower within the Tower of London and stands in the south-western corner of the fortress. This circular tower contains one floor above the ground floor. It is called the Bell Tower because it is surmounted by a small wooden turret which contains the bell which was rung to signal the curfew or raise the alarm within the fortress. It is believed that Sir Thomas More was imprisoned within the thick walls of the Bell Tower during 1534-5, and Bishop John Fisher was held in the cell above on similar charges of refusing to swear the oath of allegiance to the king and his heirs during April 1534; and later that year for declining to acknowledge Henry VIII as Supreme Head of the Church of England. During the early part of his incarceration More was permitted to walk within the grounds of the Tower of London, but as he continued to refuse to conform and swear the oath of allegiance, his privileges were gradually taken away and Henry VIII made further restrictions upon his former friend and mentor, who was now his prisoner.

Within a month of his arrival, More's daughter, Meg, was allowed to visit him. The Lieutenant of the Tower entered his room and in the presence of his daughter More was given another opportunity to swear the oath which would secure his release from captivity. Once again More declined. Alice, his wife, was permitted licence to visit More in the Bell Tower in order to persuade him to swear the oath so that he could gain his liberty and return to his home in Chelsea. Alice said:

> What the good-yere, Master More. I marvel that you that have been always hitherto taken for so wise a man will now so play the fool to lie here in this close filthy prison, and be content thus to be shut up among mice and rats, when you might be abroad at your liberty, and with the favour and good will both of the king and his council if you would but do as all the bishops and best learned of this realm have done, And seeing you have at Chelsea a right fair house, your library, your gallery, your garden, your orchid, and all the other necessaries so handsome about you, where you might in the company of me your wife, your children, your household, be merry, I muse what a God's name you mean here still thus fondly tarry.[118]

Henry wanted to keep political prisoners such as More in a state of isolation, depravation and penury, in an effort to wear down their resolve and encourage them to submit to swearing the oath. It was More's friendship with the Constable of the Tower of London which saved him from suffering the hardships experienced by fellow prisoners of state. Bishop John Fisher was also imprisoned in the Bell Tower for the same reason as More and after several months of imprisonment his health was suffering. On 22 December 1534, Fisher, who was aged 80, wrote directly to Thomas Cromwell to appeal for improved conditions, food, books and clothes or his liberty. In that letter, he provided an idea of the deprivations experienced while imprisoned in the Tower of London:

> Furthermore I beseech you to be good master unto me in my necessity; for I have neither shirt, nor suit, nor yet other clothes, that are necessary for me to wear, but that be ragged, and rent to shamefully. Notwithstanding, I might easily suffer that if they would keep my body warm. But my diet also, god knoweth how slender is it at many times. And now in my age my stomach may not away but with a few kind meats, which if I want, I decay forthwith, and fall into coughs and diseases of my body and cannot keep myself in health. And, as our lord knoweth I have no thing left unto me for to provide any better, but as my brother of his own purse layeth out for me, to his great hinderance. Wherefore good master secretary have sons, I beseech you to have pity upon me, and let me have such things as are necessary for me in my age, and specially for my health. And also that it may please you by your high wisdom, to move the King's Highness to take me unto his gracious favour again, and to restore me unto my liberty, out of this cold and painful imprisonment; whereby you should bind me to be your poor beadsman for ever unto Almighty God, who ever have you in his protection and custody.
>
> Other two things I must also desire upon you; that it may please you that one is, that I may take some priest with me in the Tower, by the assignment of the master lieutenant, to hear my confession against this holy time. That other is, that I may borrow some books to stir my devotion more effectually these holy days, for the comfort of my soul. This I beseech you to grant me of your charity.[119]

The Bell Tower, Tower of London. Sir Thomas More and Bishop John Fisher were imprisoned here during 1534–5 because they refused to accept the king as Supreme Head of the Church of England. In 1554, Princess Elizabeth, the future Queen of England, was incarcerated within the Bell Tower. (Author's Collection)

On 30 April 1535, Thomas Cromwell and members of the Privy Council, including Thomas Audley and the Dukes of Norfolk and Suffolk, visited Sir Thomas More in the Bell Tower. They wanted to give him another opportunity to swear the oath, given that the king and his future heirs were proclaimed 'the supreme head in earth of the Church of England under Christ' through an Act of Parliament and to refuse to take the oath was an act of treason. They encouraged him to confess the Supremacy or deny it. More wrote that it was 'the King's pleasure, that those of his council there assembled, should demand mine opinion, and what mind was therein'. More attempted to remain neutral declaring 'I have in good faith discharged my mind of all such matters, neither will dispute king's titles nor popes': but the King's true faithful subject I am, and will be, and daily I pray for him.... and for all the realm'. Cromwell persisted in his attempt to extract the oath from More, offering him mercy and asking More if it was fair to enforce the Act of Supremacy upon everyone in the country, but make allowance for him. When Cromwell commented upon More's obstinacy, More would not be influenced into taking the oath and in his answer he confirmed his willingness to die for his faith and principles:

> Whereto I answered, that I give no man occasion to hold any point one or other. And for conclusion I could no farther go, whatsoever pin should come thereof. I am (quoth I) the King's true faithful subject and daily bedesman, and pray for his highness and all the realm. I do nobody no harm, I say no harm, I think no harm, but wish everybody good. And if this be not enough to keep a man alive, in good faith I long not live . . . and therefore my poor body is at the king's pleasure. Would God my death might do him good.[120]

Cromwell made numerous attempts to encourage More to take the oath. On another occasion, More responded:

> For if it were that my conscience gave me against the statute (wherein how my conscience giveth me I make no declaration) then I, nothing doing nor nothing saying against the statute, it were a very hard thing, to compel me to say, either precisely with it against my conscience to the loss of my soul, or precisely against it to the destruction of my body.[121]

Henry needed More to take the oath, and his refusal was a direct action against the king's will and so long as More stood his ground his refusal could be used as a rallying point for anyone who opposed the king. Therefore, Sir Thomas More would remain imprisoned in the Bell Tower until he submitted to the king's will.

54

The Act of Supremacy, 1534

Henry VIII as Head of the Church of England

In order to completely sever ties with Rome, Henry needed Parliament to sanction the conclusions reached by the convocation of the clergy, which consented to Henry becoming Head of the Church of England during April 1533 and declared that Henry's marriage to Katherine was invalid. The Act contained a single paragraph which replaced the Pope with the king as the one with overall authority over the clergy within England. They were not giving the king additional powers but recognising that authority already belonged to him. The decisions made by the convocation of the clergy had eroded papal authority and the Act of Supremacy, during November 1534, was a mechanism for Parliament to affirm that the king and his heirs:

> shall be taken, accepted and reputed the only Supreme Head in earth of the Church of England called *Angelicana Ecclesia*, and shall have and shall enjoy annexed and united to the Imperial Crown of this realm as well the title and style thereof, as all honours, dignities, pre-eminences, jurisdictions, privileges, authorities, immunities, profits and commodities, to the said dignity of the Supreme Head of the same Church belonging and appertaining.[122]

The Act of Supremacy was passed by Parliament on 3 November 1534. As Supreme Head, the Act empowered Henry and his heirs with the mandate and consent of Parliament to make any modifications and reforms to the Church of England, independent of influence from the Vatican. The king was now responsible for ecclesiastical issues and policy by consent of the people. The Act of Supremacy went on to assert:

> That our Sovereign Lord, his heirs, his successors, kings of this realm, shall have full power and authority from time to time to visit, repress, redress, reform, order, correct and restrain, and amend all such errors, heresies, abuses, offences, contempts and enormities, whatsoever they be, which by any manner spiritual authority or jurisdiction ought or may lawfully be reformed, repressed, ordered, redressed, corrected, restrained, or amended, most to the pleasure of Almighty God, the increase of virtue in Christ's religion, and for the conservation of the peace, unity, and tranquillity of this realm: any usage, custom, foreign laws, foreign authority, prescription, or any other thing or things to the contrary hereof notwithstanding.[123]

The Act of Supremacy would allow the king control of the English Church, break from the Catholic Church in Rome and power to grant his own divorce from Katherine and to legitimise his marriage to Anne Boleyn, who he hoped would provide a male heir and secure the Tudor dynasty.

A Treasons Act was also introduced during November 1534 to deal with those individuals who opposed and refused to accept the changes made by Henry VIII to the constitution and the Reformation of the Church, including the Act of Supremacy and the legitimacy of his new marriage to Anne Boleyn. The act was designed

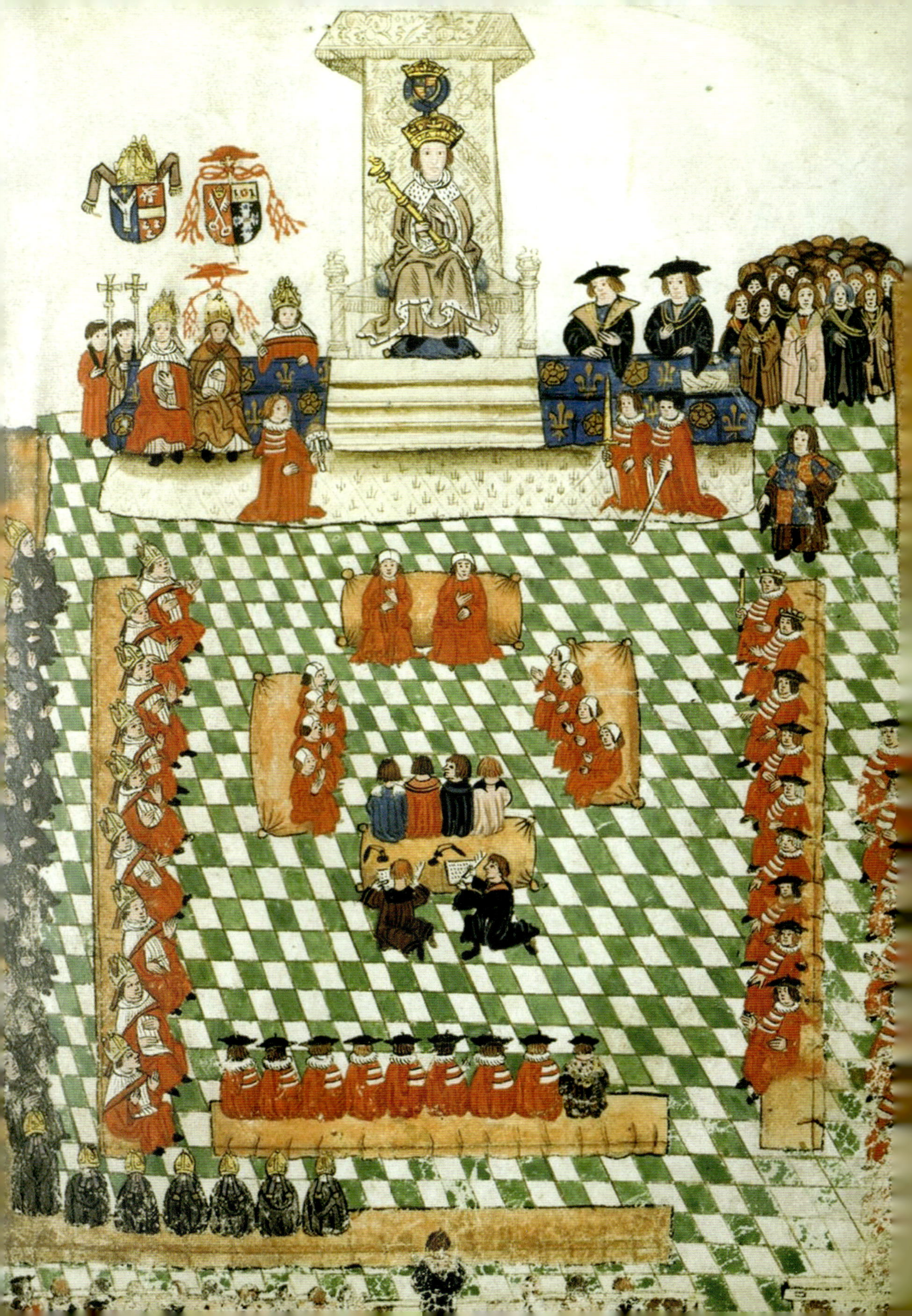

to criminalise and punish anyone who verbally contested the king as head of the Church of England, or those individuals such as Sir Thomas More and Bishop John Fisher, who refused to accept the oath of Royal Supremacy. The Act targeted persons that:

> Do maliciously wish, will, or desire by words or writing, or by crafty images invent, practise, or attempt any bodily harm to be done or committed to the King's most royal person, the Queen's, or their heirs apparent, or to deprive them or any of them of the dignity, title, or name of their royal estates, or slanderously or maliciously publish and pronounce, by express writing or words that, that the King our Sovereign Lord should be heretic, schissmatic, tyrant, infidel, or usurper of the Crown.[124]

The Act also made it a treasonable offence for anyone to withhold or refuse to surrender, castles, fortresses, ships, artillery, ordinances and munitions of war to the king. Anyone who was found guilty through this Act would 'suffer such pains of death'.

The implications of this Act were considered across Europe and fears were expressed for the safety of More, Fisher, Queen Katherine and her daughter, Princess Mary. Eustace Chapuys wrote on 5 May 1535:

> A rumour is afloat that this King has had summonses served on the bishop of Rochester (Fisher), on Master More, on a doctor, once his confessor, as well as on one of the Queen's chaplains, and on the Princess's tutor (*precepteur*), enjoining them to swear to the statutes lately promulgated here against the Pope, and against the said Queen and Princess, as otherwise they will be dealt with as were the aforesaid monks. A term of six weeks has been granted to them to advise on the matter; and I am given to understand that all, without exception, have answered that they are ready to suffer martyrdom at the King's pleasure, and that neither the six weeks' respite granted to them, nor six hundred years, if they could possibly lire through them, would work any change in their opinion. It is generally believed that they will be dispatched as were the others. And, as several worthy personages conjecture, should this King lose all shame, and get used to such cruelties, it is to be feared that the lives of both Queen and Princess will be in jeopardy, and that they will be dispatched secretly, if not in public, the King's mistress helping with all her power towards that end; for she is known to have frequently reproached the King, and told him that it was a shame for him and for the whole kingdom not to punish them as traitors and defaulters against the letter of the statutes. Indeed, the concubine is now fiercer and haughtier than ever she was, and has been bold enough to tell the King, as I hear, that he is as much indebted to her as ever man was to woman, for she has been the cause of his being cleansed from the sin in which he was living; and, moreover, that by marrying her as he had done, he had become the richest monarch that ever was in England, inasmuch

OPPOSITE: This illustration is believed to be the earliest surviving contemporary image of the opening of Parliament. It originates from the Wriothesley Garter Book of Parliament of England, and depicts Henry VIII opening Parliament in 1523. Eleven years later, the Act of Supremacy would be passed as legislation through Parliament, which acknowledged Henry VIII and his successors as the Supreme Head of the Church of England. (Royal Collection/Public Domain)

as without her he would never have been able to reform the affairs of the Church in his kingdom, to his very great personal profit and that of his kingdom.

Henry had demonstrated that he could divorce Katherine and marry Anne Boleyn. Although Princess Elizabeth had been born and this Act of Supremacy was designed to anoint her as heir apparent in precedence, he still held the firm belief that Anne would bear him a son and this Act gave power to 'his successors, kings of this realm'. He had successfully enforced his will in defiance of the Pope, who was powerless to do anything, and Emperor Charles V, who dared not challenge Henry militarily in order to safeguard his aunt's interests. The Act of Supremacy reinforced the notion that England would not be influenced by foreign governments or leaders, and asserted his authority over his subjects internally. Henry had total control over his subjects, including their souls and faith, dictating what they should believe in. Regarding himself as God's representative on earth, Henry had prevailed and effectively elevated himself to becoming the Pope and Emperor of England.

55

Tyburn Memorial

Six Carthusian Monks Executed at Tyburn

At Marble Arch in London there is a marker stone denoting the site of the Tyburn Tree, which was where traitors were executed during the reign of Henry VIII. Individuals who were found guilty were condemned to be hung, drawn and quartered. On 4 May 1535, six Carthusian monks suffered that fate at Tyburn.

They were among the victims of the Act of Supremacy and Treasons Act. More saw from the Bell Tower the departure of the monks to their execution. His daughter was visiting him at that same time and he said to her:

> Lo, dost thou not see, Meg, that these fathers be now as cheerfully going to their deaths as bridegrooms to their marriage? Wherefore thereby mayest thou see, mine own good daughter, what a great difference there is between such as have an effect spent all their days in a straight hard, penitential and painful life, religiously, and such as have in the world, like worldly wretches, as thy poor father hath done, consumed all their time in pleasure and ease of licentiously. For God, considering their long-continued life in most sore and grievance penance, will no longer suffer them to remain here in this vale of misery and iniquity, but speedily hence taketh them to the fruition of His everlasting deity.[125]

Dressed in their habits, the six monks were taken to Tyburn where they received the death of a traitor, which involved being hung by the neck, then while conscious disembowelled and then their bodies were hacked to pieces. Eustace Chapuys reported:

> Yesterday three Carthusians, and one monk of the Order of St. Brigitis, all men of good and sound doctrine, as well as exemplary life and reputation, were dragged through the streets of this capital to the place of execution, and there put to death for no other cause than their having said and maintained that the Pope was the true chief and sovereign of the universal Christian Church, and that, according to God, reason, and conscience, it did not appertain to this King to usurp the sovereignty of the Church and supremacy over the English clergy. Which declaration, for the relief of their own and the King's conscience, the said monks went of their own accord to make before Cromwell about three weeks ago; and upon the latter pointing out the danger of such uncalled-for declaration, and advising them to take warning before matters went any farther, all resolutely answered that they would rather suffer one hundred deaths than change their opinion. About a week ago the duke of Norfolk, in representation of the King, his master, assisted by the Chancellor (Audeley), Master Cromwell, the ordinary judges of the kingdom, the knights of the Garter who had attended the solemn ceremony of St. George, and several other lords, sat in court and interrogated the said monks, who made most commendable answers to all questions, and maintained their assertions until, as I have been told, it being deemed impossible to

LEFT and ABOVE: The Tyburn Tree stone is positioned on an island in the road at Marble Arch, south of the Edgeware Road. (Author's Collection)

convince them by reasoning, they were told that the statute had been made, and was not to be disputed, and that unless they retracted and spoke in other terms they had better withdraw, and come next day to hear their sentence. Accordingly, the day after the monks appeared again before the Court, and were again much exhorted to retract; and upon their refusal to do so, they were, after long disputation, condemned by lay judges, and declared guilty of treason and the crime of 'læsæ majestatis'. There was no question of degradation, nor unfrocking. The same fate was shared by a priest for having spoken and written against this King and his government.[126]

Henry wanted the execution of the Carthusian monks to serve as a warning to potential dissenters who refused to acknowledge the Acts of Supremacy and Succession.

Westminster Hall

Sir Thomas More Tried for Treason

Westminster Hall is all that remains of the Palace of Westminster, which had been the epicentre of government and the principal residence of the monarch since the eleventh century until most of it was destroyed by fire in 1512. Henry and Katherine kept a vigil in the Chapel of St Stephen during the night before their coronation and a banquet was held in Westminster Hall on 24 June 1509 after Henry and Katherine had been crowned at Westminster Abbey. In October 1529, Sir Thomas More was led by the Dukes of Suffolk and Norfolk into Westminster Hall and then up to the Chancery, where he was sworn in as Chancellor of England. Six years later, More was brought to Westminster Hall to be tried for treason and condemned to death. A small plaque within Westminster Hall is dedicated to Sir Thomas More stating that he was condemned to death there on 1 July 1535.

The Act of Supremacy had escalated More's refusal to accept the oath of Royal Supremacy as an act of treason. The line which stated 'to deprive them or any of them of the dignity, title, or name of their royal estates' had brought him from the Tower of London to Westminster Hall where, on 1 July 1535, he was charged with high treason before a special Commission of Oyer and Terminer, which translates to 'hear and determine'. The commission comprised ten peers and ten judges, presided over by Sir Thomas Audley, the Lord Chancellor. The Dukes of Norfolk and Suffolk, Thomas Cromwell and Anne Boleyn's father, the Earl of Wiltshire, and her brother George, Lord Rochford, were among those who formed the commission judging More.

All the charges revolved around More depriving the king of his title as Supreme Head of the Church of England. He was first charged with refusing to answer questions when examined by a council led by Cromwell; More exclaimed, 'I will not meddle with any such matters, for I am determined to serve God, and to think upon his passion, and my passage out of this world.' By not addressing the oath, he was refusing to acknowledge the king as Supreme Head of the Church and his marriage to Anne Boleyn.

The second charge against More related to a letter that he had written to Bishop John Fisher regarding the Act of Supremacy: 'The Act is like a two-edged sword; if I speak against it I shall cause the death of my body, and if I assent to it I shall purchase the death of my soul'.

The third indictment related to a conversation he had in the Tower when he said to Richard Rich, if a statute made the king Supreme Head of the Church, then he could not be bound to it.

After the charges were read to him, the Duke of Norfolk gave him a final opportunity to swear the oath of the king's supremacy: 'You, Master More, have gravely erred against the King; nevertheless, we hope by his clemency that if you repent and correct your obstinate opinion in which you have so rashly persevered, you will receive pardon.'

More declined this final chance to save his life and replied: 'My lords, I thank you very heartily for your good will. I pray God preserve me in my just opinion even to death.' After a chair

Westminster Hall hosted the banquets celebrating the coronation of Henry VIII in 1509 and the coronation of Anne Boleyn in 1533. Two years later, during 1535, Sir Thomas More was tried for treason in this hall. On 12 May 1536, Norris, Weston, Brereton and Mark Seaton were tried here for treason on the basis of their alleged relationships with Anne Boleyn, while married to Henry VIII, and they were found guilty. (Gimas/Shutterstock)

was brought for him to be seated, he proceeded to address each charge that was brought against him.

As to the first article, charging me with having always maliciously opposed the King's second marriage, I will only answer that what I have said has been according to my conscience. I never wished to conceal the truth, and if I had, I should have been a traitor. For this error, if error it should be called, I have been condemned to perpetual imprisonment, which I have already suffered for fifteen months, and my goods confiscated. For this reason I will only reply to the principal charge against me, that I have incurred the penalty of the Statute made in the last Parliament since I was in prison, by refusing to the King his title of Supreme Head of the Church, in proof of which you allege my reply to the Secretary and Council, that as I was dead to the world, I did not care to think of such things, but only of the passion of Christ. I reply that your Statute cannot condemn me to death for such silence, for neither your Statute nor any laws in the world punish people except for words or deeds,—surely not for keeping silence.[127]

The second charge laid against More was that he conspired against the statute. This accusation was based on eight letters that he wrote to Bishop John Fisher. The prosecution confirmed that these letters had been burnt by Fisher and it was left to More to prove to the court that they were not the basis for a conspiracy against the Act of Supremacy. More testified:

> Some were about private matters connected with our old friendship. Another was a reply to one of his asking how I had answered in the Tower to the first examination about the statute. I said that I had informed my conscience, and so he also ought to do the same. I swear that this was the tenor of the letters, for which I cannot be condemned by your statute.[128]

On the third charge, More responded:

> Touching the third article, that when I was examined by the Council, I answered that your Statute was like a two-edged sword, for he who approved it would ruin his soul, and he who contradicted it, his body; and that the bishop of Rochester answered similarly, showing that we were confederates, I reply that I only answered thus conditionally, that if the Statute cut both ways like a two-edged sword, how could a man behave so as not to incur either danger? I do not know how the Bishop replied, but if he answered like me, it must have been from the agreement between us in opinion, but not because we had ever arranged it between us. Be assured I never did or said anything maliciously against the Statute, but it may be that this has been maliciously reported to the King.[129]

More pleaded not guilty after addressing each charge. He was confident that he could hold his ground, however it was the evidence of Richard Rich that condemned him. Rich had served as Solicitor General since 1533 and had participated in the prosecution of those who had refused to swear the oath of supremacy. He had already condemned to death Bishop John Fisher and the Carthusian monks a month before More was brought to trial for the same crime.

Rich had visited More in the Bell Tower to confiscate his books, during which time he engaged in a conversation that would incriminate More. According to Rich, More denied the king's title as Supreme Head of the Church of England. More disputed this accusation and it is not mentioned in Roper's book. However, Rich's words would incriminate and bring a successful conviction against More. After Richard Rich presented his evidence, More responded:

> If I were a man, my lords, that did not regard an oath I needed not, as it is well known, in this place, and at this time, nor in this case to stand here as an accused person. And if this oath of yours, Master Rich, be true, then I pray that I never see God in the face, which I would not say, were it otherwise, to win the whole world, . . . In good faith Master Rich, I am sorrier for your perjury than for mine own peril, and you shall understand that neither I nor no man else to my knowledge, ever took you to be a man of such credit as in any matter of importance I or any other would at any time vouchsafe to communicate with you.[130]

An usher then ordered twelve men on the jury to consider if More had maliciously contravened the statute in his denial to swear the oath in accordance with the Act of Supremacy. More was standing in front of judges that were not impartial. There existed a serious conflict of interest for they represented the king. The Earl of Wiltshire was Anne Boleyn's father and the Duke of Norfolk was her uncle. It was in their own interests to ensure that Anne's position as queen was secure, which would ultimately sure up their own positions within Henry's court. After 15 minutes of deliberation, More, was found guilty and was condemned to death. After sentencing, More responded: 'Since I am condemned, and God knows how, I wish to speak freely of your Statute, for the discharge of my conscience. For the seven years that I have studied the matter, I have not read in any approved doctor of the Church that a temporal lord could or ought to be head of the spirituality.'

Thomas Audley, the Lord Chancellor, interjected with a question, 'What, More, you wish to be considered wiser and of better conscience than all the bishops and nobles of the realm?'

More answered: 'My lord, for one bishop of your opinion I have a hundred saints of mine; and for one parliament of yours, and God knows of what kind, I have all the General Councils for 1,000 years, and for one kingdom I have France and all the kingdoms of Christendom'.

More was isolated as he sat in Westminster Hall. As he tried to respond to the sentence, he received another interruption from Duke of Norfolk, who asserted that More's last sentence was an indication of his malice. More continued:

> What I say is necessary for discharge of my conscience and satisfaction of my soul, and to this I call God to witness, the sole searcher of human hearts. I say further, that your Statute is ill made, because you have sworn never to do anything against the Church, which through all Christendom is one and undivided, and you have no authority, without the common consent of all Christians, to make a law or Act of Parliament or Council against the union of Christendom. I know well that the reason why you have condemned me is because I have never been willing to consent to the King's second marriage; but I hope in the divine goodness and mercy, that as St. Paul and St. Stephen whom he persecuted, are now friends in Paradise, so we, though differing in this world, shall be united in perfect charity in the other. I pray God to protect the King and give him good counsel.[131]

Sir Thomas More, painted by Hans Holbein the Younger in 1527, around the time that the artist was lodging at More's home in Chelsea. More is pictured wearing the chain of the Royal Servant. The SS design represents the livery of the House of Lancaster and the Beaufort Porticulus forms the clasp from which the Tudor rose is suspended. (Frick Collection)

After being condemned to death, More was returned to the Tower of London to await his execution. His daughter, Margaret, waited for him to pass through Tower Wharf before he entered the fortress. Passing through guards armed with halberds and bills, she embraced her father one final time before he entered the Tower of London.

57

Bishop John Fisher and Sir Thomas More, Execution Memorial Plaque, Tower Hill

Executed for Defying Henry VIII

A plaque on Tower Hill commemorates the execution of Bishop John Fisher and Sir Thomas More in 1535. Both men had refused to acknowledge King Henry VIII as Supreme Head of the Church of England and to swear an oath. They resolutely upheld their faiths and their allegiance to the Pope in Rome, but they were both tried and condemned for treason; both would ultimately die martyrs for their faith and values.

Preserving his faith and his allegiance to the Pope, Fisher had grown weak while imprisoned in the Tower of London. In recognition of his suffering for his support and loyalty to the Catholic Church and its authority, Pope Paul III appointed Fisher a cardinal, which further antagonised Henry VIII. This gesture would hasten Fisher's fall, because he was tried on 17 June 1535 and found guilty of treason. Sir Thomas Audley, Lord Chancellor and presiding judge, ordered that he be returned to the Tower of London from where he would be paraded through the streets of the city and taken to Tyburn, where he would be hung, brought down to have his bowls removed and burnt in front of him and finally beheaded. He decreed that his body be divided into four parts and sent

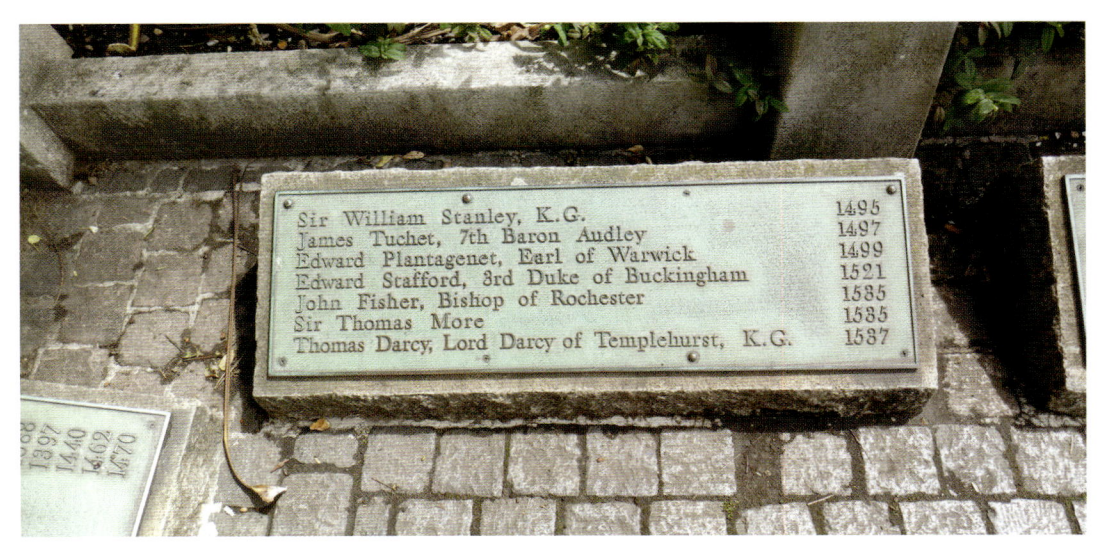

A close-up of the plaque that commemorates the executions of Sir Thomas More and Bishop John Fisher. It also remembers two other executions that took place during the reign of Henry VIII, the execution of Edward Stafford, Third Duke of Buckingham, in 1521 and Lord Thomas Darcy in 1537. (Author's Collection)

to parts of the kingdom as the king desired as a warning to others across the nation not to defy him. Henry VIII considered the frailty of Fisher and commuted the sentence to beheading which was carried out on this site at Tower Hill on 22 June 1535. Fisher did not live to receive the cardinal's cap, which was sent to Rome, for it had reached Calais on the day of his execution. His body was initially buried in All Hallows Church and his head impaled upon a spike on London Bridge. Fisher's remains were later reinterred in St Peter ad Vincula Church, within the confines of the Tower of London.

After he was found guilty of treason and condemned to death on 1 July 1535, Sir Thomas More had to wait seven days before his execution. On 5 July 1535, the day before his execution, More wrote his last letter to his daughter, Margaret, using a piece of coal, in which he wrote, 'I cumber you, good Margaret, much, but would be very sorry if it should be any longer than tomorrow. For tomorrow is Saint. Thomas Eve, and the Utas of Saint. Peter, and therefore tomorrow long I to go to God; it were a day very meet and convenient for me.'[132] This letter and the hair shirt that he wore were sent to Margaret after his execution.

More's wish for the sentence to be carried out came to fruition when during the early hours of the morning of 6 July 1535, his friend, Sir Thomas Pope, brought a message from the king, advising that he was to die before 9am that same day and that he was to prepare himself for that end. Aware that he had only hours to live, More spoke fondly of the king:

> Master Pope, for your good tidings I heartily thank you. I have always been much bounden to the King's highness for the benefits and honours that he had still from time to time most bountifully heaped upon me; and yet more bounden am I to his grace for putting me into this place, where I have had convenient time and space to have remembrance of my end. And so help me God, most of all, Master Pope, am I bounden to his highness that it pleaseth him so shortly to rid me out of the miseries of this wretched world, and therefore will I not fail earnestly to pray for his grace, both here, and also in the world to come.[133]

Pope also warned More not to say too many words at the scaffold, to which More assured him that he was 'ready obediently to conform . . . to his grace's commandment'. More was probably mindful that if he spoke words against the king on the scaffold, then Henry VIII might punish his family as an act of reprisal. Pope was advising More on behalf of the king. The public would witness the execution and the king did not want More to speak against him and so incite dissent or inflame a rebellion. More requested that his family and friends be present at his burial to which the weeping Pope assured him that this request would be granted by the king. Later that morning the Master Lieutenant led the condemned More from the Tower of London to this spot on Tower Hill for execution. As he approached the scaffold, More was accosted by a lady who accused him for holding some deeds while he was in office. More replied, 'Good woman, have patience a little, for the King is so gracious to me, that, within, this half hour, he will discharge me of all my business, and help thee himself.'[134]

As he was about to ascend the unstable wooden stairs that led to the scaffold that had been constructed for his execution, More jovially commented, 'Master Lieutenant, see me safe up, and for my coming down let me shift myself.'

Once on the scaffold, according to his son-in-law, William Roper, More addressed the crowds, 'then he desired all the people there about to pray for him, and to bear witness with him, that he should now there suffer death in and for the faith of the holy Catholic Church'. Edward Hall, who served as an under-sheriff in the City of London during that year and witnessed the execution, does not mention his appeal for prayers to the onlookers, but both he and Roper recall that More kneeled at the block and after saying his final prayers, he turned to the executioner and said, 'Pluck up thy spirits, man, and be not afraid to do thine office: my neck is very short, take heed, therefore, thou strike not awry, for saving of thine honesty'.

As More stretched out his hands to signal that he was ready to receive his punishment, the executioner swung his heavy axe towards the block and with one strike More was decapitated. Hall mentioned that 'even when he should lay down his head on the block, he having a great grey beard, striked out his beard and said to the hangman, I pray you let me lay my beard over the block least you should cut it, thus with a mock he ended his life'. The executioner picked up More's head and raised it to the crowd declaring, 'behold the head of a traitor'. More's decapitated body was transferred from the scaffold and taken to St Peter ad Vincula for burial, within the Tower of London. His head was boiled and taken to London Bridge where the head of Fisher was removed from a spike and replaced with the head of Sir Thomas More. After a month, the executioner was responsible for removing the head from London Bridge and discarding it in the River Thames, however, it is believed that More's daughter bribed him to pass it to her and that his skull was eventually interred in the Roper family vault at St Dunstan's Church, Canterbury.

More had died for his faith and was beatified as a martyr on 19 May 1935 by Pope Pius XI, exactly 400 years after his execution, alongside Bishop John Fisher, who was also beatified as a saint on that same day.

A picture painted by William Frederick Yeames in 1872 depicting the meeting of Sir Thomas More with his daughter, Margaret, after being condemned to death. He is seen being returned to the Tower of London to await his execution.

58
Title Page of the Valor Ecclesiasticus

Report of the Assets and Revenue of Religious Houses in England

The Valor Ecclesiasticus was the result of the survey of the lands and wealth of the religious houses of England carried out in 1535. It was used to determine which religious esablishments were to be closed during the dissolution of the monasteries.

Once Henry VIII had become the Supreme Head of the English Church and had separated from the Pope and Catholic religion in 1534, he imposed taxes upon the churches and monasteries within England. Money that would have been paid to the Pope in Rome would now be paid to the King of England. Henry implemented a new annual income tax upon these religious institutes of 10 per cent per annum towards the end of 1534. In order to assess how much was owed by religious institutes across the country, Henry needed to know the wealth of those organisations.

In January 1535, Henry appointed Thomas Cromwell, Vicar-General of the Church, and ordered him to conduct a census of assets and wealth owned by the Church for the purpose of tax collection, as well as assessing the condition of the monasteries across England and to assert the Royal Supremacy. Commissioners were appointed to collect financial information about each religious house, determine the value of the property and the annual income generated; through this

Illuminated title page of the Valor Ecclesiasticus. (The National Archives)

audit clergymen would declare their revenue and the commissioners would examine documentation to support their claims and the value of the properties. This census was the equivalent of the census conducted during the eleventh century to compile the Domesday Book. The Commissioners executing this audit were local noblemen, mayors and sheriffs who were unpaid and they were given until May 1535 to complete the task.

Once this census had been completed by July 1535, Cromwell commissioned six canon lawyers to visit the monasteries to evaluate religious practices and to identify if reform was required. This was a cover to masquerade their real intentions which were to find evidence of abuses of the Church that were incriminating and would warrant a suppression of the monasteries and enable Henry VIII to seize their wealth. During the last six months of 1535, Henry VIII began confiscating Church property and assets in order to improve the royal finances; this process became known as the dissolution of the monasteries.

This is the illuminated title page of the document known as the Valor Ecclesiasticus, which was the result of the survey of the lands and wealth of the religious houses of England. It is significant because it determined which monasteries should be closed and became the template for the dissolution of the monasteries during the period 1536–40 when approximately 800 churches, abbeys, monasteries and friaries, accommodating 10,000 friars, monks and nuns, were dissolved. King Henry VIII dominates the image sitting with his arms and legs stretched out, asserting his authority as his courtiers cower around him.

Portrait of Henry VIII, 1535

Middle-Aged Henry

This portrait painted by Joos van Cleve in 1535 shows a middle-aged, handsome Henry VIII aged 44. Henry VIII is depicted holding a scroll inscribed 'Go ye into all the world, and preach the Gospel to every creature' (Mark 16.15). By the time this portrait was painted, Henry had devoted the previous eight years to attempting to prove that Katherine was not his lawful wife. Since marrying a second time, in 1533, he had spent the following two years attempting to obtain recognition and acknowledgement for Anne Boleyn as his wife and respect for her as his queen.

By 1535, despite making himself Supreme Head of the English Church in an effort to usurp the Pope's authority and by introducing various Acts through Parliament to force his subjects to demonstrate acknowledgement of Anne Boleyn as Henry's wife and queen and executing those that refused, Henry was experiencing difficulty in winning support at home and abroad. His actions had resulted in religious dissension and suppression across England, with him persecuting anyone who would not accept him as Supreme Head of the English Church. The Valor Ecclesiasticus had audited the assets and wealth of the churches, abbeys and friaries in England during 1535 and Henry was beginning the process of seizing those assets. Henry's actions against the Church in England were frowned upon overseas. On the international stage he had politically isolated England from European nations which accepted papal authority. He had placed England in danger of invasion from a coalition of those nations, sponsored by the Pope to free England from Henry's tyranny and religious suppression.

Henry was also under pressure from Anne Boleyn, who was anxious to ensure that Princess Elizabeth, her daughter, was next in the line of succession. So long as Katherine and Mary were alive, they would attract empathy from many people in England and from overseas. They could be the pivot and rallying point for revolt, which would place her position in jeopardy. Anne and the Boleyn family would have felt more secure in court if Katherine and Mary had suffered the same fate as More and Fisher, but Henry was not prepared to order the execution of his first wife and eldest daughter, although he had not forgiven Katherine for her refusal to accept their divorce.

It is ironic that after several years of pursuing Anne Boleyn and all the efforts made to engineer a divorce with Katherine that by the end of 1535 Henry's relationship with Anne Boleyn had started to deteriorate. She had failed to bear him a son and he was in desperate need of a male heir to ensure stability within England and preserve the Tudor dynasty. Anne was openly critical of Henry, especially when he was embarking upon extra-marital affairs with mistresses. Henry may have desired to be rid Anne Boleyn from his life, but he did not want to lose prestige in the eyes of those that dissented against him.

In January 1536, Henry was knocked from his horse resulting in him receiving an incurable, ulcerous wound to his leg which would affect him for the remainder of his life. Without a male heir, Henry's mood was black and as the new year began, he was thinking of finding another suitor to give him a son.

Henry VIII by Joos van Cleve 1535. (Royal Collection/Public Domain)

60

Tomb of Katherine of Aragon, Peterborough Cathedral

Queen Katherine's Death

Katherine continued to resist the king's will, refusing to take the oath of allegiance and not accepting that her marriage had ended. In May 1534, Henry sent Katherine to Kimbolton Castle where he had removed the privileges of royalty from her, forcing her into a life of impoverishment. She devoted herself to prayer and needlework. Although she refused Cardinal Campeggio's attempts to persuade her to live in a nunnery at Blackfriars in 1529, her existence was similar to life in such an establishment.

At Kimbolton Castle Katherine was surrounded by people that were loyal to the king. Dr Pedro Ortiz, Charles V's ambassador in Rome, wrote on 16 December 1535:

> The Imperial ambassador writes that he has not leave to visit or send any person to see the Queen and Princess. Those with the Queen are guards and spies, not servants, for they have sworn in favour of Anne, not to call her highness Queen, nor serve her with royal state. So, not to give them cause to sin, the Queen has not left her chamber for two years; and perhaps if she wished to, it would not be allowed, '*y que no manda un ducado*', nor has she any of her old servants except her confessor, physician, and apothecary. The King always asks those who wish to join him (*se quisieren juntar con el*) to renounce obedience to the Apostolic See, and he who formerly appealed to a Council now wishes it not to be held.[135]

While living in seclusion at Kimbolton Castle, Katherine was aware of those championing her cause and papal authority and it grieved her that people like More, Fisher and the Carthusian monks were so committed to their faith that they were willing to die for their convictions. She became very concerned that more lives were to be lost for that cause. On 10 October 1535, in a letter to Pope Paul III she wrote 'for, if a remedy be not applied with all speed, there will be no end to the loss of souls or to the making of martyrs. The good will be constant and suffer, the lukewarm perhaps fall away, and the rest stray like sheep without a shepherd.' Katherine was also in fear that she and her daughter would suffer the same fate as More and Fisher. Dr Ortiz reported: 'The ambassador in England writes of the incredible cruelties prepared in Parliament. The King has twice said that the Queen and Princess are traitors, and despise the statutes, and that though he lose his crown they shall suffer the same penalty as others. The ambassador declares most seriously that they are in great danger'.[136]

The stress of the divorce and the threat of execution as a mechanism to intimidate her to swear the oath of succession and accept the separation severely affected Katherine's health. By early December 1535 she had become ill, but rallied. Her nephew, Emperor Charles V, wrote to Chapuys on 29 December 1535:

> The ill will of the King of England to the Queen and Princess is cruel and horrible.

TOMB OF KATHERINE OF ARAGON, PETERBOROUGH CATHEDRAL

The tomb of Queen Katherine of England, surrounded by the banners of Henry VIII. (Author's Collection)

The tomb of Queen Katherine of Aragon, surmounted by pomegranates. Katherine's coat of arms features a crowned pomegranate, the heraldic emblem of the city of Granada and also a symbol of fertility and marriage. Visitors leave pomegranates on the tomb as a mark of respect. (Author's Collection)

It is impossible to believe that he would be so unnatural as to put them to death, considering his ties to them, their descent, their virtues and long sufferings. He probably intends by threats to make them swear to and approve his statutes.[137]

On that same day Chapuys received a letter from Katherine's physician advising that Katherine had relapsed, she was vomiting, suffering stomach pains, unable to eat and was unable to walk or sit upright in bed. Her condition had worsened considerably since earlier that month. Chapuys immediately visited Henry at Greenwich Palace to seek permission to visit Katherine at Kimbolton Castle. Chapuys wrote:

At last he said that he believed the Queen, whom he only called Madame, would not live long, and that if she died you would have no cause to trouble yourself about the affairs of this kingdom, and might refrain from stirring in this matter. I said the death of the Queen could do no possible good, and that in any event the sentence was necessary. After I had taken leave of the King he recalled me by the duke of Suffolk to tell me news had just come that the Queen was *in extremis*, and that I should hardly find her alive; moreover, that this would take away all the difficulties between your Majesty and him.[138]

It is apparent from this meeting that Henry was not concerned for the health of his first wife and that he was looking forward to the prospect of her death in the hope that it would improve his political relationship with Charles V. The king allowed Chapuys to visit Katherine on provision that a friend of Thomas Cromwell accompanied him. His remit was to spy upon Chapuys and record what was said between the Spanish Ambassador and Katherine. They hastily rode northwards, arriving at Kimbolton on 2 January 1536. Chapuys reported that Katherine believed that 'if it pleased God to take her, it would be a consolation to her to die under my guidance (*entre mes braz*) and not unprepared, like a beast'.

Chapuys attempted to comfort Katherine, even resorting to an untruth 'that the King was very sorry for her illness; and on this I begged her to take heart and get well'. Chapuys had raised Katherine's spirits and morale during his four-day visit. Her condition had improved and she was able to eat without vomiting and he reported that she was cheerful before he returned to London. However, her health deteriorated two days after his departure. It was reported to Chapuys that after he left her:

The Queen appeared to be better; and even on the day of the Kings (Epiphany), on the evening of which she, without any help, combed and tied her hair and dressed her head. Next day, about an hour after midnight, she began to ask what o'clock it was, and if it was near day; and of this she inquired several times after, for no other object, as she at length declared, but to be able to hear mass and receive the sacrament. And although the bishop of Llandaff, her confessor, offered to say mass before 4 o'clock, she would not allow him, giving several reasons and authorities in Latin why it should not be done. When day broke she heard mass and received the sacrament with the utmost fervour, and thereafter continued to repeat some beautiful orisons, and begged the bystanders to pray for her soul, and that God would pardon the King her husband the wrong he had done her, and that the divine goodness would lead him to the true road and give him good counsel. Afterwards she received extreme unction, applying herself to the whole office very devoutly.[139]

Katherine died at 2pm on 7 January 1536. Katherine's physician indicated to Chapuys the cause of her death was due to poison. If this was the case, the king, Anne Boleyn and her family would benefit from her demise. Chapuys reported to Charles V:

The Queen's illness began about five weeks ago, as I then wrote to your Majesty, and the attack was renewed on the morrow of Christmas day. It was a pain in the stomach, so violent that she could retain no food. I asked her physician several times if there was any suspicion of poison. He said he was afraid it was so, for after she had drunk some Welsh beer she had been worse, and that it must have been a slow and subtle poison for he could not discover evidences of simple and pure poison; but on opening her, indications will be seen.[140]

However, Chapuys later stated that Katherine's physician was not present at her autopsy and the person who carried it out was not medically qualified, which indicates that foul play may have been the cause of her death. Chapuy continued his report:

The Queen died two hours after midday, and eight hours afterwards she was opened by command of those who had charge of it on the part of the King, and no one was allowed to be present, not even her confessor or physician, but only the candle-maker of the house and one servant and a 'compagnon', who opened her, and although it was not their business, and they were no surgeons, yet they have often done such a duty, at least the principal, who on coming out told the bishop of Llandaff, her confessor, but in

Peterborough Cathedral, burial place of Queen Katherine of England. (Chris Dorney/Shutterstock)

great secrecy as a thing which would cost his life, that he had found the body and all the internal organs as sound as possible except the heart, which was quite black and hideous, and even after he had washed it three times it did not change colour. He divided it through the middle and found the interior of the same colour, which also would not change on being washed, and also some black round thing which clung closely to the outside of the heart. On my man asking the physician if she had died of poison, he replied that the thing was too evident by what had been said to the Bishop her confessor, and if that had not been disclosed the thing was sufficiently clear from the report and circumstances of the illness.[141]

Twentieth-century physicians confirmed that the black colour of Katherine's heart was most likely a result of cancer, caused by the stress of the breakdown of her marriage. Her corpse was placed in a lead coffin containing spices and laid in a chapel at Kimbolton Castle for three weeks. However, the reaction of the king did not stop rumours circulating within England and Europe that he might have played a role in her death for Henry was not shaken or showed any signs of bereavement. Both Henry and Anne were joyful at the news. Henry exalted on the day of hearing the news 'God be praised that we are free from all suspicion of war.' It was believed within the English court that with Katherine gone, the grievance between Charles V and

Henry was removed, and so the prospect of war with Spain diminished. After dinner, on the night after receiving notification of her death, Henry and Anne danced. Chapuys thought that Anne was disrespectful for wearing yellow that evening, however Edward Hall wore yellow 'for mourning'.

Henry VIII sought a way to seize Katherine's money and possessions, despite the fact that her will divided her wealth among Mary, her daughter, and her servants. This action conflicted with Henry's campaign during the past decade to argue that Katherine was not his lawful wife, however Richard Rich, the Solicitor-General, found a solution where Henry could claim her property without acknowledging that Katherine was his wife.

In another report written on 21 January 1536, Chapuys suggested that Anne Boleyn, who he referred to as the 'concubine' in many of his reports, was responsible for the death of Katherine:

> If they were compelled to swear all that the King wished (besides the bad effect mentioned in your Majesty's letters, that so many would lose heart and join the new heresy), the danger would be, not that the King would proceed by law to punish daily disobedience, but that, under colour of perfect reconciliation, if he were to treat them well,—I don't suppose the King but the Concubine (who has often sworn the death of both, and who will never be at rest till she has gained her end, suspecting that owing to the King's fickleness there is no stability in her position as long as either of the said ladies lives), will have even better means than before of executing her accursed purpose by administering poison, because they would be less on their guard; and, moreover, she might do it without suspicion, for it would be supposed when the said ladies had agreed to everything that the King wished and were reconciled and favourably treated after they had renounced their rights, there could be no fear of their doing any mischief, and thus no suspicion would arise of their having received foul play.[142]

Queen Katherine, seen here in this portrait by Michael Sittow, was aged 49 when she died on 7 January 1536 at Kimbolton Castle. She remained according to her motto, 'Humble and loyal' to her king and husband until the day she died. (Everett Historical/Shutterstock)

There was so much conjecture and speculation circulating around England and reaching heads of states abroad that Katherine of Aragon had died as a result of foul play. Conspiracy theories were being considered. According to Chapuys, the English people believed that king was responsible for Katherine's death: 'From all I hear the grief of the people at this news is incredible, and the indignation they feel against the King, on whom they lay the blame of her death, part of them believing it was by poison and others by grief; and they are the more indignant at the joy the King has exhibited.'[143]

Public opinion remained against Henry, and his marriage to Anne Boleyn, He did not want to inflame the situation by holding Katherine's funeral in London, so therefore she was buried three weeks after her death on 29 January 1536 at the Benedictine Abbey at Peterborough, contrary to her wish to be buried in one of the convents of the Observant Friars. She was interred as Dowager, Princess of Wales, and Henry who was not in attendance, forbade Princess Mary to attend her mother's funeral. Katherine's funeral cortège was draped in black velvet and pulled by six horses. The body was accompanied by fifty servants, dressed in black and carrying torches, together with four golden standards. The Bishops of Lincoln, Ely and Rochester received the body at the western entrance of the abbey and it was then taken to a chapel lit with a thousand candles and displaying eighteen banners, one of which was the flag of her nephew, Emperor Charles V.

Chapuys was critical that she was not buried as queen:

> There were present four bishops and as many abbots, but no other man of mark except the comptroller of the King's Household. The place where she is buried in the church is far removed from the high altar, and much less honourable than that of certain bishops buried there; and even if they had not taken her for princess dowager as they have done in death and life, but only as simple baroness, they could not have given her a less honourable place, as I am told by men acquainted with those matters.[144]

Peterborough Abbey was dissolved in 1539, but survived as a church when Henry selected it to become a cathedral in 1541, perhaps as a memorial to his first wife. Katherine's tomb was desecrated by Oliver Cromwell's troops in 1643 and the current black slab covering it was installed in 1895, having been funded by an appeal for donations from women named Katherine. Although she was denied the title of queen at her burial, today her tomb bears the name 'Katherine Queen of England'.

Site of the Great Hall, Tower of London

Anne Boleyn Tried for Treason

Here is the site of the Great Hall and the queen's quarters, where Anne Boleyn resided and was tried for alleged adultery in 1536. The queen's lodgings were positioned between the Wardrobe Tower and Lanthorn Tower which formed part of the royal apartments. The Lanthorn Tower was referred to in a survey conducted in 1532 as the New Tower after Henry VIII ordered renovation work on it. Anne previously stayed here before her coronation in 1533, but three years later she returned as a prisoner. The Great Hall stood in between Wakefield Tower and Lanthorn Tower, parallel to the southern wall of the fortress. These buildings no longer exist as they were destroyed by fire in 1774.

On 29 January 1536, the same day as Katherine's funeral, Anne Boleyn suffered a miscarriage. The foetus was male and Anne was believed to have been three-and-half months pregnant. Anne blamed rumours of Henry's affairs and the news of his recent accident, when he fell from his horse on the tiltyard at the Greenwich, as a reason for losing the child. Instead of comforting Anne after the miscarriage, Henry was more concerned with the prospect of not fathering a male heir. Chapuys, referring to Queen Anne as the 'concubine', reported:

> I learn from several persons of this Court that for more than three months this King has not spoken ten times to the Concubine, and that when she miscarried he scarcely said anything to her, except that he saw clearly that God did not wish to give him male children; and in leaving her he told her, as if for spite, that he would speak to her after she was 'releuize' [back on her feet].[145]

Anne was in a precarious situation and the prospect of her giving birth to a male heir was becoming increasingly remote. It seemed that Henry was considering finding another wife who could bear him a son. Chapuys confirmed that 'some think it was owing to her own incapacity to bear children, others to a fear that the King would treat her like the late Queen, especially considering the treatment shown to a lady of the Court, named Mistress Semel, to whom, as many say, he has lately made great presents.' 'Mistress Semel' was a reference to Jane Seymour, a lady-in-waiting to Anne and whom Henry was already infatuated with at the time of Anne's miscarriage in January 1536.

Henry openly doubted the validity of his marriage to Anne within his court. Chapuys heard confirmation from a courtier that:

> He had made this marriage, seduced by witchcraft, and for this reason he considered it null; and that this was evident because God did not permit them to have any male issue, and that he believed that he might take another wife, which he gave to understand that he had some wish to do. The thing is very difficult for me to believe, although it comes from a good source. I will watch to see if there are any indications of its probability.[146]

When Henry heard accusations that Anne Boleyn had had sexual relations with several other men, including court organist Mark Smeaton,

The queen's lodgings were between Wardrobe Tower and Lanthorn Tower, marked by the row of benches. Anne Boleyn stayed here in 1533 prior to her coronation and three years later as a prisoner. (Author's Collection)

Henry Norris, Chief Gentleman of the Privy Chamber and Groom of the Stool, Sir Frances Weston, William Brereton and her own brother, George, Lord Rochford, he ordered Thomas Cromwell to investigate. After undergoing torture on the rack for 4 hours in the Tower of London on 1 May 1536, Smeaton confessed to Cromwell that he had committed adultery with Anne. On 2 May, Anne was arrested at Greenwich, and brought by barge to the Tower of London. She was escorted into the Tower of London by her uncle, the Duke of Norfolk, and two chamberlains. She was permitted to take four ladies to attend upon her. There was no fanfare, no artillery salute and no king to greet her at Queen's Stairs, unlike three years previously when she made the same journey for her coronation. Sir William Kingston, Constable of the Tower of London, received Anne and reported her arrival to Thomas Cromwell:

> On my lord of Norfolk and the King's Council departing from the Tower, I went before the Queen into her lodging. She said unto me,

'Mr. Kingston, shall I go into a dungeon?' I said, 'No, Madam. You shall go into the lodging you lay in at your coronation.' 'It is too good for me', she said; 'Jesu have mercy on me'; and kneeled down, weeping a good pace, and in the same sorrow fell into a great laughing, as she has done many times since. She desired me to move the King's hymns that she [might] have the sacrament in the closet by her chamber, that she might pray for mercy, for I am as clear from the company of man as for sin as I am clear from you, and am the King's true wedded wife. And then she said, Mr. Kingston, do you know where for I am here? and I said, Nay. And then she asked me, when saw you the King? and I said I saw him not since I saw him in the tiltyard. And then, Mr. K., I pray you to tell me where my Lord, my father, yes? And I told her I saw him after dinner in the Court. O where is my sweet brother? I said I left him at York Place; and so I did. I hear say, said she, that I should be accused with three men; and I can say no more but nay, without I should open my body. And there with opened her gown. O, No, hast thou accused me? Thou are in the Tower with me, [and thow and I shall] die together; and, mark, thou art here to.[147]

Anne, Norris and Rochford did not admit to adultery. Two other men, Weston and Brereton, were also arrested. In a letter to Henry VIII written on 6 May 1536, Anne pleaded for a fair trial:

Your Grace's displeasure and my imprisonment are things so strange unto me as what to write or what to excuse I am altogether ignorant. Whereas you sent unto me, willing me to confess a truth and so to obtain your favour, by such an one whom you know to be my ancient professed enemy, I no sooner received this message by him than I rightly conceived your meaning; and if, as you say, confessing a truth indeed may procure my safety, I shall with all willingness and duty perform your command. But do not imagine that your poor wife will ever confess a fault which she never even imagined. Never had prince a more dutiful wife than you have in Anne Boleyn, with which name and place I could willingly have contented myself if God and your Grace's pleasure had so been pleased. Nor did I ever so far forget myself in my exaltation but that I always looked for such an alteration as now; my preferment being only grounded on your Grace's fancy. You chose me from a low estate, and I beg you not to let an unworthy stain of disloyalty blot me and the infant Princess your daughter. Let me have a lawful trial, and let not my enemies be my judges. Let it be an open trial, I fear no open shames, and you will see my innocency cleared or my guilt openly proved; in which case you are at liberty both to punish me as an unfaithful wife, and to follow your affection, already settled on that party for whose sake I am now as I am, whose name I could some while since have pointed unto, your Grace being not ignorant of my suspicion therein. But if you have already determined that my death and an infamous slander will bring you the enjoyment of your desired happiness, then I pray God he will pardon your great sin, and my enemies, the instruments thereof. My innocence will be known at the Day of Judgment. My last request is that I alone may bear the burden of your displeasure, and not those poor gentlemen, who, I understand, are likewise imprisoned for my sake. If ever I have found favour in your sight, if ever the name of Anne Boleyn has been pleasing in your ears, let me obtain this request, and so I will leave to trouble your Grace any further. From my doleful prison in the Tower.[148]

Brereton, Norris, Smeaton and Weston were brought to Westminster Hall for trial on 12 May 1536 when they were charged with 'high treason against the King, for using fornication with the Queen Anne, wife to the King, and also for conspiracy of the Kings death'. Mark Smeaton pleaded 'guilty of violation and carnal knowledge of the Queen'. Smeaton admitted committing adultery with the Queen on three occasions, but Brereton, Norris and West affirmed their innocence. All were found guilty and condemned to death. Their punishment was to be hung, drawn and quartered. Chapuys thought that the convictions of Brereton, Norris and Weston were unsafe, 'condemned upon presumption and certain indications, without valid proof or confession'.

In the interests of security, Anne and her brother George were tried within the Great Hall at the Tower of London on 15 May 1536. Anne was charged with treason against the king, with conducting sexual relations with Brereton, Norris, Smeaton and Weston and an incestuous relationship with her brother, George, Lord Rochford.

The Duke of Norfolk, George and Anne's uncle, officiated as Lord High Steward and presided over the trial in front of a panel of judges that included twenty-six peers of the realm. Among those passing judgement were the king's friend, Charles, Duke of Suffolk, Henry, Earl of Northumberland, a former suitor of Anne, and their father the, Earl of Wiltshire, who was remarkably willing to participate in that judgement.

The charges were probably unfounded and used as a mechanism for Henry to remove Anne from his life so that he was free to marry Jane Seymour in hope of conceiving a son and heir. Chapuys heard that 'even before the arrest of the Concubine, the King, speaking with Mistress Jane Semel of their future marriage'.

Henry would place his second wife in a situation where her virtue was in question, which would be judged by a commission in front of a large gathering of 2,000 spectators, who viewed proceedings from specially constructed stands within the Great Hall. Anne was tried before her brother and had to defend herself. It was an impossible task, for she had already been condemned by verdicts made upon her alleged lovers three days previously at Westminster Hall. There were many witnesses who claimed to have seen the queen commit adultery, who provided testimonies relating to situations and circumstances which were most likely misconstrued, which ultimately condemned the Queen. Achieving a successful conviction upon her brother George for incest was difficult to prove without witnesses, so he was tried after Anne. The following indictments were brought against the Queen:

Queen Anne has been the wife of Henry VIII. for three years and more, she, despising her marriage, and entertaining malice against the King, and following daily her frail and carnal lust, did falsely and traitorously procure by base conversations and kisses, touchings, gifts, and other infamous incitations, divers of the King's daily and familiar servants to be her adulterers and concubines, so that several of the King's servants yielded to her vile provocations; viz., on 6th Oct. 25 Hen. VIII., at Westminster, and divers days before and after, she procured, by sweet words, kisses, touches, and otherwise, Henry Norris, of Westminster, gentle man of the privy chamber, to violate her, by reason whereof he did so at Westminster on the 12th Oct. 25 Hen. VIII.; and they had illicit intercourse at various other times, both before and after, sometimes by his procurement, and sometimes by that of the Queen. Also, the Queen, 2 Nov. 27 Hen. VIII. and several

The Great Hall was located between Lanthorn Tower (left) and Wakefield Tower (right), and was where Anne Boleyn and her brother, George Rochford, were tried in 1536. (Author's Collection)

times before and after, at Westminster, procured and incited her own natural brother, George Boleyn, lord Rochford, gentleman of the privy chamber, to violate her, alluring him with her tongue in the said George's mouth, and the said George's tongue in hers, and also with kisses, presents, and jewels; whereby he, despising the commands of God, and all human laws, 5 Nov. 27 Hen. VIII., violated and carnally knew the said Queen, his own sister, at Westminster; which he also did on divers other days before and after at the same place, sometimes by his own procurement and sometimes by the Queen's. Also, the Queen, 3 Dec. 25 Hen. VIII., and divers days before and after, at Westminster, procured one William Brereton, late of Westminster, gentleman of the privy chamber, to violate her, whereby he did so on 8 Dec. 25 Hen. VIII., at Hampton Court, in the parish of Littlehampton, and on several other days before and after, sometimes by his own procurement and sometimes by the Queen's. Also, the Queen, 8 May 26 Hen. VIII., and at other times before and since, procured Sir Francis Weston, of Westminster, gentleman of the privy chamber, &c., whereby he did so on the 20 May, &c. Also, the Queen, 12 April 26 Hen. VIII., and divers days before and since, at Westminster, procured Mark Smeaton, groom of the privy chamber, to violate her, whereby he did so at Westminster, 26 April 27 Hen. VIII.

Moreover, the said lord Rochford, Norris, Brereton, Weston, and Smeaton, being thus inflamed with carnal love of the Queen, and having become very jealous of each other, gave her secret gifts and pledges while carrying on this illicit intercourse; and the Queen, on her part, could not endure any of them to converse with any other woman, without showing great displeasure; and on the 27 Nov. 27 Hen. VIII., and other days before and after, at Westminster, she gave them great gifts to encourage them in their crimes. And further the said Queen and these other traitors, 31 Oct. 27 Hen. VIII., at Westminster, conspired the death and destruction of the King, the Queen often saying she would marry one of them as soon as the King died, and affirming that she would never love the King in her heart. And the King having a short time since become aware of the said abominable crimes and treasons against himself, took such inward displeasure and heaviness, especially from his said Queen's malice and adultery, that certain harms and perils have befallen his royal body.[149]

Anne's alleged indiscretions were probably misinterpretations of her affectionate and playful nature, but they provided Henry with the opportunity of ending his second marriage. Anne was found guilty and condemned to death by burning or beheading on Tower Green within the confines of the Tower of London. The method of her death was to be decided by the king. The sentence was pronounced by her uncle the Duke of Norfolk who said:

> Because thou have offended our Sovereign, the King's grace, in committing treason against his person and her attainted of the same, the law of the realm is this, that thou has deserved death, and thy judgement is this: that thou shall be burnt here within the Tower of London on the Green, or to have thy head smitten off as the King's pleasure shall be further known.

It must have caused both Anne and George so much pain that their uncle and father, their own flesh and blood, were willing to sacrifice their own family in order to stay in favour with the king and preserve their positions within the court.

Either Chapuys or one of his representatives was present, for he produced this detailed report of the trial:

> Neither the *pertain* nor her brother was brought to Westminster like the other criminals. They were condemned within the Tower, but the thing was not done secretly, for there were more than two thousand persons present. What she was principally charged with was having cohabited with her brother and other accomplices; that there was a promise between her and Norris to marry after the King's death, which it thus appeared they hoped for; and that she had received and given to Norris certain medals, which might be interpreted to mean that she had poisoned the late Queen and intrigued to do the same to the Princess. These things she totally denied, and gave to each a plausible answer. Yet she confessed she had given money to Weston, as she had often done to other young gentlemen. She was also charged, and her brother likewise, with having laughed at the King and his dress, and that

she showed in various ways she did not love the King but was tired of him. Her brother was charged with having cohabited with her by presumption, because he had been once found a long time with her, and with certain other little follies. To all he replied so well that several of those present wagered ten to one that he would be acquitted, especially as no witnesses were produced against either him or her, as it is usual to do, particularly when the accused denies the charge.[150]

Rochford was also found guilty by the panel, with the exception of the Earl of Northumberland, who had to withdraw as a result of becoming ill, probably due to the shock of condemning his former love, Anne. Rochford was sentenced to be transferred from the Tower through the City of London to the gallows at Tyburn, where he was to be hung. Chapuys continued:

> They were judged separately, and did not see each other. The Concubine was condemned first, and having heard the sentence, which was to be burnt or beheaded at the King's pleasure, she preserved her composure, saying that she held herself 'pour toute saluee de la mort', and that what she regretted most was that the above persons, who were innocent and loyal to the King, were to die for her. She only asked a short space for shrift. Her brother, after his condemnation, said that since he must die, he would no longer maintain his innocence, but confessed that he had deserved death.

Queen Anne remained in her lodgings at the Tower waited upon by Lady Kingston, the wife of the Constable of the Tower, and her aunt, Lady Boleyn. On the day after her trial, she held the desperate hope that the king would not allow her death sentence to be carried out. Her jailer, Sir William Kingston, reported to Thomas Cromwell, 'Yet this day at dinner the Queen said she would go to "anonre" [a nunnery], and is in hope of life.'

Any hopes of a reprieve were futile for the king had ordered a swordsman from Calais to execute the queen. He had commuted her sentence from beheading by axe to decapitation by sword. Death by sword was quicker, requiring just one strike at the neck. An axe could take three strikes before the head was decapitated. While waiting for her sentence to be carried out, she was informed that on 17 May 1536 Archbishop Cranmer, presiding over a court of ecclesiastical lawyers, in the presence of Sir Thomas Audley and Charles, Duke of Suffolk at Lambeth Palace, pronounced Anne's marriage invalid. Henry purposely delayed the annulment of his second marriage because if the divorce had been passed before the trial, Anne could not have been convicted of adultery and he would have been unable to declare that Princess Elizabeth was illegitimate alongside her step-sister, Princess Mary, therefore removing her from the line of succession.

62

Tower Green

The Site of Anne Boleyn's Execution

Only a small number of executions took place on Tower Green within the walls of the Tower of London. Most prisoners who were condemned as traitors were executed on Tower Hill. Three queens and several high-profile prisoners, mainly nobility, were executed in the privacy of Tower Green, out of sight of public spectators, because they were easy to control. Anne Boleyn, Margaret Pole, Countess of Salisbury, Queen Catherine Howard and Jane Boleyn were executed here during the reign of Henry VIII.

Queen Victoria was so affected by the story of Anne Boleyn that she ordered a memorial be dedicated to those who suffered such brutal deaths on Tower Green during the reign of Henry VIII. Today, a memorial sculptured by Brian Catling commemorates the site where prominent prisoners were executed. Inaugurated in 2006, a glass cushion raised above a green glass pane which bears the names of those executed here and their dates of death is secured upon a black marble base with the following words inscribed: 'Gentle visitor pause a while, where you stand death cut away the light of many days. Here jewelled names were broken from the vivid thread of life. May they rest in peace while we walk the generations around their strife and courage under these restless skies.'

However, some historians have disputed that this is the actual site where Anne Boleyn and other prisoners were executed and have identified the position as being between the entrance to the Waterloo Barracks where the Crown jewels are displayed and the north face of the White Tower. Charles Wriothesley, who may have witnessed the execution, states: 'Anne Boleyn was brought to execution on the green within the Tower of London, by the Great White Tower'.

Anne had hoped for clemency from the king and that her execution would not take place. Sir William Kingston, Constable of the Tower, wrote to Thomas Cromwell on 16 May 1536 'yet this day at dinner the Queen said she would go to "anonre" (a nunnery) and is in hope of life.'

Rochford, Brereton, Norris, Smeaton and Weston were executed on 17 May 1536. They were not taken to Tyburn to be hung as sentenced during their trial at Westminster Hall, but were executed outside the walls of the Tower of London on Tower Hill. Rochford, Brereton, Norris and Weston were beheaded and Smeaton was hanged. Sir William Kingston had arranged the construction of the scaffold. In a letter to Thomas Cromwell he wrote: 'I shall send at once to Master Eretage for carpenters to make a scaffold of such a height that all present may see it'. Chapuys reported that Anne saw them executed from the Tower, however, since the queen's lodgings where she was being held were south-east of the White Tower, it would have been impossible to see the execution site at Tower Hill.

The date of Anne's execution was deferred for two days while divorce proceedings were conducted, to declare Princess Elizabeth illegitimate and to give adequate time for the executioner to arrive from Calais. Sir William Kingston wrote to Cromwell on 18 May 1536: 'I am very glad to hear of the "executur" of Cales [Calais], for he can handle that matter.'

TOWER GREEN

The Execution Memorial commemorates the site on Tower Green where prominent prisoners were executed. (Author's Collection)

The Execution Memorial, looking towards the actual site of where Anne Boleyn was executed, in between the entrance to Waterloo Barracks (left) and the White Tower (right). (Author's Collection)

Anne was awake for most of the night before the day of execution on 19 May 1536. Sir William Kingston wrote to Thomas Cromwell reporting the conversation with Queen Anne during her final hours:

> This morning she sent for me, that I might be with her at such time as she received the good Lord, to the intent I should hear her speak as touching her innocency always to be clear. And in the writing of this she sent for me, and at my coming she said, 'Mr Kingston, I hear I shall not die afore noon, and I am very sorry therefore, for I thought to be dead at this time and past my pain.' I told her it should be no pain, it was so little. And she said, 'I heard say the executioner was very good, and I have a little neck,' and put her hands about it, laughing heartily. I have seen many men and also women executed, and that they have been in great sorrow, and to my knowledge this lady has much joy and pleasure in death. Sir, her almoner is continually with her, and had been since two o'clock after midnight.[151]

Foreign ambassadors and representatives were denied access to the Tower of London to observe the execution of the queen. However, Chapuys

The Execution Memorial stands before the Chapel of St Peter ad Vincula, where the bodies and heads of Anne Boleyn and her brother, George, Lord Rochford, were buried. Brereton, Norris, Smeaton and Weston were buried within the confines of the Tower of London. Other prominent prisoners executed outside the walls of the Tower of London, on Tower Hill, were buried here including Sir Thomas More and Bishop John Fisher. (Author's Collection)

did learn from Lady Kingston that Queen Anne asserted her innocence in private until the end for he reported: 'The lady who had charge of her has sent to tell me in great secrecy that the Concubine, before and after receiving the sacrament, affirmed to her, on the damnation of her soul, that she had never been unfaithful to the King.'

Anne was brought from her lodgings to the scaffold at 8am on the 19 May 1536. She was led by a captain and accompanied by four ladies. Anne was looking behind her as she approached the scaffold. Maybe she was hoping for a last-minute reprieve with the king's mercy and the sentence reduced to banishment to a nunnery. Sir Thomas Audley, Charles Duke of Suffolk and most of the King's Council were in attendance together with the Mayor of London and sheriffs and alderman from the city. The king was not present to witness the execution. After ascending the scaffold, she asked to speak a few words to the onlookers, promising to talk favourably of the king, fearing that any negative lambast would endanger the life of her daughter. Anne was permitted to address the crowd and according to Edward Hall, she spoke the following words:

> Good Christian people, I am come hither to die, for according to the law, and by the law I am judged to die, and therefore I will speak nothing against it. I am come hither to accuse no man, not to speak anything of that, whereof I am accused and condemned to die, but I pray God save the King and save him long to reign over you, for a gentler nor a more merciful prince was there never: and to me he was ever a good, a gentle and sovereign lord. And if any person will meddle of my cause, I require them to judge the best. And thus, I take my leave of the world and of you all, and I heartily desire you pray for me. O Lord have mercy on me, to God I commend my soul.[152]

Anne then removed her hood and cloak, which was furred with ermines. One of the ladies in attendance presented her with a linen cap with which she covered her head and ensured that her hair did not obscure her neck, so that the executioner could take clear aim. Another lady covered her eyes with some cloth. As she knelt down she said the words 'To Christ I commend my soul, Jesus receive my soul', and then with one strike of the sword the French executioner with precision beheaded Queen Anne. Her decapitated body and head were wrapped in white cloth and buried within the chapel of St Peter ad Vincula.

According to Chapuys, the public welcomed the demise of Anne Boleyn and the possible reinstatement of the Princess Mary to court for he confirmed that 'the joy shown by this people every day not only at the ruin of the Concubine but at the hope of the Princess' restoration, is inconceivable, but as yet the King shows no great disposition towards the latter; indeed he has twice shown himself obstinate when spoken to on the subject by his Council'.

In 1542, Henry VIII's fifth wife, Katherine Howard, suffered the same fate on Tower Green.

Roundel from the Ceiling of the Great Watching Chamber, Hampton Court Palace

Emblems of Henry VIII and Jane Seymour

On the day of Queen Anne's execution, Thomas Cranmer, Archbishop of Canterbury, granted Henry a dispensation to marry Jane Seymour. Wriothesley confirmed that they married in secret in Chelsea the following day, 20 May 1536. However, other historians, including Edward Hall, assert that the ceremony, conducted by Bishop Stephen Gardiner, took place on 30 May at Whitehall Palace.

On 4 June 1536, Jane Seymour was proclaimed queen at Greenwich Palace. Work to erase Anne Boleyn's emblems within all the royal palaces and replace them with the arms of Jane Seymour swiftly took place during that year. Jane's arms comprised a phoenix and a hawthorn tree surmounted above a gateway. Evidence of this change can be seen on the ceiling of the Great Watching Chamber where the roundels are decorated with the emblems of Henry VIII and Jane Seymour and the Tudor rose. Henry Blankston and John Hethe were commissioned to paint and gild 130 roundels on the ceiling of the Great Watching Tower during 1536.

Jane Seymour was a descendant of Edward III and served as a lady-in-waiting to Anne Boleyn. Chapuys first mentioned Henry's interest in Jane Seymour in January 1536, but it is believed that the king's romantic feelings for her developed during the royal progress as it passed through Marlborough in Wiltshire during October 1535. At that time the king stayed at the Seymour family home, Wolfhall, for five days. Jane was placid and submissive and completely different from the assertive and opinionated Anne Boleyn. Jane Seymour's duty as queen was emboldened on her badge, 'bound to obey and serve'. Chapuys described Jane to be:

> Of middle stature and no great beauty, so fair that one would call her rather pale than otherwise. She is over twenty-five years old. I leave you to judge whether, being English and having long frequented the Court, 'si elle ne tiendroit pas a conscience de navoir pourveu et prevenu de savoir que cest de faire nopces'. Perhaps this King will only be too glad to be so far relieved from trouble. Also, according to the account given of him by the Concubine, he has neither vigour nor virtue; and besides he may make a condition in the marriage that she be a virgin, and when he has a mind to divorce her, he will find enough of witnesses. The said Semel is not a woman of great wit, but she may have good understanding (*un bel enigm*, qu. *engin?*). It is said she inclines to be proud and haughty. She bears great love and reverence to the Princess.[153]

It was Jane's compassion and affection for Princess Mary that encouraged Henry to initiate a

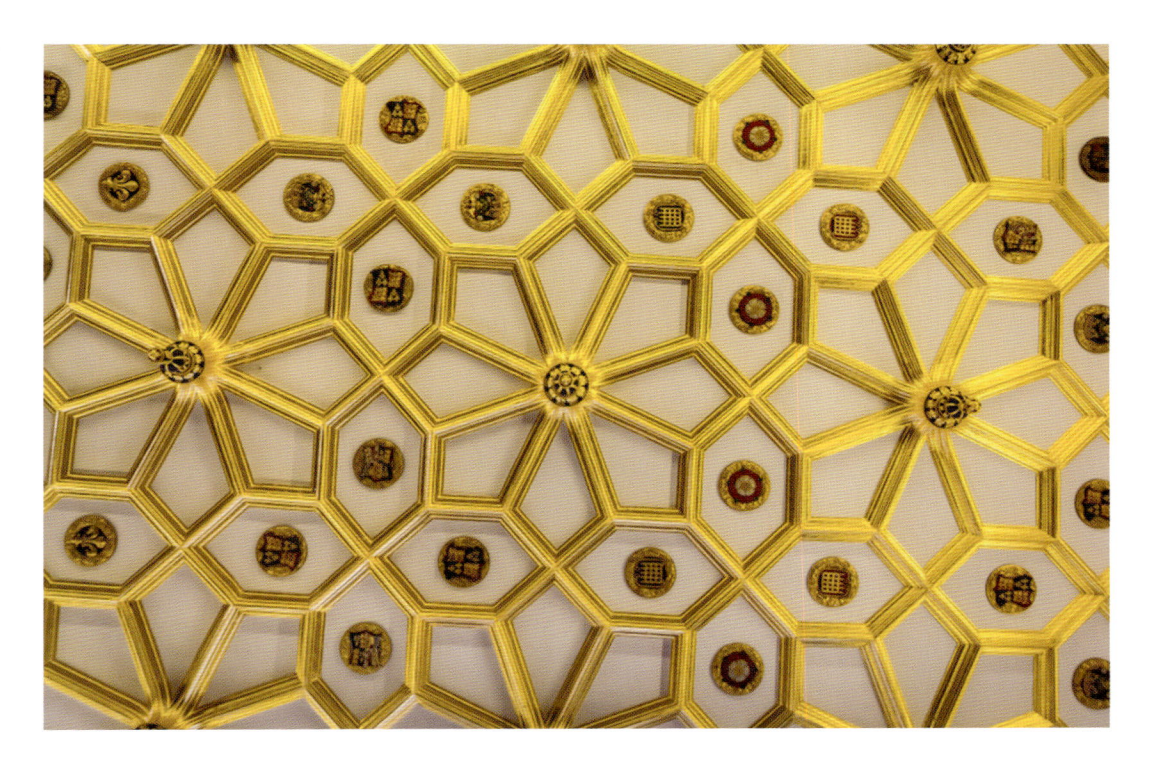

ROUNDEL FROM THE CEILING OF THE GREAT WATCHING CHAMBER

Emblems of Henry VIII and Jane Seymour in the ceiling of the Great Watching Chamber at Hampton Court Palace. This room was positioned between the Great Hall and the king's state apartments, where he ate, slept and received guests. The king's private chambers were demolished when William III expanded the palace. It was here in this chamber that the Yeoman of the Guard watched and controlled access to Henry VIII. (Shutterstock)

A roundel featuring the emblem of Jane Seymour, a phoenix rising from a castle, decorates the ceiling of the Great Watching Chamber. The roundels were made of leather mâché and some of the original ones survive today, although others have been replaced with copies. (Author's Collection)

reconciliation and allow her back to court. The death of Anne Boleyn brought hope to the nation that Princess Mary might be restored to the succession and, before the execution, Jane made efforts to bring Princess Mary back into the king's favour and to court, albeit causing some initial resentment. Eustace Chapuys wrote on 19 May 1536:

> I hear that, even before the arrest of the Concubine, the King, speaking with Mistress Jane Semel of their future marriage, the latter suggested that the Princess should be replaced in her former position; and the King told her she was a fool, and ought to solicit the advancement of the children they would have between them, and not any others. She replied that in asking for the restoration of the Princess she conceived she was seeking the rest and tranquillity of the King, herself, her future children, and the whole realm; for, without that, neither your Majesty nor this people would ever be content. Will endeavour by all means to make her continue in this vein. . . . Several have already told me, and sent to say that, if it cost them their lives, when Parliament meets they will urge the cause of the Princess to the utmost (*il pourteront jusques au boult laffaire de lad. princesse*).[154]

Jane Seymour persisted and she was able to convince the king to reconcile with Princess Mary. Her Catholic faith and her lack of enthusiasm for the Reformation may have been the motivation for assisting the princess gain Henry's favour once again.

Henry agreed to Mary's restoration to court, once she signed declaration that she accepted that his marriage with her mother, Katherine, was unlawful and acknowledged his position as Supreme Head of the English Church. Mary was initially reluctant, but later complied on 22 June 1536.

The rebellions that took place in northern England bewteen October 1536 and January 1537 caused Henry to postpone Jane's coronation. Once the rebellions had been crushed, Jane was pregnant and it was thought unwise to crown her as Queen of England until after the birth. Jane was married for seventeen months, but it is believed that Henry loved her the most of all his six wives. After her death, Henry commissioned paintings that featured her image and the Seymour family badges and emblems, with a phoenix rising from a castle, would continue to be displayed in royal palaces. The badges that are seen adorning the ceiling of the Great Watching Chamber at Hampton Court Palace are testament to Henry VIII's love for Jane Seymour, his third wife.

Portrait of Jane Seymour painted by Hans Holbein the Younger, 1536. It is on display at the Kunsthistorisches Museum in Vienna. (Courtesy of the Kunsthistorisches Museum)

64

St James's Palace, London

The Death of Henry Fitzroy, Illegitimate Son of Henry VIII

Henry obtained St James's in the Field Hospital during November 1531. A leper hospital surrounded by countryside, situated north-west of Westminster, Henry ordered its demolition on 1532 and a palace to be built on the site. Construction was completed in 1540. The palace contained many of the common features incorporated within other palaces, such as courtyards, a tiltyard, tennis court, accommodation for guests, but there was no great hall.

Henry did not stay at St James's, but it was the London residence of his illegitimate son, Henry Fitzroy, 1st Duke of Richmond. His tenure at St James's Palace was short because he died from tuberculosis at the palace on 22 July 1536, before the building was completed. The day after Fitzroy's death Chapuys recognised the position it placed Princess Mary in relation to the line of succession, for he reported: 'I have just this moment heard that the duke of Richmond died this morning; not a bad thing for the interests of the Princess. She, thank God, is very well, and I think her father's affection for her increases daily.'

Fitzroy was buried in secret at Thetford Priory, in order to prevent fear regarding the succession. The death of the illegitimate Fitzroy meant that Princess Mary became the next in line to the throne. Charles V would welcome the news and his ambassador, Chapuys, reported:

> That the duke of Richmond, whom the King had certainly intended to succeed to the Crown, after being dead eight days, has been secretly carried in a wagon (*charette*), covered with straw, without any company except two persons clothed in green, who followed at a distance, into Norfolk, where the Duke his father-in-law will have him buried, 'et Dieu scet comme je vous laisser [*sic*] penser quel honneur, &c.' Few are sorry for his death because of the Princess. Even Secretary Cromwell has congratulated her in his letters, and thank God she now triumphs, and it is to be hoped that the dangers are laid with which she has been surrounded to make her a paragon of virtue, goodness, honour, and prudence: I say nothing of beauty and grace, for it is incredible. May God raise her soon to the Crown for the benefit of his Majesty and of all Christendom! London, 5 Aug. 1536.[155]

Fitzroy's remains were later transferred from Thetford Priory and buried at Framlingham church.

St James's Palace. On its completion in 1540, Henry VIII was making plans to marry Anne of Cleves and her emblems together with their initials were incorporated within the final designs for the interior of the palace. (Author's Collection)

ST JAMES'S PALACE, LONDON

St James's Church, Louth

The Lincolnshire Rising

A church existed on the site of St James's Church in Louth, Lincolnshire, from the eleventh century, but construction of the spire was only completed during the reign of Henry VIII in 1515. On 1 October 1536, the Lincolnshire Rebellion started from St James's Church. It was the first direct insurgence against Henry VIII.

Poor harvests in 1535/6 led to raised prices and the implementation of Church reforms as a result of the Reformation and the dissolution of monasteries caused anxiety and concern across the country. Thomas Cromwell had sanctioned the visitation of monasteries to assess their assets and wealth, as well as to investigate the culture and lifestyle of the monks. The visitations began in 1535 and it was reported that some monks' lives were 'manifest sin, vicious, carnal and abominable living'. As a result, in 1536 Parliament passed the Act of Suppression of smaller monasteries, which sanctioned the closure of religious houses with less than twelve monks or nuns and income under £200.

Towards the end of summer 1536, rumours circulated in the north that hefty taxes were to be imposed, including taxation on burials, marriages and christenings. Henry VIII was desperate to obtain money in order to maintain his affluent lifestyle and Cromwell was searching for ways of boosting the coffers of the realm. Other measures to be enforced included the marking of the cattle and the payment of a levy to the king for all livestock owned and marked. Livestock that was unmarked was forfeited to the Crown. The number of parish churches was reduced, with churches within 5 miles of each other being dissolved, and their assets, including jewels, were confiscated by the king. On 20 September 1536, the parson at Farforth, Lincolnshire, reported that the silver chalices of the church were to be handed over in exchange for tin chalices. These events caused dissension in northern England, especially in Lincolnshire where Louth Abbey had been closed in September 1536 and the disenfranchised and homeless monks forced to seek refuge in nearby churches.

On 1 October 1536 the Lincolnshire Rising began in Louth, when Thomas Kendale, Vicar of St James's Church, warned his parish that the king's commissioners were about to visit and intimated that the valuable ornaments that belonged to the church were at risk of being confiscated. It prompted Thomas Foster, a yeoman and member of the choir, to declare as parishoners assembled before walking behind the three silver crosses of St James's Church, 'Go we to follow the crosses for and if they be taken from us we be like to follow them no more.'

News of the threat spread throughout Louth and nearby villages and the words of Kendale and Foster helped to galvanise resistance against the rumoured attempt to confiscate the church's property. After evensong John Wilson, a sawyer, requested the keys to the jewels from the churchwardens at the choir door. On gaining possession of the keys of the jewels, the church bells were rung to rally support further. Wilson brought the keys to Nicholas Melton, who led a company of armed villagers outside the church.

Melton was the villager shoemaker, known as Captain Cobbler, and he organised a watch on the church during that night and on consecutive nights until the end of the rising to protect the treasures inside.

On 2 October 1536, John Frankishe, the Bishop of Lincoln's registrar, and his colleague, John Henneage, arrived at Louth to conduct a visitation to assess the assets at Louth church. Frankishe was seized by John Taylor, a webster, and other villagers in Louth, who confiscated his assessment books and burnt them in the market place, together with copies of the New Testament, which was regarded by those opposing the Reformation as a heretical work.

The insurgents from Louth did not support the policies instigated by Cromwell and other unscrupulous individuals that had ascended to positions within the King's Privy Council. They also sought the removal of new bishops that did not hold the values of the old Church. They refused to pay levies and were only willing to pay subsidies in times of war. Finally, they requested the restoration of suppressed monasteries. The rebels swore an oath to 'God, the King, and the commons for the wealth of Holy Church'.[156] The church bells in Louth were rung to rouse people in surrounding villages to rise up against the visitations of the king's commissioners. Nicholas Melton led forty rebels from Louth to a small nunnery at Legbourne, 2 miles away, where they confronted John Bellowes, a representative of Thomas Cromwell who was conducting a visitation and was much detested by locals. When he was brought to Louth, there were calls to kill him, but instead he was put in the village stocks. Rumours that Bellowes had been killed circulated and were reported to the king, but proved to be untrue because he was later held in prison for two weeks, until released on the orders of Charles, Duke of Suffolk.

News of the Lincolnshire Rising arrived at court, as reported by Chapuys on 7 October 1536:

Five days ago, in Lincolnshire . . . a great multitude of people rose against the King's commissioners, who levied the taxes lately imposed by Parliament and put down the abbeys. It is said some of the commissioners have been killed; others who allowed themselves to be taken have been compelled to swear fidelity first to God, secondly to the Church, and thirdly to the King, and that they would not consent to the demolition of the churches or the exaction of the taxes demanded by the King. They have given the same oath to their band and to three or four gentlemen whom they take with them. Their numbers are reckoned by some at 10,000; by some more, by others less; but, to judge by the preparations made against them, the numbers must be very great and apparently increasing, for there is not a gentleman or man of influence whom the King has not ordered to be ready with his power.[157]

On 3 October, the rising spread to Caistor where a visitation was obstructed. Chapuys' approximation of 10,000 rebels was a gross over estimation and probably something in the region of 3,000 armed men from Louth descended upon Caistor. As they approached Caistor the king's commissioners fled. As the rebels from Louth discussed the situation with unarmed villagers from Caistor, they saw twenty men on horseback head for the home of Sir William Askew, who was one of the king's commissioners. Askew and several other commissioners in the county were apprehended and taken to Louth where they were persuaded to write a petition to explain their grievances and request a pardon, which would be sent to Henry VIII. This petition, signed by

St James's Church, Louth. (Shutterstock)

Sir Robert Tyrwhit, Sir William Askew, Edward Madeson and Thomas Portyngton, read:

This 3rd October we, by your commission for levying your second payment of your subsidy, were assembled at Caster, Linc. There were, at our coming, within a mile of the town 20,000 of your 'true and faithful subjects' assembled because the report went that all jewels and goods of the churches were to be taken away to your Grace's Council, and the people put to new charges. They swore us to be true to your Grace and to take their parts and then conveyed us from Caster to Louth, 12 miles distant, where we remain till they know further of your gracious pleasure. Desire a general pardon, 'or else we be in such danger that we be never like to see your Grace nor our own houses', as the bearer can show, for whom we beg credence. Your said subjects have desired us to write that they are at your command 'for the defence of your person or your realm'.[158]

Henneage left Louth on 3 October and delivered the petition to the king at Windsor Castle at 9am the following day. The news caused Henry great distress for this was a serious national crisis. He immediately prepared for war, assembling men and horses from London to strengthen his army and arming them with weapons from the Tower of London. He feared for the safety of his two daughters, the Princesses Mary and Elizabeth, and summoned them to court. A French diplomat reported to Cardinal du Bellay that:

At the beginning of the insurrection the Queen threw herself on her knees before the King and begged him to restore the abbeys, but he told her, prudently enough, to get up, and he had often told her not to meddle with his affairs, referring to the late Queen, which was enough to frighten a woman who is not very secure.[159]

News of the rising spread across the county and beacons were lit to rouse support. By 6 October, the insurgents had assembled at Lincoln and it was reported to the Lord Chancellor, Sir Thomas Audley, that 'they are over 40,000 harnessed men and naked men clad in bends of leather, and say they will die in God's quarrel and the King's'.

They demanded that the Church of England's old, accustomed privileges be reinstated together with the restoration of all suppressed houses. They sought the dismissal of several bishops who did not share the values of the old Church and finally they demanded 'that the King shall not now or hereafter demand any money of his subjects except for defence of the realm in time of war'.

Henry VIII was furious that the common people would challenge the rule and will of the king. He directly responded to the grievances of the Lincolnshire insurgents in a letter which was read to them in Lincoln Cathedral:

How presumptuous then are ye, the rude commons of one shire, and that one of the most brute and beastly of the whole realm and of least experience, to find fault with your prince for the electing of his counsellors and prelates? Thus, you take upon yourself to rule your prince. As to the suppression of religious houses we would have you know it is granted to us by Parliament and not set forth by the mere will of any counsellor. It has not diminished the service of God, for none were suppressed but where most abominable living was used, as appears by their own confessions signed by their own hands in the time of our visitations. Yet many were allowed to stand, more than we by the act needed; and if they amend not their living, we fear we have much to answer for. As to the relief of poor people, we wonder you are not ashamed to affirm that they have been a great relief, when many or most have not more than four or five religious persons in them and divers but one; who spent the goods of their house in nourishing vice. As to the Act of Uses we wonder at your madness in trying to make us break the laws agreed to by the nobles, knights, and gentlemen of this realm, whom the same chiefly toucheth. Also, the grounds of those uses were false and usurped upon the prince. As to the fifteenth, do you think us so faint hearted that ye of one shire, were ye a great many more, could compel us to remit the same, when the payments yet to come will not meet a tenth of the charges we must sustain for your protection? As to First Fruits, it is a thing granted by Parliament also. We know also that ye our commons have much complained in time past that most of the goods and lands of the realm were in the spiritual men's hands; yet, now pretending to be loyal subjects, you cannot endure that your prince should have part thereof. We charge you to withdraw to your houses and make no more assemblies, but deliver up the provokers of this mischief to our lieutenant's hands and submit yourselves to condign punishment, else we will not suffer this injury unavenged. We pray God give you grace to do your duties and rather deliver to our lieutenant 100 persons than by your obstinacy endanger yourselves, your wives, children, lands, goods, and chattels, besides the indignation of God.[160]

The king, who was residing at Windsor Castle was incandescent and dispatched two armies northwards to supress the Lincolnshire Rising. He wrote to Lord Darcy on 8 October claiming that the reports of levies and confiscation of Church property were false:

By letters sent us from the rout of those traitors assembled in Lincolnshire, suing for their pardon, it appears that this insurrection grew by crafty persons reporting that we would take the goods of all the churches, and levy unheard of impositions. In order that the people may see the malice of these persons, you are to read these letters to those about you, and to show that we never intended to take one pennyworth of parish church goods, or to levy more than has been given by an Act of Parliament which charges no man that is not worth 20*l*. in goods, and those worth more with only 6*d*. in the pound. So a man worth 40*l*. is a very traitor that for 20*s*. would rebel against his prince. 'By this declaration, which we assure you is true, our good subjects may perceive the wretched and devilish intents of those false traitors and rebels.' Given under our signet at our castle of Windsor, [the 8th day of October] in the 1536j. year of our reign.[161]

Henry showed no mercy and wanted to make examples of those that questioned his authority. While rebellion was taking place in Lincolnshire and Yorkshire, in Windsor, Henry punished those in southern England who sympathised with the insurgents. On 9 October 1536, a butcher was hanged at the court gate and a priest was hung from a tree close to the River Thames for vocally supporting their cause. Edward Hall explained the circumstances that brought them to their deaths:

There was a butcher dwelling within five miles of Windsor, where the King then lay, who caused a priest to preach that all such as took part with the Yorkshire rebels, whom he named God's people, did fight and defend God's quarrel; and, further, the said butcher, in selling of his meat, answered a customer

Plaque commemorating the start of the Lincolnshire Rebellion at St James's Church, Louth. (Courtesy of Michael Garlick; www.geograph.org.uk)

who bid him a less price 'Nay, by God's soul, I had rather the good fellows of the North had it among them, and a score more of the best I have'.[162]

By 10 October, the army of less than a thousand men, led by the Duke of Suffolk, had reached Stamford. They were poorly armed, had no money and were not in a position to successfully quell the revolt, which numbered 40,000 men. Henry sent reinforcements, supplies and munitions to his friend.

The rebels had heard the king's dismissive and disdainful message and were aware that an army was approaching Lincoln to confront them. They were unaware that they outnumbered Suffolk's army, however, the insurgents lacked leadership and direction. By 13 October, this mass of insurgents dispersed before the arrival of the Duke of Suffolk and his army. He experienced no opposition as he entered Lincoln, but the townsfolk refused to doff their caps as he passed through the streets. Henry sanctioned him to take measures to punish the insurgents, especially in Louth. In a letter dated 19 October, Henry wrote the following to Suffolk.

It appears that the rebels of Lincolnshire are not yet fully stayed, but some attempt as much as they dare to renew the rebellion by setting up beacons, putting themselves in harness, and appointing new assemblies. You are to use all dexterity in getting the harness and weapons of the said rebels brought in to Lincoln or other sure places, and cause all the boats on the Humber or means of passage into Yorkshire to be taken up. After this, if it appear to you by due proof that the rebels have since their retires from Lincoln attempted any new rebellion, you shall, with your forces run upon them and with all extremity 'destroy, burn, and kill man, woman, and child the terrible example of all others, and specially the town of Louth because to this rebellion took his beginning in the same'.[163]

The king spared most of the Lincolnshire nobles who took part in the rebellion, provided they policed the county to ensure that there was no further resurgence of an uprising. The commoners were also spared punishment but only if they surrendered their leaders.

Forty-six Lincolnshire rebels, including Thomas Kendale, the Vicar of Louth, were tried at the Guildhall in the City of London on 27 March 1537, when they were condemned to death. The sentence was carried out two days later when they were hauled from the Tower of London and taken to Tyburn where they were hung, drawn and quartered. Sir Thomas Audley reported to Thomas Cromwell: 'Today the prisoners go to their execution. As the gates of London are full of quarters not yet consumed, has ordered the heads of these prisoners to be set up at London Bridge and at every gate, and the bodies to be buried.'

The Lincolnshire rebellion failed because it lacked strong leadership and was devoid of definite objectives. The rising was ignited by a mixture of objections to religious, agricultural and political policies instigated by Henry VIII. They were protesting against the king's reformation of the church, unfair taxes, unpopular bishops and ministers such as Thomas Cromwell. The presentation of their dissent was inconsistent, especially when they were protesting against the dissolution of the monasteries, but mentioned the question of Royal Supremacy only once, but then contradicted themselves when they recognised the king as Supreme Head of the English Church. It was quite understandable for Henry VIII to have considered their grievances vague.

Pilgrimage of Grace Banner

The Pilgrimage of Grace March on York

This embroidered badge showing the five wounds of Christ was used by Yorkshire rebels to symbolise the Pilgrimage of Grace uprising. Christ's hands and feet represent four of those wounds, which are depicted in each corner of the badge. A bleeding heart, positioned over a chalice, denotes the fifth wound in the centre.

Although the Lincolnshire rising had failed, news of this insurrection spread into Yorkshire, where the mantle of their cause was taken up under the leadership of Robert Aske, a Yorkshire landowner and London barrister. The Yorkshire rebellion was better organised and was a more serious challenge to the authority of the king, causing a national crisis that had the potential to escalate into a civil war on a scale similar to the Wars of the Roses. Aske transformed this rebellion into a religious cause, branding it the Pilgrimage of Grace and proclaiming its supporters as pilgrims. He assumed the role of grand captain of the pilgrimage. The imagery of the five wounds of Christ inspired people of Yorkshire of all classes, including the nobility, to rally behind the cause. The Pilgrimage of Grace was a response to the Henry VIII's Reformation of the Church and the policies of Thomas Cromwell which implemented those changes to religious institutions within England. It became the most serious domestic crisis during Henry's reign. The grievances of the Yorkshire rebels reflected the concerns raised during the Lincolnshire rising. Their principal aim was to preserve the old values of their religion which were rapidly becoming eroded by the Reformation. They were apprehensive towards 'the suppression of so many religious houses the service of God is not well performed and the people unrelieved'. They sought a 'repeal of the Act of Uses, which restrains the liberty of the people in the declaration of their wills concerning their lands, as well in payment of their debts, doing the King service, and helping their children'. They challenged the levies charged on sheep and cattle which impoverished farmers were unable to afford. They also expressed concern at the unsuitability of the corrupt advisors to the king claiming that 'the King takes of his Council, and has about him, persons of low birth and small reputation, who have procured these things for their own advantage, whom we suspect to be lord Cromwell and Sir Ric. Riche, Chancellor of the Augmentations'. Finally, the rebels were 'grieved that there are bishops of the King's late promotion, who have subverted the faith of Christ, viz., the bishops of Canterbury, Rochester, Worcester, Salisbury, St. David's, and Dublin. Think the beginning of all this trouble was the bishop of Lincoln.'

Although the insurgents carried weapons and opposed the king's policies, they still proclaimed their allegiance to the king addressing him as 'our sovereign lord'. Everyone who joined the Pilgrimage of Grace was made to swear the following oath:

> Ye shall not enter to this our pilgrimage of Grace for the common wealth, but only for the maintenance of God's Faith and Church militant, preservation of the King's person and issue, and purifying the nobility of all

Pilgrimage of Grace Banner.

villains' blood and evil counsellors; to the restitution of Christ's Church and suppression of heretics' opinions, 'by the holy contents of this book'.[164]

The insurgents began their march upon York on 12 October 1536 from Howden. They sang hymns and songs as they marched behind banners displaying the five wounds of Christ. As they got closer to the city of York they were joined by men from Hull and the Lords Neville, Lumley and Latimer sent their soldiers wearing armour to support the rising. Sir Thomas Percy brought 5,000 men from Northumbria to join the cause. Aske arrived at York on 16 October 1536.

When Henry VIII heard of this second insurgency in northern England, he ordered his armourers at Greenwich Palace to restore rusting armour held in the Royal Armoury and for this to be used to counter the insurgents. He dispatched the Earl of Shrewsbury and Duke of Norfolk to confront this rebellion. Henry sent the following instruction to Shrewsbury on 17 October:

Forasmuch as we have heard that divers traitors have assembled in Yorkshire, though we do not believe the matter dangerous yet we marvel, considering your accustomed circumspection, you have not ere this by espial or otherwise investigated, and—it being so long since you first heard of the matter—advertised us of the truth. We require you therefore to find means to inform us of the whole truth by your letters to which we would give credence before many others. Intending to punish that insurrection to the example and terror of all others hereafter, however the matter may stand at your receipt hereof we require you to act as follows:— First, if you find there is indeed such a rebellion as reported, you shall according to our former letters of the 15th inst., 'advance yourselves with all your forces' against the said rebels, &c. Second, if you learn that the said rebels were once up but have retired again, you shall, with no greater forces than you think requisite and necessary with due consideration of our honour your persons and also our charges, proceed to the parts where the rebellion first began. There you shall find out the authors thereof and, calling before you the chief offenders of every town and village, administer such execution and punishment to the said authors, gentlemen or otherwise, that others shall beware of like attempt in time coming. And you shall punish not only those who were openly in rebellion but all who you find were counsellors, procurers, and abettors of them or would have joined or aided them. If you advance only for the punishment of the traitors after their dispersal you shall send home such of your forces as you do not require. Finally, we marvel that the nobles and gentlemen of those countries, knowing you so nigh them with such puissance, do not more diligently advertise you of the rebellion; and we think that on your arrival there you should have special regard to their slackness in this and trust them the less.[165]

After a six-day siege, the port of Hull capitulated to the insurgents on 19 October. On that same day, Aske and the rebels reached Pontefract Castle. Lord Darcy, constable of the castle, with only 300 soldiers, was unable to resist the rebel force. Six days earlier, on 13 October, Darcy had requested arms, bows, arrows and gunpowder from the king. Henry wrote a letter on that same day rebuking Darcy's ineffectual efforts to quash the rebellion. When Darcy received this strongly worded letter from the sovereign without the necessary arms to defend Pontefract Castle, he was left in a difficult situation. He had to choose between defending the castle in a battle that he would almost certainly lose and himseld die or surrender Pontefract Castle to the insurgents. Some historians believe that he was sympathetic to the rebels, while others think that he may have held his opinion depending on who reached the castle first, the rebels or the king's army, in an act of self-preservation. Surrendering to the rebels had aroused Henry VIII's concerns that Darcy might be disloyal and it would eventually result in Darcy's execution.

The capture of Pontefract Castle had given the Pilgrimage of Grace further momentum. Aske was a capable soldier, an effective politician and leader. He had galvanised the support of 6 northern counties and led 30,000 men south towards Doncaster. The Earl of Shrewsbury was also heading towards Doncaster with a small force on behalf of the king. On 17 October he

Illustration depicting the Pilgrimage of Grace. Banners can be seen being carried by participants in the procession. (Author's Collection)

reached Newark where he reported to the Duke of Norfolk: 'it appears that the rebels number 40,000 and daily increase, while I and those with me, who intend to advance thither tomorrow are little over 7,000; I beg you will march towards Doncaster and we will do the best we can, either to set some stay, or keep them in play till you come.'

The Duke of Norfolk with only 8,000 men joined the Earl of Shrewsbury to defend Doncaster. The forces belonging to the Duke of Norfolk were clearly outnumbered and were heading for certain defeat if they engaged in battle with the insurgents, who were in control of York, Hull and Pontefract Castle. Fortunately for Henry VIII, the risk of another English civil war was averted at Doncaster where both sides decided to negotiate a truce on 26 October.

Initially the king refused to receive a petition containing the grievances and demands of the rebels, but eventually he instructed Norfolk to accept it and invite two representatives to present their petition in London on the condition that there was a temporary armistice. Sir Ralph Ellekar and Sir Robert Bowes were the designated representatives of the insurgents. The king entertained these two rebels in London, but Henry was biding his time, waiting for the cold winter to set in, which he hoped would cool the anger of the rebels and disperse them.

The king also agreed to comply with Aske's demands. On 3 December, Aske and the rebels compiled a list of grievances and objectives on behalf of the pilgrims, which included the reversal of the king's religious reforms, addressing economic issues and the establishment of a parliament in the north. The king requested that Aske write down the events of the rising so as to better understand the cause of this insurrection. In reality Henry was seeking detailed information about those that supported the rebellion so that when he had sufficient power, and at the right moment, he would exact his revenge. Henry continued with his displays of superficial friendship with Aske by granting him a pardon on 8 December and inviting him to court as his guest during the Christmas period. Henry played a great deception upon Aske, for he lured him into a false sense of security. The king gave the impression that they were close, even presenting Aske with a crimson coat as a gift. Aske wrote of these gifts, which were 'a gown of tawny satin faced with velvet, a jacket of crimson satin that the King's Grace gave me, a crimson satin doublet and a pair of scarlet hose and other trifles'.

Henry sent Aske back to Yorkshire with assurances that the rebels' aims would be met. These were hollow words, for when Aske returned to Yorkshire, commissioners continued to visit monasteries assessing their assets. Instead of receiving a warm welcome when he returned, his fellow rebels treated him with suspicion because their demands had not been met and Aske's relationship with the king aroused suspicion. Aske was in a dangerous position because the king was preparing for his fall and the relationship that Aske had with the king caused the rebels to distrust Aske.

Hussey Tower, Boston

Lord John Hussey Executed for Treason

Hussey Tower was part of a manor house built in 1460 and in the eighteenth century was named after John Hussey, who purchased the property in 1475. Hussey was a wealthy landowner and also a soldier. He participated in the Battle of Blackheath in 1497 when the army of Henry VII defeated the Cornish Rebellion, and was subsequently knighted.

Hussey acted as a loyal courtier to Henry VIII and fought during the French campaign in 1513. He accompanied the king to the Field of the Cloth of Gold in 1520. Elected Member of Parliament for Lincolnshire in 1523, six years later he was elevated to the House of Lords. Hussey was appointed Chamberlain to Princess Mary and his, wife Lady Ann, assigned as her attendant. It was forbidden to call Mary by her title Princess, however, and when Lady Ann addressed Mary as 'Princess' in 1534 she was imprisoned in the Tower of London. Lord Hussey had appealed for the king's pardon to secure her release. Although Hussey was a friend of the king, his role as Chamberlain brought him closer to Mary and his sympathy for her predicament developed.

Hussey had previously counselled Chapuys to encourage Charles V to take military action against Henry VIII and assured him that any invasion would be supported by the people of England who wanted the religious reforms introduced by Henry VIII reversed and his tyrannical reign brought to a conclusion. Chapuys reported to Emperor Charles V on 30 September 1534:

The lord Usey [Hussey], chamberlain of the Princess, who for his good sense and prudence was one of the principal councillors of Henry VII; desiring of late to go home to the North, sought a secret interview with me before his departure, when he told me plainly what he had before expressed more covertly, that he and all the honest men of the kingdom were very much dismayed that your majesty did nothing to remedy affairs here, as it could be done so easily,—that the thing concerned the lives and interests of the Queen and Princess and the honour of your majesty, and that it was God's cause, which you, as a Catholic prince and chief of other princes, were bound to uphold, especially out of pity for all this people, who regard you with as much affection as if they were your own subjects. I told him you were desirous of the peace and union of Christendom, and to preserve the ancient friendship with this king, for which there was no better means than to maintain the rights of the Queen and Princess, and wait the other terms of justice in discharge of the oath you had made to this king; and I thought that even if your majesty had every opportunity to remedy affairs by war, nevertheless you might object to do so for fear of oppressing this innocent people; and as he was a wise and experienced man, I begged him to declare what he would do if he were in your majesty's place. He said, as to the disposition of this kingdom, I might know it in part as well as he; nevertheless he would assure me that almost everybody was expecting your majesty would begin to move

Hussey Tower. (Courtesy of David Hallam-Jones; www.geograph.org.uk)

to their assistance, and you need have no fear of oppressing them by making war, because the indignation of the people was so great that everything would be reformed immediately before any resistance could be offered. As to

the form of the war, as you had experienced soldiers, he would not enlarge upon it, especially as he knew that lord Darcy, whom he called his brother, would explain the matter for me much better than he could, being a

A view of the side of Hussey Tower showing the pathway that leads to Skirbeck Road. (Courtesy of David Hallam-Jones; www.geograph.org.uk)

A portrait of Lord John Hussey. (Author's Collection)

person of long experience in the business. One thing he would not forget to say, that your majesty ought first of all to make the said war, which might at once remedy everything, by the insurrection of the people, who would be joined immediately by the nobility and the clergy also, which is powerful and half in disorder.[166]

Although Hussey tried to encourage Charles V to invade England to overthrow Henry VIII, he had to appear loyal to his king. On 3 October 1536, Lord John Hussey wrote to Robert Sutton, Mayor of Lincoln:

Heard at 9 o'clock this morning from the Dean of Lincoln that there is a company of false rebellious knaves risen in Lyndsey. Commands him to see the city of Lincoln surely kept, so that no such evil disposed rebellious persons can pass through it; to be ready with such company as he can make, to suppress them; to take up the bows and arrows in the bowyers' and fletchers' hands at a reasonable price; to handle the matter secretly, and if he thinks he is unable to resist, to send word to Hussey, who will come to his aid.[167]

Lord John Hussey wrote to Cromwell on 5 October 1536: 'The country is becoming more and more rebellious. They are today coming towards Lincoln, but not in such great numbers, I believe, as it is noised. I have called my countrymen, and most part say they will be glad to defend me, but I shall not trust them to fight against the rebels'.

It is believed that Lord Hussey sympathised with the insurgents of the Lincolnshire Rebellion. Henry thought that his lacklustre attempt to suppress this revolt was evidence that he supported them and he was therefore tried for treason alongside Lord Darcy at Westminster Hall, by the Marquis of Exeter. Hussey pleaded not guilty at his trial in May 1537 in London, but was found guilty of treason. Hussey was taken to Lincoln Castle where he was beheaded.

Hussey's property and lands, including Hussey Tower, was forfeited to the Crown. Hussey Tower was sold to the Boston Corporation in 1545. It was never used as a home after the demise of Lord Hussey and maintenance of the manor house was neglected. The gatehouse was demolished in 1565 and its bricks were reutilised for other buildings constructed within the town of Boston. The town still owns Hussey Tower, which is administered by Heritage Lincolnshire.

68

Clifford's Tower, York

Site of the Execution of Robert Aske

When a further rising erupted in East Riding during January 1537, led by Sir Francis Bigod, and there were further insurgencies in Westmoreland and Cumberland, Henry VIII was prepared and in a strong position to suppress the rebels. He ordered the Duke of Norfolk to crush the revolt in the north and exact his vengeful punishment upon those who took part in the Pilgrimage of Grace, including Robert Aske.

Aske was invited to London by the king, and he knew that when he arrived in the capital on 24 March 1537 he was heading for danger. On 7 April, Aske was committed to the Tower of London along with other leading rebels. They were to be judged on the revolts that took place after 8 December 1536 and not for the insurgency for which they were pardoned. Despite Aske not being involved in any revolts after that pardon was granted by the king, Henry wanted to make an example of him.

Aske was tried on 17 May at Westminster Hall and found guilty of treason. He was initially sentenced to be hung at Tyburn. Aske was fearful for his fellow Yorkshiremen who had taken part in the Pilgrimage of Grace, and wanted a quick death. He appealed to the king, probably through Cromwell. 'I humbly ask the King, and his Council and Lords, forgiveness for any offences or words against them; and to save my life to be in perpetual prison 'or else to let me be full dead ere I be dismembered.'

Henry showed mercy and commuted the sentence from being hung, drawn and quartered to hanging. The king wanted to assert his authority in Yorkshire and make an example of Aske to prevent further insurrections and sent Aske to York for execution. On 12 July 1537, on market day when many people were in the city to shop, Robert Aske was executed in the presence of the Duke of Norfolk and John Aske, his brother. During that morning Robert Coren tried to get a confession from Aske that would reveal the identity of sympathisers of the Yorkshire Rebellion in the south of England. Aske refused. Aske was tied to a hurdle and taken through the streets of York to York Castle where he was executed. Richard Coren, the Government Chaplain, confirmed:

> When he 'should be' laid on the hurdle to be drawn he openly confessed he had offended God, the King, and the world. After this he declared that the King was so gracious that none should be troubled for offences comprised in the pardon. He was then laid on the hurdle and drawn through the notable places of the city 'desiring the people ever as he passed by to pray for him'.[168]

Aske was taken to Clifford's Tower, where he waited for the Duke of Norfolk's arrival. He spoke of his grievances, and Coren reported that:

> There were two things, wherewithal he was aggrieved. The one was, that he said my lord Privy Seal [Thomas Cromwell] spoke a sore word and affirmed it with a stomach, swearing that all the Northern men were but traitors: where-withal he was somewhat offended.

ABOVE and BELOW: Clifford's Tower was originally perched on a motte above the castle in the city of York. It was a suitable location to execute Robert Aske, where he could be hanged in full view of the people who lived in York, serving as a warning to anyone who defied the king. (Author's Collection)

The second was that my lord Privy Seal sundry times promised him a pardon of his life, and at one time he had a token from the King's Majesty of pardon for confessing the truth. These two things he showed to no man in these North parts, as he said, but to me only; which I have and will ever keep secret.[169]

When the Duke of Norfolk arrived, Aske ascended the gallows and begged forgiveness of the king and commended his soul to God. He was then hung in chains from Clifford's Tower until he died, in full view of the people of York, who could see the tower from outside the castle walls.

Aske was one of over a hundred traitors to die for their part in the rebellion. Henry VIII wanted revenge and to ensure that no further revolts would threaten his reign. In a letter to the Duke of Norfolk on the 27 February 1537, Henry wrote:

> The course of our laws must give place to martial law; and before you close it up again you must cause such dreadful execution upon a good number of the inhabitants, hanging them on trees, quartering them, and setting their heads and quarters in every town, as shall be a fearful warning, whereby shall ensue the preservation of a great multitude.[170]

The Pilgrimage of Grace failed to reverse the reforms to the Church and the removal of unsuitable court advisors and bishops. Instead it strengthened the king's position and buoyed up his efforts to dissolve larger monasteries during 1538/9.

69

Portrait of Henry VIII, 1537

Henry in His Prime

This portrait shows Henry before his decline and the strong image it presents made it ideal for diplomatic purposes, to send as a political gift to establish and maintain relationships at home and abroad, as well as to deter anyone who thought of challenging his rule. Such portraits of the sovereign were commissioned by wealthy courtiers and noblemen to display in their great halls to demonstrate their allegiance and loyalty to the king. It is believed that this well-known portrait of King Henry VIII was commissioned by a wealthy courtier intent on affirming support for the king. His stance in this picture is similar to that of the Whitehall Mural, which shows Henry VIII with his parents and Jane Seymour and was also painted by Hans Holbein the Younger in 1537. This mural was destroyed in a fire in 1698 at Whitehall Palace, where the painting hung, but was later reproduced as an oil painting by Remigius van Leemput for Charles II. The courtier who commissioned the painting of Henry VIII seen here may have had access to the Whitehall Mural. It is the image that transformed Henry into an iconic king.

Throughout his life Henry was a slim and athletic man, but after a fall during a joust at Greenwich Palace in 1536 he had injured his leg and this became ulcerous eventually making him becoming immobile. Unable to exercise, Henry's waistline expanded from 32in to 52in and during his last years he became so obese and heavy that he had to be hoisted up onto his horse with the aid of a winch.

This portrait by Hans Holbein uses Henry's bulky physique to portray a powerful, affluent and brutal monarch. It shows a complete transformation from the slim, handsome, kind, charismatic king of his youth. Henry VIII was 6ft 2in tall and is presented here as a magnificent figure, strong and resplendent. Holbein's painting immortalised Henry as one of England's most imposing monarchs. Painted by an unknown artist, possibly from the workshop of Hans Holbein the Younger between 1537 and 1547, he appears as a large, intimidating person. His eyes look intently towards the artist, commanding unconditional obedience and exuding confidence in his own omnipotence. With his legs astride, Henry VIII stands confidently with his right hand on his hip, assertive and with gravitas as he upholds his right to the throne.

The artist captures the king wearing splendid, bejewelled garments that present him as fashion-conscious, flamboyant and affluent. Each day the king would be dressed by servants in his privy chamber. The Eltham Ordinances dictated:

> It is also ordered that the King's doublet, hose, shoes, or any other garment, which his pleasure shall be to wear from day to day, the gown only excepted, shall be honestly and cleanly brought by the yeoman of the wardrobe of the robes ... to the King's privy chamber door, without entering into the same, where one of the said grooms shall receive the said garments and apparel, bringing and delivering the same to the six gentlemen to be administered unto the King's person, as shall stand with his pleasure.[171]

The painting shows Henry to be well groomed and stylish. Since the compilation of the Eltham

Ordinances in 1526 a barber was in attendance to the king each day. The ordinances stated that 'it is ordered, that the King's barber shall be daily by the King's uprising, ready and attendant in the privy chamber; there having in readiness, his water, cloths, knives, combs and scissors, and such other stuff as to his room doth appertain, for trimming and dressing the King's head and beard'.

During the past five years Henry had confronted Rome, divorced his first wife, remarried, severed ties with the Catholic Church, established the Church of England, of which he was the figure head, began the dissolution of the monasteries, divorced and executed Anne Boleyn and married a third wife, Jane Seymour. If Henry had remained married to Katherine of Aragon and not confronted the Vatican and Catholic-dominated Europe, he might have been regarded as an unremarkable, forgotten monarch, but his actions transformed him into a notorious figure in English history. This portrait encapsulates that perception of the king.

In 1537, the year that this portrait was painted, Henry had crushed the rebellions that took place in northern England from October 1536 to January 1537 and prevented the coronation of Jane Seymour. By the time Henry had suppressed those rebellions, Jane was pregnant and in order not to jeopardise the birth, her coronation was postponed until after the birth of their child. Jane had succeeded where Katherine and Anne had failed for she was also able to provide Henry with a male heir to the throne. At 2am on 12 October 1537, after a difficult labour at Hampton Court Palace, she gave birth to a son, who would become the future King Edward VI. Henry VIII was overjoyed that he was father to a legitimate son. News of the birth of the boy was rapturously received throughout the realm. Bonfires were lit in the streets and church bells were rung in celebration. The boy was christened in a midnight ceremony conducted

The portrait of Henry VIII. (Courtesy of the Walker Art Gallery)

by Thomas Cranmer, at the Chapel Royal within Hampton Court Palace with Henry VIII and his two daughters, Mary and Elizabeth, in attendance. However, the celebrations lasted for less than two weeks because on 24 October Jane Seymour died as a result of complications from the birth. She was the only wife of Henry VIII to be accorded a funeral that befitted a queen. On 8 November 1537, she was buried in a vault beneath St George's Chapel at Windsor Castle.

Nonsuch Palace Marker in Nonsuch Park, Surrey

Work Begins on the Construction of Nonsuch Palace

In 1538 Henry VIII purchased a village named Cuddington, near Ewell in Surrey. The entire village, including the church, was completely demolished so that work could begin on building a new palace called Nonsuch for the king. Its name was derived from the intention that no other building in England would rival its grandeur. Henry wanted to use this new palace, containing two courts, as a place for sport and entertainment. It was close to one of his principal hunting grounds in this area.

Work commenced on 22 April 1538, one day after Henry celebrated the thirtieth anniversary of his reign. It would take nine years to complete. The design of Nonsuch Palace was inspired by the Renaissance architecture of Chateau Chambord, which had been built for King Francis I in the Loire in France. Henry wanted this new palace to validate his status as a European monarch in terms of magnitude and style. He commissioned 500 craftsmen from across Europe to build the palace. Nicolas Bellini designed the interior. Stones from the dissolved Merton Priory were used in the construction. A large statue of Henry seated was placed in the centre of the inner court.

Despite its magnificence, Henry only visited Nonsuch Palace on three occasions. Twice in

The concrete marker denoting the position of the outer gatehouse, which was the northern entrance into Nonsuch Palace. (Author's Collection)

A two-storey banqueting house was built south-west of Nonsuch Palace, and from here Henry VIII could observe hunting and entertain his guests. These foundations are all that remain of this building. (Author's Collection)

1545 and once in 1547. The palace was given to Barabara, Countess of Castlemaine, mistress of Charles II, in 1670, but she was forced to sell the estate to pay her gambling debts in 1682 and the building was demolished. Nothing remains of the original palace, but the layout of the building is indicated in Nonsuch Park with concrete markers.

Rievaulx Abbey

The Dissolution of Rievaulx Abbey

Rievaulx Abbey was the first Cistercian monastery to be established in north Yorkshire in 1132. During the twelfth century there were 650 monks living in the abbey. By the time Henry VIII dissolved the monastery on 3 December 1538, the community had been reduced to twenty-two monks.

During 1535, Thomas Cromwell sent commissioners to assess the incomes of monasteries across the country and to try and discover if any of the residing monks were involved in anything scandalous or committing abuses within the monasteries. The results of these assessments were published in a document entitled the Valor Ecclesiasticus, which resulted in the Act of Suppression of smaller monasteries, passed by Parliament in March 1536, which sanctioned the dissolution of small religious houses with annual incomes of less than £200. The leading monk was offered a pension, while other monks were encouraged to transfer to a larger house. This Act affected approximately 300 monasteries across the country.

On 3 December 1538, Abbot Roland Blytone surrendered Rievaulx Abbey with all its possessions to the King. After seizing it Henry VIII sold the property to courtier Thomas

Rievaulx Abbey near Helmsley in North Yorkshire. (Emily Marie Wilson/Shutterstock)

The ruined interior of Rievaulx Abbey. (Shutterstock)

Manners, 1st Earl of Rutland. Henry needed to generate income to pay for the maintenance of his royal residences and the construction of new properties such as Nonsuch Palace. The Earl of Rutland dismantled the buildings of Rievaulx Abbey, stripped it of its riches and reserved the lead from the roofs and the bells within the monastery for the king.

On 18 June 1538, Pope Paul III had negotiated a ten-year truce between Emperor Charles V and King Francis I, and Henry became increasingly concerned that this alliance would result in an invasion of England to reverse the Reformation and restore the Catholic Church. By breaking from the Catholic Church, declaring himself head of the English Church, dissolving the monasteries such as Rievaulx Abbey and carrying out religious persecutions during the Reformation had politically isolated Henry VIII from Europe. The situation was further exacerbated on 17 December 1538 when Pope Paul III excommunicated Henry VIII and dispatched Cardinal Reginald Pole to European courts to form a coalition that would fight a crusade against Henry VIII. Henry would also utilise money taken from monasteries such as Rievaulx Abbey to build coastal fortifications to defend England against a potential invasion.

72

Design for a Henrican Castle on the Kent Coast

Henry VIII Orders the Construction of Defences Around the English Coast

On 10 January 1539 Emperor Charles V and King Francis I signed the Treaty of Toledo, in which they both agreed not to make any new alliances with Henry VIII, whether it was for marriages for himself or his children or any other treaties without mutual consent. This treaty thwarted Henry's efforts to marry a French or an Imperial princess in an attempt to isolate England from the Holy Roman Empire and France. The threat of invasion by France and the Holy Roman Empire to restore the Catholic Church forced Henry to strengthen the existing fortifications and build new defences along the English coast during 1539.

Raphael Holinshed confirmed in his chronicle that 'the King, being informed that the Pope . . . had moved and stirred great princes and

Deal Castle on the Kent coast. (Author's Collection)

A diagram of the layout of Deal Castle, showing the design of a Henrican castle on the Kent coast.

potentates of Christendom to invade the realm of England, without delay rode himself toward the sea coasts, and sent orders of his nobles and councillors to secure all ports and places of danger on the coast'.[172] These defences stretched from Milford Haven along the southern coastline in Cornwall, Hampshire, including the dockyard facility at Portsmouth, Sussex, Kent and along the eastern coast from Essex to Hull in Yorkshire. They were built specifically to defend harbours, anchorages and beaches that might be used by an invading force. This major construction programme was financed with valuable assets stripped from monasteries during the dissolution.

In February 1539 Henry ordered the construction of three new castles at Walmer, Deal and Sandown to protect the vulnerable beaches and anchorages on the Downs situated between Goodwin Sands, 6 miles offshore, and the east Kent coastline. This stretch of coastline was extremely vulnerable because of its close proximity to mainland Europe and the deep water close to the long shingle beach made it an ideal place for hostile forces to land.

It was an enormous challenge for the surveyor, master mason and master carpenter from the king's works who were responsible for supporting two appointed commissioners, Sir Edward Ryngeley and Thomas Wingfield (who was a local from Sandwich), in delivering and completing this project because the building of fortifications for war was different to designing and building palaces for the king. Clement, the master carpenter, and Christopher, the master mason, had worked on the construction of Hampton Court Palace.

It is probable that this fortification plan entitled 'A Castle for the Downes' was drawn up very soon after the order and presented to the king for his approval. The design is identical to the layout of Deal Castle, which comprises a keep surrounded by a series of six connected semi-circular bastions which were built upon a base of six larger outer bastions which were also semi-circular in shape and built symmetrically. The flat roofs of the outer bastions could accommodate four guns which could fire through parapet embrasures. Three guns could be fired through gun-ports in the lower chambers of the outer bastions. Deal Castle had the capacity to accommodate sixty-four guns. The structure of the castle meant the guns had a 360-degree range enabling it to defend against attacks from both sea and land.

Construction of the three castles began in April 1539 with a workforce numbering 1,400 craftsmen and labourers. Work was temporarily interrupted when those working at

Walmer Castle, built between 1539 and 1540, was Henry VIII's southernmost castle and specifically built to defend the Downs. It was similar in design and construction to Sandown Castle, comprising a central circular keep surrounded by four semi-circular bastions which were surmounted by canons. The castle was surrounded by a dry, deep moat, which could be crossed by a wooden drawbridge. Both Walmer and Sandown castles were controlled by the captain commanding the larger Deal Castle. (Author's Collection)

Deal went on strike demanding a pay rise, but Sir Edward Ryngeley sent nine ringleaders to gaol and persuaded the others to continue the work. Ryngeley reported to Thomas Cromwell in 11 June 1539:

This week we had business with the King's labourers here, saying they would have 6*d*. a day, but after I had spoken with them, I caused them to return to work, as Robert Lord, who was present at Deal, can inform your Lordship. I have sent the nine first beginners, five to Canterbury Castle, and four to Sandwich Gaol.[173]

When Anne of Cleves arrived at Deal Castle at about 5pm on 27 December 1539 it was deemed 'newly built' according to Edward Hall, however it was likely that work was completed in 1540. She was welcomed by the Duke and Duchess of Suffolk and local Kent dignitaries with a banquet before being taken to Dover Castle, where she rested before proceeding to Canterbury.

The ruins of Sandown Castle photographed in 1875. The castle fell into disrepair and was eventually lost to the savage sea, any remains being encased within the modern sea defences. (Author's Collection)

By the time that Deal Castle and other castles had been built, the threat of an invasion had receded. Walmer Castle was expanded and became the official residence of the Cinque Ports. Sandown Castle was demolished. Only Deal Castle remains unchanged from its original design. These fortifications are visual reminders of the legacy that Henry VIII left to the nation and these structures continued to be used throughout the following centuries in the defence of the nation. Some were employed as artillery platforms during the Second World War.

Camber Castle

The Strengthening of Fortifications Along the Southern English Coastline

A circular tower was built 1 mile south of Rye, a Cinque Port, between 1512 and 1514 by Sir Edward Guldeford, to protect the Camber anchorage and the approaches to Rye harbour, where the navy of Henry VIII would stop to replenish with victuals. However, Rye was surprised in February 1539, when four French ships passed through the Camber undetected to reach the town. Thomas Byrchet, Mayor of Rye, wrote to Thomas Cromwell on 11 February 1539:

> Twelve or thirteen days since, four great galleys of the French King, 'being more than ballast with wheat', came into the Camber to tarry a wind to sail to a French city nigh about the Straits, and to receive more ordnance out of France, which has been delivered them by a hoy and a crayer, 'and lyeth in them of from the Whelys'. They said they came only for harbourage and to receive the said ordnance, and the captains have been several times on land and demeaned themselves peaceably. Has taken precautions (described) against any surprise of the town, not from fear, but that men should be ready to resist enemies.[174]

The tower near Rye would be incorporated into a new fortress, known as Camber Castle, constructed between 1539 and 1544. Due to the lack of English engineers, Henry commissioned the German engineer Stefan von Haschenperg to supervise the building of the new series of fortifications including Camber Castle. Commonly known as Stephen the Almain, he was influenced by designs used in the construction of castles in Italy, which were built low. Work commenced on the development of Camber Castle in 1539. Local sandstone, wood and limestone, together with stone retrieved from the ruins of monastic buildings in nearby Winchelsea, were used as material to build four outer towers and a rectangular entrance, which were connected by an octagonal containing a concealed passage. Artillery could be placed on the towers to defend this concentric castle, but the structure it had serious flaws. The low height of the castle and the high water table meant that the castle suffered from dampness. The rectangular gatehouse was positioned north and obstructed the line of fire in the direction of Rye, the angles of fire being restricted, making it impossible to fire upon enemy vessels approaching Rye or the Camber. When construction was completed in 1540, Henry was not pleased with the castle and he commissioned further work.

By the time this renovation work began in 1542, the threat of a French invasion had diminished and renovations on Camber Castle were implemented. The floor was elevated to overcome the damp problems. As the coastline moved southwards, the artillery within the castle did not have the range above the shingle and upon the shoreline. Therefore, the height of the keep and the stirrup towers was raised and the curtain wall was buttressed. The four outer towers were demolished and replaced with four larger semi-circular bastions, which were used as artillery positions. The rectangular entrance was replaced with a semi-circular gatehouse and the

Camber Castle. (Author's Collection)

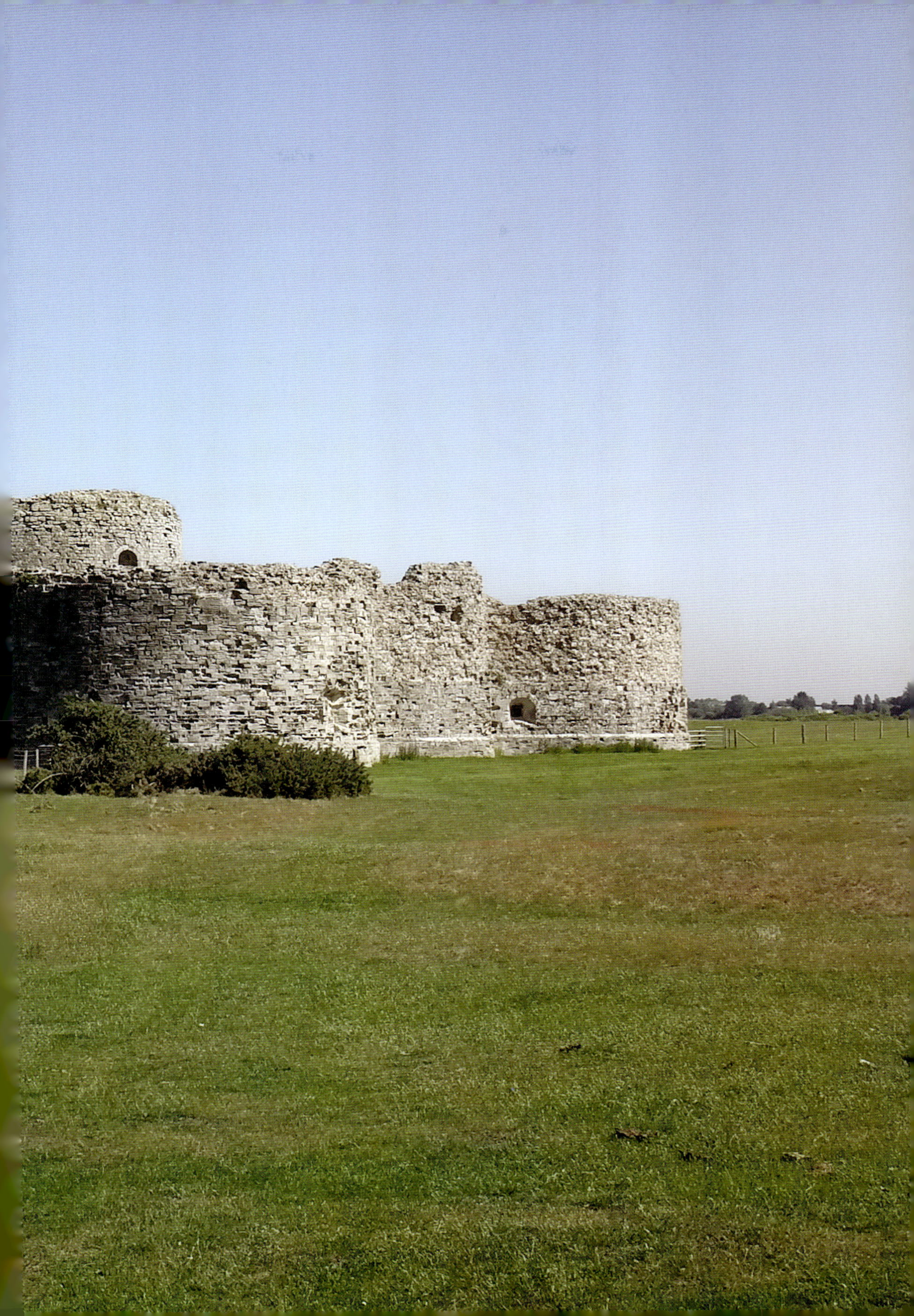

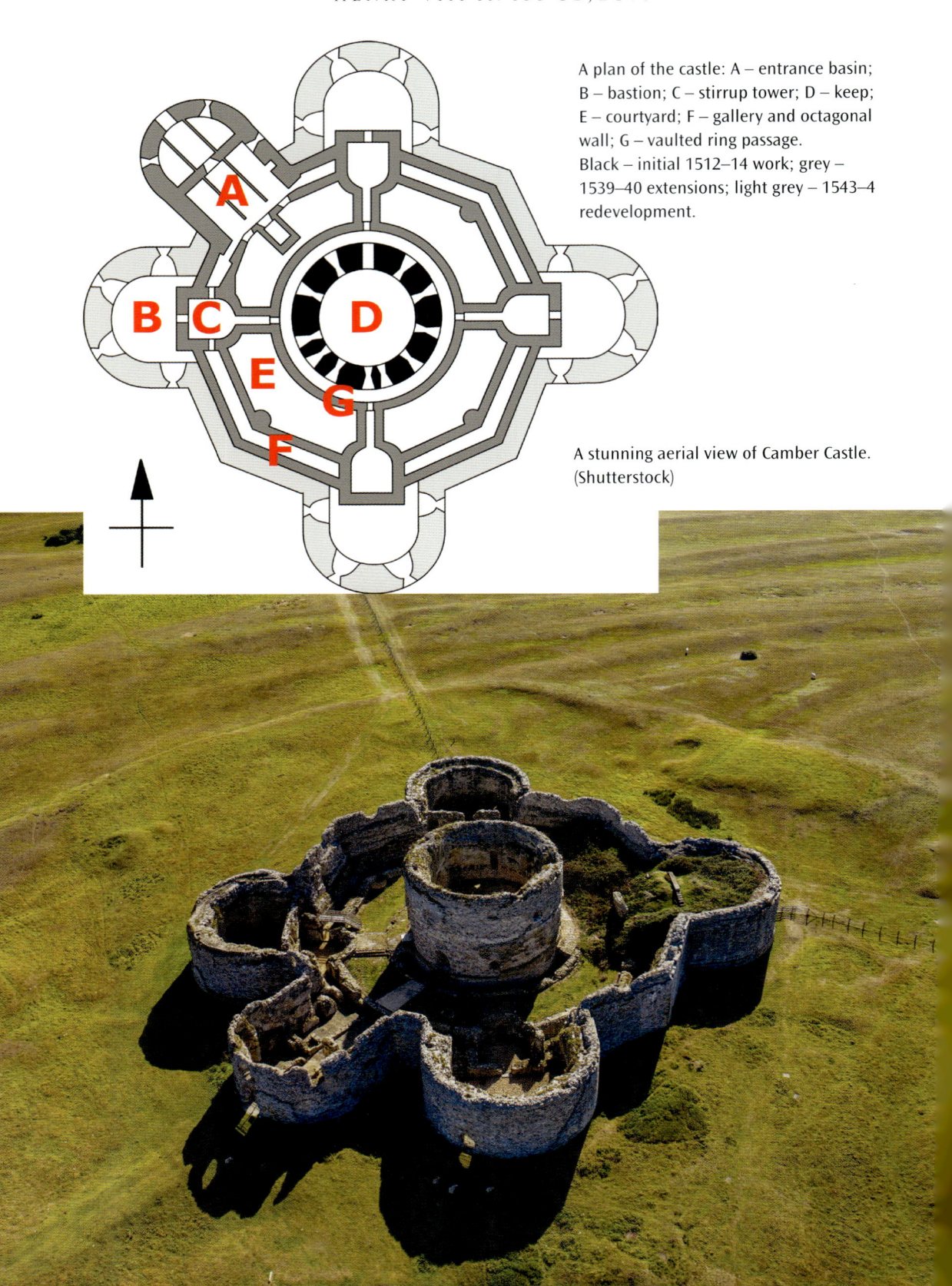

A plan of the castle: A – entrance basin; B – bastion; C – stirrup tower; D – keep; E – courtyard; F – gallery and octagonal wall; G – vaulted ring passage. Black – initial 1512–14 work; grey – 1539–40 extensions; light grey – 1543–4 redevelopment.

A stunning aerial view of Camber Castle. (Shutterstock)

space to accommodate the forty-two soldiers garrisoned within the castle was improved.

Despite the renovations, some flaws in the design remained, but Henry VIII approved the work carried out. Following the raising of the artillery platforms, some areas of ground surrounding the castle could not be reached by the guns. Therefore, the soldiers within the garrison had to rely on longbows to defend the castle's vulnerable blind spots.

The soldiers that were garrisoned at all the fortifications modified or built in 1539, including Camber, Sandgate, Deal, Sandown and Walmer castles, had to serve under regulations stipulated in the orders of Henry VIII. A document dated 21 April 1540 entitled 'Ordinances and statutes devised by the King's Majesty for the rule, establishment, and surety of his Highness's castles, bulwarks, and other fortresses appointed to the survey of the lord Admiral' provides details of daily life and routines within these Henrican forts.

1. The captain of a castle must not be absent more than 8 nights in a month without special licence from the King, on pain of forfeiting one month's wages for the first offence, 3 months' for the second, and his office on the third, with further punishment according to the King's pleasure.
2. The deputy is not to be absent more than four nights a month, and never when the captain is away, under similar penalties;
3. nor the porters more than three nights, and when absent each must find a substitute.
4. Every day certain of the gunners and soldiers must keep guard, the numbers to be determined by the Admiral. Absentees must find a substitute to keep guard, or forfeit double wages to the man whom the captain puts in their place.
5. Two gunners and soldiers are to keep watch every night, and if found sleeping or absent from their circuit, to forfeit, the first time, two days' wages, the second, a fortnight's, and the third, their place.
6. The captain or deputy, with the whole ward for the day, must be present daily at the opening and shutting of the gates, morning, noon, and night. The gate is to be opened from All hallow tide to Candlemas at 8 a.m. and shut at 4 p.m., from Candlemas to Easter, 6 a.m. and 6 p.m., from Easter to Bartholomew tide, 5 a.m. and 8 p.m., and from Bartholomew tide to All hallow tide, 7 a.m. and 6 p.m. It must likewise be shut from 11 a.m. to 1 p.m. The gate is not to be opened at any other time, unless it is thought proper by the captain or deputy, or the porter in the captain's absence if there is no deputy. The keys are always to be kept by the captain, deputy, or the porter in the captain's absence if there be no deputy.
7. That no 'stranger born, as nigh as they can', be allowed to enter the hold. That no greater number of persons than half the garrison be allowed to enter at one time except for the King's service or necessary works.
8. No captains or others of the garrison are to make any exaction, or accept anything from ships passing or lying in the roads, nor trouble or hinder them to make them offer any of their merchandise. They shall pay truly for what they have from the country on pain of losing their place, and imprisonment.
9. None of the garrison are to hunt or course deer, hares or conies, or hawk, take or shoot hawks, pheasants, partridges, or shovellers, under the same penalty.
10. Every man must furnish himself with convenient weapons, as a dagger and

sword, a halberd or bill, and harness, and every gunner a handgun or hagbush at his own charge, between this and midsummer, and for every day without them after that time to forfeit 3 days' wages.

11. No gunner to shoot off ordnance or hale any ship without license of the captain or deputy in his absence, on pain of losing his place. The captain must not waste the King's powder.
12. All suits against any of the garrison to be made to the lord Admiral.
13. Every pay day, proclamation must be made for the payment of victuals, &c., taken by any of the garrison, before they shall receive their wages, and the captain or deputy must see that the parties are duly paid.
14. The captain must never allow more than two soldiers to be absent at once, and only for three days a month.
15. Allowances of powder for exercise, and for halsing of ships, and trying of pieces, will be made by the lord Admiral's discretion to the captains.
16. Each of the captains, deputies, gunners, and porters are to have their bills signed by the King.
17. Musters are to be taken quarterly by the lord Admiral or such as he shall appoint, at which each man must declare on oath how these orders have been kept.
18. Inventories of munitions are to be taken at the first muster, and they must be viewed every quarter.
19. Certificate of the death of any of the garrison must be made to the lord Admiral.
20. No soldier must leave or be discharged except at musters, or by permission in writing from the lord Admiral.
21. Any man making any affray at the gates, or on the walls, or at night, to lose his place and be imprisoned.
22. Any man not keeping his oath, will be imprisoned for disobedience in addition to the penalties mentioned above.[175]

The garrison at Camber Castle was placed on high alert on 7 August 1545 when 200 French warships sailed off the coast at Rye, although the French landing at Seaford on 25 August was a disaster. Further silting, towards the end of the sixteenth century, made the castle obsolete and it was finally abandoned in 1627.

74

Sandgate Castle

Further Reinforcement of Coastal Fortifications

Sandgate Castle is unique in comparison with other fortifications built during 1539 because it was not built to defend a port or anchorage, but solely to defend a vulnerable stretch of coastline between Folkestone and Hythe, which was approximately 27 miles from the French coast. The shingle beach and the low ground made it a suitable landing position for a French invasion.

Work on Sandgate Castle commenced during March 1539. The German engineer Stefan von Haschenperg devised and supervised the construction of the castle. Details of salary payments for that month provide an insight into the initial work to build the castle:

Masons, 'working not only on berkyng skapelyng, but also laying of stone for the foundation and buildings of the foresaid castle at Sandgate', Robt. Lynsted at 10*d*. a day, 10 at 8*d*., and 34 at 7*d*. Labourers to the masons 'carrying of water, slaking of lime, making of morter', and serving the said masons, 59 at 6*d*. a day. Skavell men and rock breakers, digging and casting 'beeche' from the foundation, breaking rocks and carrying them from the sea, and lading rocks and earth, 59 at 6*d*. Carpenters, making wheelbarrows, handbarrows, 'bossis', hods and morter tubs, and helving mattocks and other tools, 1 at 8*d*., and 3 at 6*d*. Sawyers, cutting boards for the wheelbarrows, &c., and 'planks for the stayes going up to the castle walls', 2 at 6*d*., and 2 others paid by

A general view of the site of Sandgate Castle. (Author's Collection)

the piece. Wood-fellers, felling scaffold timber and 'tallyng' wood for lime kilns, 28 at 6*d*. Limeburners at St. Radegond's digging a kiln out of the main chalk and also cutting chalk to serve the kiln, 1 at 7*d*., and 6 at 6*d*.; ditto, at St. Enswyth, 2 at 7*d*., and 8 at 6*d*. Carters, one carrying lime from St. Radegund's, and 24 carrying stone from the quarry. Cartage of wood and elm-board from Lymmynge Park, Swynfeld Mynewis, and Pulton Wood, of wheelbarrows, &c., from St. Radegund's, and of iron from Canterbury.[176]

Thomas Crocke, controller of Sandgate Castle, sent a progress report to Thomas Cromwell on 3 September 1539: 'The castle at Sandgate, within your lordship of Folkestone, is well brought forward. Three towers are ready to be covered; which Stephen the Almain, deviser of the said castle, would have covered with canvas, pitch, and tar. Thinks lead would be better, of which there is enough to cover the whole castle'.

The castle was completed in October 1540. At high tide the southern buttress would have been in the sea. The artillery had the range to fire upon any French vessel that approached Folkestone or the 5-mile stretch of coastline between Sandgate and Hythe.

Henry VIII visited Folkestone on 2 May 1542 to inspect the harbour defences and it is possible that he visited Sandgate Castle. The southern section of Sandgate Castle has been lost to the sea over the past five centuries and the original keep was transformed into a Martello Tower in the early nineteenth century, but the outer wall of the northern parts of the original Henrican castle remain. A blue plaque on the wall of the castle states 'Queen Elizabeth rested here 28 August 1575. Queen Victoria and Prince Consort visited 8 August 1855'.

Fish caught along this stretch of coastline was bought from a Hythe fishmonger, Thomas Hewitt, and served in the royal palaces in London.

Sandgate Castle looking south-east towards Folkestone. The castle was modified during the period 1805–8 in anticipation of a French invasion led by Napoleon and the keep was transformed into a Martello Tower. (Author's Collection)

75

Glastonbury Abbey

Glastonbury Abbey Dissolved and Abbott Richard Whiting Executed

By January 1539, Glastonbury Abbey was the only remaining monastery in Somerset that had not surrendered its assets and wealth to the Crown. Abbot Richard Whiting refused to relinquish control on the grounds that it did not meet the criteria as detailed in the Act of Suppression of lesser houses.

Richard Pollard, Thomas Moyle and Richard Layton, royal commissioners acting on behalf of the king, made an unannounced and impromptu visit to Glastonbury Abbey on 19 September 1539 with the intention of closing it down. Expecting to find vast amounts of wealth, they found very little within the abbey. When they visited the home of Abbot Whiting, a mile away at Sharpham, they found items of wealth that incriminated the abbot, including a book that supported Queen Katherine of Aragon. In a joint letter to Thomas Cromwell, they reported on 22 September 1539:

> Came to Glastonbury on Friday last at 10 a.m. Went to the abbot, at Sharpham, about a mile from the abbey, and examined him on certain articles. As his answer was not to our purpose, advised him to call to mind what he had forgotten and tell the truth. Visited the abbey, searched his study, and found a book against the King's divorce from the lady Dowager, and divers pardons, copies of bulls, and the counterfeit life of Thomas Becket in print; but could not find any letter that was material. Examined him again on the articles received from Cromwell. His answers which we send will show his cankered and traitorous heart. 'And so, with as fair words as we could, we have conveyed him from hence unto the Tower, being but a very weak man and sickly.' Will now proceed to discharge his servants and the monks. We have in money over 300*l*., and how much plate precisely we cannot yet say. Have found a gold chalice and other articles which the abbot hid from previous commissioners, and as yet he knows not we have found it. Desire to know to whom to deliver the custody of this house. It is the goodliest house of the sort we ever saw,—meet for the King and no man else; and we trust there shall never come any double hood within it again. There is never a doctor within that house, but three bachelors of divinity, meanly learned.[177]

On 28 September 1539 Pollard, Moyle and Layton continued their search of the monastery and homes of the abbott and monks and discovered that they had hidden a substantial number of valuable items from Glastonbury Abbey in manor houses belonging to the abbey. Whiting had withheld these riches and was deemed by the commissioners to have pilfered from the king. Pollard, Moyle and Layton reported:

> Since writing last from Glastonbury, have found money and plate hid in walls, vaults, and other secret places, and some conveyed to divers places in the country, and they expect to find more if they wait here a fortnight. Have committed to jail, for arrant robbery,

The ruins of Glastonbury Abbey. (Shutterstock)

the two treasurers of the church, monks, and the two clerks of the vestry, temporal men. At their first entry into the treasury and vestry found neither jewels, plate, nor ornaments, sufficient for a poor parish church, but recovered it by diligent enquiry and search. Have had no time to weigh it but think it, of great value. The abbot and monks had embezzled and stolen as much plate and ornaments as would have sufficed for a new abbey. Asks whether it is the King's pleasure for justice to be executed on these four persons.[178]

Reports of the resistance of the abbot and monks at Glastonbury Abbey were being sent to Europe. On 25 October 1539 Marillac, the French Ambassador, wrote:

> It will then be seen what will be treated anew, and what will be done with the abbot of Glastonbury, who has recently been put in the Tower, because, in taking the abbey treasures, valued at 200,000 crowns, they found a written book of the arguments in behalf of queen Katherine, the Emperor's aunt, against the marriage of queen Anne, who was afterwards beheaded.

The frail Abbot Richard Whiting was interrogated by Thomas Cromwell in the

Glastonbury Tor, where Abbot Robert Whiting was executed. (Mark Higgins/Shutterstock)

Tower of London. He was then sent back to Glastonbury with Pollard. On reaching Wells on 14 November 1539, Whiting was arrested, tried and found guilty of stealing from Glastonbury Abbey. On the following day, 15 November, Whiting was taken to Glastonbury Tor, which was close to the abbey, and executed. Lord Russell reported to Thomas Cromwell:

> On Thursday, the 14th inst., the abbot of Glastonbury was arraigned and next day executed on the Torre Hill beside Glastonbury, with two of his monks, for robbing Glastonbury church. The abbot was beheaded and quartered. One quarter stands at Wells, another at Bath, the rest at Ilchester and Bridgwater, and his head upon the abbey gate at Glastonbury. As for the rape and burglary committed, those parties are all condemned and four of them executed at a place called the Were, where the act was done.

Richard Pollard also wrote about the execution to Cromwell:

> The late abbot of Glastonbury went that day from Wells to Glastonbury, was drawn through the town upon a hurdle, and executed on the Tor Hill. He took his death patiently, asking pardon of God and the King for his offences, and desiring Pollard's servants to ask him and my lord President to mediate with the King for his forgiveness. His head and body were bestowed as I wrote in my last. The two other monks likewise desired forgiveness and took their deaths patiently.

Portrait of Anne of Cleves

Henry's Search for a Fourth Wife

During July 1539, Henry commissioned Hans Holbein to paint a portrait of Anne of Cleves and her sister, Amelia, so he could look upon their features before deciding to make a proposal of marriage or not. Since Jane Seymour's death, Henry considered finding a fourth wife with the hope of conceiving another son as a spare heir. The Treaty of Toledo, signed by Charles V and Francis I, prevented Henry from finding a suitable wife in France or within the Holy Roman Empire. Thomas Cromwell saw Henry's desire to seek another wife as an opportunity to forge an alliance with Germany in an effort to realign the balance of power within Europe.

The influential Duke John III of Cleves governed a German Lutheran principality and had two unmarried daughters named Anne and Amelia, who were considered suitable candidates to become the English King's next wife. John was not a Lutheran, but he had rejected papal authority. Henry sent his envoys, Richard Beard and Dr Nicholas Wotton, to Düsseldorf in Germany to see if the Cleves daughters were a suitable match during March 1539. Henry needed to see their faces before he could agree to marriage. The envoys were offered portraits, but Anne and her sister were wearing German court dress in the images and veils obscured their faces, so they were deemed unsatisfactory. Beard returned to England to report to Henry VIII in July 1539 and during that same month he was dispatched to Germany with Hans Holbein, the king's artist, who would paint a portrait of Cleve's daughters for Henry's review. It was recorded that in the King's Payments for that month:

'Richard Bearde, a groom of the Privy Chamber, and Hans Holbein, painter, "sent into the parts of High Almain upon certain his Grace's affairs", for their costs, 40*l*.; and "to Hans Holbein for the preparation of such things as he is appointed to carry with him".'

Hans Holbein arrived at the Cleves home at Duren in August 1539 and painted both daughters. He was under enormous pressure to capture their features in these images, because this would determine whether the king would find them attractive or not and would form the basis for his decision to propose marriage. Henry VIII received the following letter from Dr Nicholas Wotton, his ambassador, dated 11 August 1539, in which he refers to these paintings: 'Your Grace's servant Hans Holbein has taken the effigies of my lady Anne and the lady Amelye and hath expressed their images very lovely.'

The images of Amelia have not survived. Only this portrait of Anne, which is a watercolour on parchment mounted on canvas displayed in the Louvre in Paris, and a miniature belonging to the Victoria & Albert Museum in London exist. It is believed that the images were presented to the king to see if he would make one of the daughters his queen. Henry preferred to marry Anne because she was deemed more suitable being aged 24. Wotton described Anne's personality and qualities in his letter dated 11 August 1539.

She occupieth her time most with the needle, where withall . . . she can read and write . . . French, Latin, or other language she [hath no] knowledge, nor yet she cannot sing nor play any instrument, for they take it here in Germany for a rebuke and an occasion of lightness that great ladies should be learned or have any knowledge of music. Her wit is good and she will no doubt learn English soon when she puts her mind to it.[179]

Hans Holbein returned to England towards the end of August and showed the king his painting of Anne of Cleves. Thomas Cromwell was taking an enormous risk in trying to arrange a marriage to a woman that the king had never met and basing a proposal on this image. Henry was

Anne of Cleves, by Hans Holbein, 1539. Holbein painted this portrait and a miniature so Henry could see if he found her attractive. It would be decisive in his decision whether to marry her or not.

impressed by the image of Anne of Cleves and authorised Thomas Cromwell to organise the marriage with envoys sent by Anne of Cleves' brother, William, Duke of Julliers. Marillac, the French ambassador wrote on 1 September to Francis I:

> Having followed this King in his progress as far as this place, Grapton [sic], 50 miles from London, has learnt that an excellent painter [Hans Holbein] whom this King sent to Germany to bring the portrait of the sister of the duke of Cleves, recently arrived in Court, and, immediately afterwards, a courier bringing, among other news which is still kept secret, news that the said Duke's ambassadors have started to come hither to treat and conclude the marriage of this King and the said lady.[180]

Arrangements for the marriage were finalised on 6 October 1539 and Anne left Cleves for England during November, travelling via Antwerp and Bruges. Arriving in Calais on 6 December 1539, she was received by the Earl of Southampton, Lord High Admiral, who was accompanied by Sir Thomas Seymour, Gregory Cromwell, son of Thomas Cromwell, and Thomas Culpepper, a junior member of the Privy Council, who had sailed across the English Channel in three ships, the *Lyon*, *Primrose* and *Genette*. It was originally planned that Anne would arrive in London on 10 December, but bad weather prevented her from crossing the English Channel and she spent fifteen days in Calais waiting for favourable winds and calm seas.

Anne and her entourage landed at Deal in Kent at 5pm on 27 December 1539. They were welcomed by Charles Brandon, Duke of Suffolk, and his wife with a banquet at Deal Castle before proceeding to Dover Castle later that night. It would take several days to reach London using horses and carts. Anne continued her journey via Canterbury where she was received by Archbishop Cranmer and stayed at the newly constructed royal apartments within St Augustine's Abbey, before proceeding to Sittingbourne. Anne of Cleves arrived at the Archbishop's Palace at Rochester on 31 December. It had been arranged that Henry would first set eyes upon his bride at Greenwich three days later, but he was impatient and decided to abandon protocol and ride from London by horse in a chivalric dash through the night with five gentlemen from the Privy Council to meet Anne at Rochester. Before he departed from Greenwich Palace, he told Cromwell that he intended to 'nourish love'.

77

The Bishop's Palace, Rochester

Henry and Anne Meet for the First Time

Henry arrived at Rochester during the afternoon of New Year's Day, 1540, but his intention to surprise his bride-to-be backfired disastrously.

Disguised as a courtier, dressed in a cloak and hood, Anne did not recognise this old, rugged, obese man as the king and rebuked his advances. Wriothesley recorded:

> On New Year's day, at afternoon, the King's Grace, with five of his Privy chamber being disguised with cloaks of marble with hoods, and they should not be known, came privately to Rochester, and so went up into the chamber, where the said Lady Anne looked out at a window to see the bull beating that was that time in the court, and suddenly he embraced her and kissed, and shewed her a token that the King had sent for her New Year's gift, and she being abashed, not knowing who it was, thanked him, and so he communicated with her; but she regarded him little, but always looked out of the window on the bull bating, and when the King perceived she regarded his coming so little, he departed into another chamber and put off his cloak and came in again in a coat of purple velvet, and when the Lords and knights did see his Grace, they did him reverence; and then she, perceiving the lords doing their duties, humbled her grace lowly to the King's Majesty.[181]

Their initial meeting was embarrassingly awkward. Anne was being embraced and kissed by a bearded, old and unattractive man who was a complete stranger, whose intrusive behaviour was unwelcomed by such a refined lady who was reported to have been 'marvellously astonished and abashed'.

When the king did reveal his true identity, it was difficult for either of them to salvage the situation because Anne could not speak English. There was no physical attraction, no chemistry and no ability to converse with each other, and so the marriage was destined to fail. Furthermore, Henry was furious that Anne of Cleves did not look as beautiful as depicted in Holbein's painting. Henry commented to an attendant, 'I see nothing in this woman as men report of her and I marvel that wise men would make such report as they have done'.

Other courtiers noticed that Holbein's painting did not reflect the true likeness of Anne of Cleves. Marillac reported on 5 January 1540, that 'the Queen of England has arrived who, according to some who saw her close, is not so young as was expected, nor so beautiful as everyone affirmed. She is tall and very assured in carriage and countenance, showing that in her the turn and vivacity of wit supplies the place of beauty.'

Henry returned to Greenwich on 2 January and Anne was left to continue her journey to London alone. When Cromwell asked the king how he liked the lady Anne, he responded, 'Nothing so well as she was spoken of', adding that if he had known before as much as he then knew, she should never have come within the realm. The king swiftly convened a Privy Council meeting to discuss how he was to avoid marrying

HERE LIVED FOR THIRTY ONE YEARS JOHN FISHER. BISHOP OF ROCHESTER CHANCELLOR OF THE UNIVERSITY OF CAMBRIDGE AND CARDINAL WHO LAID DOWN HIS LIFE FOR HIS FAITH ON TOWER HILL JUNE 22ND 1535

The Bishop's Palace, Rochester. This was the home of the Bishop of Rochester, John Fisher, for thirty-four years and where Henry VIII and Anne of Cleves had their first disastrous encounter. (Author's Collection)

A plaque commemorating Bishop Fisher's occupancy of this building. (Author's Collection)

Anne of Cleves, but he was in a difficult situation, for if he did not marry her, then he would damage Anglo-German relations, which might encourage a German alliance with Francis I and Charles V. Henry said to Cromwell, 'Is there none other remedy but that I must needs, against my will, put my neck in the yoke?'

Henry received Anne at Blackheath on 3 January 1540 and they rode together to Greenwich Palace where a banquet was held in her honour. Despite behaving graciously towards Anne, Henry was determined not to marry her. The wedding was scheduled to take place the following day at Greenwich Palace, but he postponed it in order to bide himself time to extricate himself from this delicate situation, but there was no solution. If he was to prevent England from being totally isolated in Europe, then he had no choice but to marry Anne. This painting of Anne of Cleves had ensnared the King of England into a commitment of marriage to a woman that he felt no physical attraction towards, and neither could they speak each other's language. Henry VIII and Anne of Cleves married at 8am on 6 January 1540 at Greenwich Palace in a ceremony conducted by Thomas Cranmer, Archbishop of Canterbury.

Henry, the reluctant groom, lamented to Cromwell: 'My lord, if it were not to satisfy the world and my realm, I would not do that I must do this day for none earthly thing.' During their wedding night they played cards on the bed and on the following morning Henry confided to Cromwell and said 'that I was not all men. Surely, my Lord, as ye know, I liked her before not well, but now. I like her much worse.'

The marriage was not consummated that night. Thomas Cromwell wrote of the King's appraisal of his wedding night, 'for I had felt her belly and breasts, and thought she was no maid; that I was struck to the heart, and left her as good a maid as I found her.'

It is ironic that the unpleasant King, who had married three wives and had at least one mistress is disparaging about the figure of Anne of Cleves and questions whether she was a virgin, but it was fine for him to treat women, use them as pleasurable pursuits and then to discard them at his will. Sir Thomas Hennage also testified that, 'ever since the King saw the Queen he had never liked her; and said as often as he went to bed to her, he mistrusted the Queen's virginity, by reason of the looseness of her breasts and other tokens; and the marriage had never been consummated.'

Henry sought guidance from court physicians, but they could not find any evidence of impotency. Despite these consultations, Henry never had any intentions of initiating sexual relations with Anne, because if he had consummated the marriage, it would have made it difficult for him to annul the union.

Thomas Cromwell wrote that 'after Candlemas and before Shrovetide, he once or twice said that he had never known her carnally, although he had lain nightly or every second night by her … and after Easter and in Whitsun week he lamented his fate that he should never have any more children if he so continued, declaring that before God he thought she was not his lawful wife. Since Whitsuntide he has said he had done as much to move the consent of his heart and mind as ever man did, but the obstacle would not out of his mind'.

Anne's coronation was planned for 2 February 1540, but Henry had almost immediately come to the conclusion that this marriage would not work and abandoned plans to crown her Queen of England. Instead, she was brought to the Palace of Westminster, where she spent the days playing card and dice with her attendants. Henry was not in a position to divorce Anne, so he waited until he could form an alliance with a European power before getting the marriage annulled.

Anne of Cleves Public House, Melton Mowbray

Cromwell Falls from Favour and Henry Obtains an Annulment of Marriage to Anne of Cleves

The Anne of Cleves public house in Burton Street, Melton Mowbray, Leicestershire, was built in 1384 as a hall for chantry priests of the Cluniac order. There were nine priests living there when Henry VIII dissolved the priory in Melton Mowbray. In February 1538, Henry gave this house to Thomas Cromwell and it is believed that he resided there during the two years it was in his possession while he was heavily involved with the dissolution of the larger monasteries in 1539 and in arrangements for the marriage between Henry VIII and Anne of Cleves. On 17 April 1540, Cromwell's stature continued to

The Anne of Cleves public house, home of Thomas Cromwell and Anne of Cleves. (Author's Collection)

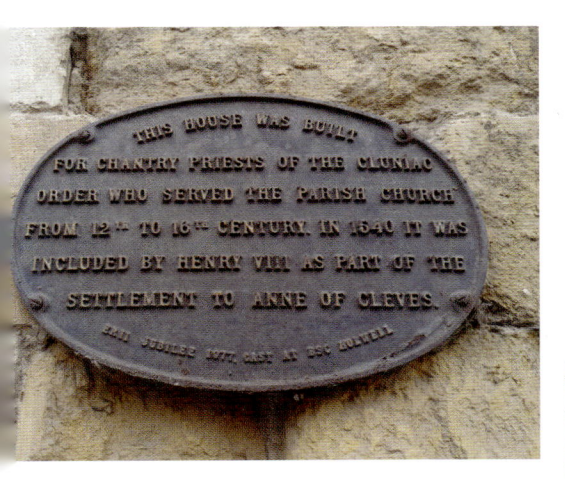

Plaque recognising that the Melton Mowbray building was built for chantry priests of the Cluniac order and was given to Anne of Cleves by Henry VIII as part of her divorce settlement. (Author's Collection)

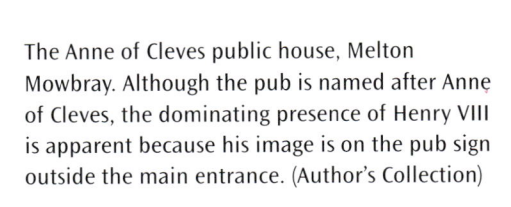

The Anne of Cleves public house, Melton Mowbray. Although the pub is named after Anne of Cleves, the dominating presence of Henry VIII is apparent because his image is on the pub sign outside the main entrance. (Author's Collection)

rise when he was created Earl of Essex and Lord Great Chamberlain. Despite these accolades, the king had not forgiven him for his mishandling of the disastrous marriage to Anne of Cleves. In addition, Cromwell had many enemies at court who would influence Henry into mistrusting his advisor and this would result in his ultimate downfall in 1540.

The king seized this property in 1540 and during that same year it became part of the divorce settlement with Anne of Cleves. His fourth wife had been living at the Palace of Westminster since February 1540. During March, the threat of an invasion had become less remote and Henry began to initiate a conclusion to his fourth marriage. In June 1540, Anne was requested to leave the court and, on 9 July, Archbishop Cranmer granted an annulment on the grounds that there had been a precontract of marriage between Anne and the Marquis of Lorraine in her own country and that the marriage between Henry and Anne was 'unwillingly entered into and never consummated'. Both the king and Lady Anne were at liberty to remarry.

Anne was given a generous divorce settlement which included an annual income of £500 (worth £150,000 today), Richmond Palace, Hever Castle, a house in Lewes and

Another 'Anne of Cleves House', this time in Lewes, East Sussex. This timber-framed Wealden Hall house was another of the properties given to Anne by Henry VIII as part of their divorce settlement. It is said that Anne never visited the house. (Courtesy of Charles Drake)

Thomas Cromwell's former home in Melton Mowbray.[182] Henry maintained good relations with his former fourth wife and she was referred to as the 'King's beloved sister'. When Anne of Cleves died in 1557 she was buried on the south side of the high altar within Westminster Abbey on the recommendation of Queen Mary I.

Tower Hill Execution Site

The Execution of Thomas Cromwell

Tower Hill stands within close proximity of the Tower of London. No other English monarch had sanctioned more executions in one reign than Henry VIII. It was here that over 125 individuals over the reigns of a series of monarchs were executed in public, including the Duke of Buckingham, Bishop John Fisher and Sir Thomas More during the reign of Henry VIII. Among them was Thomas Cromwell who is one of the few whose name is listed on a commemorative plaque on Tower Hill.

When Cromwell, who held the role of Keeper of the Privy Seal, was appointed Lord Great Chamberlain of England on 17 April 1540 he held four of the six prestigious offices of state. Among his litany of titles, he was Vicar-General, Vice-Regent, High Chamberlain of England and Chancellor of the Exchequer. The following day he received another title, Earl of Essex. Despite the debacle surrounding his involvement with the marriage of Anne of Cleves, the king still favoured Cromwell and these new awards reflected that. However, there were factions within the court working against him, mainly those from the old nobility, such as Thomas Howard, Duke of Norfolk, and religious traditionalists who would have been jubilant if he fell out of favour. They disapproved of his policies, ruthlessness and his powerful influence over the realm. They also strongly resented the fact that Cromwell had risen to the high ranks of power from humble origins, being the son of a blacksmith. In May 1540, Cromwell sent several bishops to the Tower on charges of reverting back to old religious traditions and that they refused to accept the supremacy of the king in an effort to destroy his enemies before they destroyed him.

The Bishop of Winchester, Stephen Gardiner, persuaded Henry VIII to secretly raise a parliamentary bill on 8 June 1540, denouncing Cromwell for undermining the king's aim of a religious settlement. Cromwell's fate was sealed two days later when he was arrested at a meeting of the Privy Council at the Palace of Westminster. As Cromwell approached his seat at the end of the table, the Duke of Norfolk revelled in berating him: 'Cromwell! Do not sit there! That is no place for you! Traitors do not sit with gentlemen.'[183]

Cromwell was astonished by Norfolk's tone and responded, 'I am not a traitor' as he was approached by Sir Anthony Wingfield, Captain of the Guard, who seized his arm, accompanied by six halberdiers. When asked 'What for?', Wingfield retorted, 'That, you will learn elsewhere' before Cromwell was dispatched to the Tower of London.

Marillac, the French Ambassador, reported:

> As soon as the Captain of the Guard declared his charge to make him prisoner, Cromwell in a rage cast his bonnet on the ground, saying to the duke of Norfolk and others of the Privy Council assembled there that this was the reward of his services, and that he appealed to their consciences as to whether he was a traitor; but since he was treated thus he renounced all pardon, as he had never thought to have offended, and only asked the King not

The site of the scaffold is commemorated by this memorial garden at Tower Hill, which is north-west of the Tower of London. (Author's Collection)

Another view of the execution site at Tower Hill. (Author's Collection)

to make him languish long. Thereupon some said he was a traitor, others that he should be judged according to the laws he had made, which were so sanguinary that often words spoken inadvertently with good intention had been constituted high treason. The duke of Norfolk having reproached him with some 'villennyes' done by him, snatched off the order of St. George which he bore on his neck, and the Admiral, to show himself as great an enemy in adversity as he had been thought a friend in prosperity, untied the Garter. Then, by a door which opens upon the water, he was put in a boat and taken to the Tower without the people of this town suspecting it until they saw all the King's archers under Mr. Cheyney at the door of the prisoner's house, where they made an inventory of his goods, which were not of such value as people thought, although too much for a 'compaignon de telle estoffe'. The money was 7,000*l.* st., equal to 28,000 crowns., and the silver plate, including crosses, chalices, and other spoils of the Church might be as much more. These movables were before night taken to the King's treasury—a sign that they will not be restored.

Next day were found several letters he wrote to or received from the Lutheran lords of Germany. Cannot learn what they contained except that this King was thereby so exasperated against him that he would no longer hear him spoken of, but rather desired to abolish all memory of him as the greatest wretch ever born in England. To commence, this King distributed all his offices and proclaimed that none should call him lord Privy Seal or by any other title of estate, but only Thomas Cromwell, shearman (*tondeur de draps*), depriving him of all his privileges and prerogatives, and distributing his less valuable moveables among his [Cromwell's] servants, who were enjoined no longer to wear their master's livery. From this it is inferred that he will not be judged with the solemnity accustomed to be used to the lords of this country, nor beheaded; but will be dragged up as an ignoble person, and afterwards hanged and quartered. A few days will show; especially as they have determined to empty the Tower at this Parliament, which finishes with this month.[184]

On the night of his arrest the Privy Council rejoiced at the demise of Cromwell. He was so despised by the people that they celebrated by lighting bonfires on the streets of London. The news of Cromwell's arrest was also welcomed abroad. Francis I wrote that King Henry 'shall know how much the getting rid of this wicked and unhappy instrument will tranquillise his Kingdom, to the common welfare of Church, nobles, and people'.

Cromwell was condemned on attainder without a trial, the method employed by Cromwell to imprison and eventually condemn the Countess of Salisbury, who was executed on 27 May 1541. Without a trial, Cromwell was declared a traitor and a heretic, a felon and extortionist, as well as guilty of forwarding his own Protestant agenda by manipulating the king into marrying Anne of Cleves. Henry did not question the validity of these charges or the judgement. Thomas Cranmer, Archbishop of Canterbury, wrote to the king in a futile bid to seal Cromwell's release. Cromwell also wrote directly to the king to plead for a pardon, 'Most gracious Prince, I cry for mercy, mercy, mercy', but he received no clemency.

On 28 July 1540, Cromwell awakened at dawn and as he ate his breakfast, there was a knock on his cell door. It was Sir William Laxton and Martin Bowes, sheriffs of London. They informed him that his execution would take place that morning and that the King had shown mercy, commuting his sentence from hung, drawn and quartering to death by decapitation. Cromwell was taken from the Tower of London and paraded through the crowds of spectators as he walked towards the scaffold on Tower Hill, where the memorial stands. There were a thousand halberdiers guarding his route, because Cromwell did have some supporters who might have launched a desperate bid to rescue him. As he approached the scaffold, he glimpsed his friend Thomas Wyatt, who had tears in his eyes. Wyatt had been imprisoned for an affair he had with Anne Boleyn before she married the king. Cromwell said, 'O, gentle Wyatt, good bye and pray to God for me. Do not weep for me, for if I were no more guilty than thou were when they took thee, I should not be in this pass.'

To exacerbate his humiliation, he was executed on the same day as Walter, Lord Hungerford, who, according to Marillac, was condemned 'of sodomy, of having forced his own daughter, and having practised magic and invocation of devils'. Hungerford was to follow Cromwell to the block and he was in a frenzied state. Cromwell had to calm him down.

Before the execution was carried out, Cromwell delivered a speech to the crowd and addressed some of the charges that were brought against for which he had been denied the chance to defend in a court of law. Edward Hall recorded what he said:

> I am come hither to die, and not to purge myself, as may happen, some think that I will, for if I should so do, I were a very wretch and miser: I am by the law condemned to die, and thank thy my lord God that hath appointed me this death, for my offence. For since hence the time that I have had years of discretion, I have lived a sinner, and offended my lord God, for the which I ask him heartily forgiveness. And it is not unknown to many of you, that I have been a great traveller in this world, and being but of a base degree, was called to high estate, and since then the time I came there unto, I have offended my prince, for which I ask him heartily forgiveness, and beseech you all to pray with me, that he will forgive me. O father forgive me, O son forgive me, O holy ghost forgive me. O the persons in one God forgive me. I now I pray you that be here, to hear me record, I die in the Catholic faith, not doubting in any article of my faith. No nor doubting in any Sacrament of the Church. Many hath slandered me, and reported that I have been a bearer, of such has maintained evil opinions, which is untrue, but I confess that like as God by his holy spirit, doth instruct us in the truth, so the devil is ready to seduce us, and I have been seduced; but be my witness that I die in the Catholic

A portrait of Thomas Cromwell. (The Frick Collection)

faith of the holy Church. And I heartily desire you to pray for the King's grace, that he may long live with you, in health and prosperity.... And once again I desire you to pray for me, that so long as life remain in this flesh, I waiver nothing in my faith.[185]

Cromwell spoke these words in front of a sombre crowd, some he may have recognised as adversaries in the court. He was determined to maintain his dignity. In his final words, Cromwell accepted his fate, acknowledged his roots and how high he ascended during his life, he appealed for forgiveness from the king and asserted that he was not a Lutheran. There was speculation that in his half-hearted attempt to confess his sins, Cromwell might have been coerced, even threatened to do this at the scaffold. Richard Hilles wrote: 'Others, however, say that he was threatened with burning at the stake instead of death by the axe if he did not confess his crimes at execution, and that he then said he was a miserable sinner against God and the King, but that what he said of having offended the King he said carelessly and coldly.'

Before kneeling down by the block, he asked the executioner: 'Pray if possible, cut off the head with one blow, so that I may not suffer much'. After praying and committing his soul into the hands of God, he placed his neck upon the block. Hume asserts that Cromwell was decapitated with one strike of the axe, however, according to Hall, the axeman bungled the execution, commenting that Cromwell 'so patiently suffered the stroke of the axe, by a ragged and botched miser, which very ungoodly performed the office'. Other accounts confirm that two executioners were 'chopping the Lord Cromwell's neck and head for nearly half-an-hour'.[186] The decapitated heads of Cromwell and Hungerford were placed upon spikes on London Bridge and their bodies were buried within St Peter ad Vincula.

80
Surviving Wall of Oatlands Palace

Henry VIII's Marriage to Katherine Howard

The entrance and front wall of Oatlands Palace is all that remains. It is located within a quiet residential area of Weybridge in Surrey, along the aptly named Tudor Walk. The construction of Oatlands Palace began in 1537 together with a road that linked Hampton Court Palace. The construction of Nonsuch Palace was also underway that year and was intended to become the residence of Edward, Prince of Wales, while Oatlands would be regarded as the queen's home. Henry VIII married his fifth wife, Katherine Howard, cousin of Anne Boleyn and niece of the Duke of Norfolk, Cromwell's enemy, here on 28 July 1540.

Henry and Katherine's marriage ceremony took place on the same day that Thomas Cromwell was executed. The ceremony was conducted by Bishop Edmund Bonner, but there are no recorded details of any celebrations, so it can be assumed that the king wanted the wedding to be a quiet, low-profile affair. Henry VIII and Katherine Howard would have walked through this actual entrance in order to enter the palace for the wedding ceremony.

Katherine was born in Lambeth in about 1523–5, which meant that she was probably aged between 17 and 19 when she married Henry, who was aged 49. Katherine entered court as a maid of honour within Anne of Cleves' household towards the end of 1539 and at the beginning of 1540 she swiftly attracted the attention of the king and became his mistress. When his marriage to Anne was annulled in July 1540, Henry was free to take another wife.

Speculation circulated throughout Europe regarding the astonishing circumstances in the English court. Manuell Cyrne reported to King John III of Portugal:

> There is strange news from England—that the King has left the sister of the duke of Cleves whom he married in January last. . . . The cause is not yet certain; some say that there was a previous contract with the duke of Lorraine, some that the King would marry an English lady, niece of the duke of Norfolk, daughter of his brother, and that she is already with child.[187]

Henry visited Anne of Cleves on 6 August 1540 to ensure that she was happy with her domestic arrangements and to inform her that he had married Katherine Howard. Two days later, Henry presented his new wife at court at Hampton Court Palace. Queen Katherine was never crowned because Henry could not afford a lavish ceremony and he probably wanted to see if the marriage was a success before confirming a coronation.

The king was, however, smitten with his young wife. Marillac reported to Montmorency on 3 September 1540 that Queen Katherine was 'rather graceful than beautiful, of short stature. . . . The King is so amorous of her that he cannot treat her well enough and caresses her more than he did the others.'

Henry felt invigorated by his new young bride; however, he was not aware that Katherine had been involved with three other men before their marriage. Henry Mannock, her music master,

The entrance to Oatlands Palace at Tudor Walk, Weybridge. (Author's Collection)

A plaque marking the site of Oatlands Palace. (Author's Collection)

A seventeenth-century painting of Oatlands Palace. Note that the front wall and entrance gate is all that stands today. The palace was within close proximity of Hampton Court and Nonsuch Palaces and could be approached by the River Thames. Construction began in 1537 and building material was sourced from the dissolved monasteries at Chertsey, Bisham and Merton. The palace's name derived from a previous owner of the land in the thirteenth century, Robert dc Ottelond. The palace was demolished in 1650.

Katherine Howard. The jewelled band around her neckline may have been given to her by Henry VIII as a marriage gift. (Courtesy of the Kunsthistorisches Museum, Vienna)

claimed that she had promised to be his mistress, Francis Dereham referred to her as his wife and there were reports that she was already engaged to Thomas Culpepper, her cousin and a junior member of the Privy Council. Historians have either defined these relationships as loving or depicted Katherine as promiscuous, but these men were much older than Katherine Howard and possibly took advantage of her youth. Mannock potentially abused his position as her music teacher by trying to entice his pupil. Culpepper was a violent sexual predator, who in 1539 had viciously raped the wife of a park keeper while four of his associates held her down. When a villager challenged him about this vile act, Culpepper murdered him. Henry VIII was made aware of these horrid crimes, but pardoned him. It is highly likely that the opportunist Culpepper may have intimidated and manipulated Katherine into a sexual relationship by threatening her with violence or blackmail by revealing her past liaisons. When Henry eventually found out the truth about Katherine's past, it was from Oatlands Palace on 8 December 1541 that he wrote the order to the Privy Council. This stated that those close to Katherine who had allegedly withheld this information were to be arrested for misprision of treason and sent to the Tower of London, and that Culpepper and Dereham were to be executed.

81

Tudor Graffiti, Beauchamp Tower, Tower of London

Thomas Abel Executed

There are over sixty examples of graffiti carved on the interior walls of the first-floor apartment within the Beauchamp Tower. Political prisoners, opponents of Henry VIII's regime and in particular the Reformation, were responsible for some of these inscriptions. This particular example of Tudor graffiti features the name Thomas above a bell with the letter 'A' inscribed within it, which was the Abel family insignia. Note that the surname is sometimes spelled as Abell. The image was carved by Friar Thomas Abel who was imprisoned in the Beauchamp Tower for his support for Queen Katherine, the first wife of Henry VIII.

Abel was Queen Katherine's chaplain and in January 1529 she sent him to her nephew, Emperor Charles V, on a secret mission to prevent him from giving English ambassadors a document that would have hindered her opposition to Henry's claim for divorce. In 1531, Henry ordered the publication of views of scholars that supported Henry's argument for divorce with the book *Determination of the Most Famous Universities*. Abel continued to support the cause of Queen Katherine and made a direct challenge to Henry's book with the publication of a treatise in May 1532, which was entitled *Invicta veritas. An answere, That by no manner of law, it may be lawfull for the most noble King of England, King Henry the eighth to be divorced from the queens grace, his lawfull and very wife. B.L.*, which opposed the sovereign's attempts to obtain an annulment. The main title of the book, translated as *The Invincible Truth*, was inflammatory and defiant. Edward Hall, who supported the king, wrote, 'One Thomas Abel, clerk, both preached and wrote a book, that the marriage was lawful, which caused many simple men to believe his opinion'. Henry deemed the publication such a threat that he tried to purchase every copy in order to destroy them all. For writing this work that challenged the king, Abel was incarcerated in the Tower of London in August 1532. Queen Katherine felt concern for her imprisoned Chaplain. Chapuys reported:

> The Queen is in a house of the bishop of Ely, 17 miles from London, and it is not known whether the King will remove her. She is much grieved at the arrest of a chaplain of hers, who has been sent to the Tower for printing a book in English in her favour. The King is trying to procure all the copies which have been sold, and has had the book examined by the university of Oxford, but they do not know what to take hold of, and it is certain that if the book had not been prohibited there would have been a danger of commotion.[188]

Abel was released in December 1532 on the condition that he did not interfere with the king's 'great matter' and prohibited from preaching until April. Henry wanted to silence those who criticised his relationship until he had married Anne Boleyn. After Henry married Anne and

Inscription on the wall of the Beauchamp Tower, inscribed by political prisoner Chaplain Thomas Abel. Beauchamp Tower was built in 1281 during the reign of King Edward I and named after Thomas de Beauchamp, Earl of Warwick in 1397. (Author's Collection)

Thomas Abel inscribed this carving inside the alcove to the left of the window. (Author's Collection)

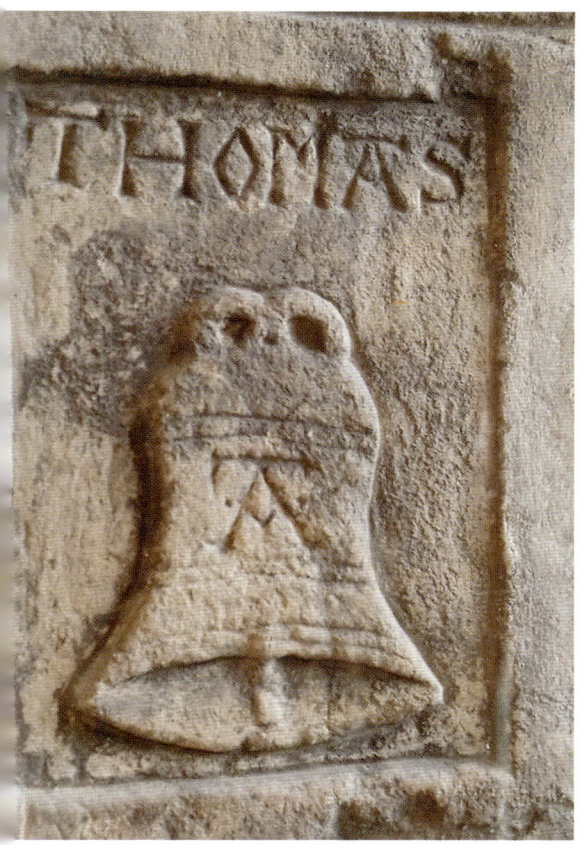

she was crowned queen in 1533, Abel refused to be suppressed. He continued to voice his opposition to the divorce and continued to address Katherine as 'Queen' instead of Princess Dowager. In December 1533, Henry sent Charles Brandon, Duke of Suffolk, accompanied by soldiers to Buckden to force Katherine to accept the divorce and Anne Boleyn as queen. On 19 December 1533, in a letter to the king, Brandon reported Thomas Abel's influence upon Katherine's household and the devotion of her servants:

> Her servants are loth to take the new oath, as they were sworn to her as Queen, and they think the second oath would be perjury; and they continued stiffly in this opinion until we had gotten with difficulty from them that they had that knowledge from Abel and Barker, her chaplains. We examined them, and found them stiffly standing in their conscience that she was your Queen, and no man sworn to serve her as Queen might change that oath without perjury. As they

persist in that opinion, we have committed them to the porter's ward, there to remain without speaking with any one till your pleasure be known.[189]

Subsequently, Abel was persecuted for defending Queen Katherine's cause and defying Brandon. Henry VIII ordered that he be imprisoned in the Tower of London in December 1533. After spending two months in confinement, Abel was implicated with Elizabeth Barton, the nun of Kent, who had prophesied the king's death if he married Anne Boleyn. Henry regarded this as treason and she was executed at Tyburn in April 1534. Abel had never met Barton, but Henry used this false charge as a mechanism to keep him imprisoned. Henry tried to break his spirit by detaining him in filthy, cold conditions where he was kept isolated and restricted with no access to books and limited food in the hope that he would conform and submit to the king's will. While imprisoned, Abel would hear of the death of Katherine in 1536, but he was not released and nor was he tried for the charges laid against him. Abel's frustrations that he was unjustly imprisoned were conveyed in this letter to Thomas Cromwell, written in March 1537, in which he appeals for his release:

'My lord, I beseke our Saviour Jesus Christ to give your Lordship after this life, life everlasting in Heaven. Amen.' I beseech you move the King's grace to give me licence to go to church and say mass here within the Tower, and for to lie in some house upon the Green. I have now been in close prison three years and a quarter come Easter, and your Lordship knows that never man in this realm was so unjustly condemned as I am, 'for I was never, since I came hither, asked nor examined of any offence that should be laid unto my charge; also Master Barker, my fellow, was commanded hither with me, and both of us for one thing and deed, and he was examined and delivered and I was never spoken to, and yet condemned and lie here still in close prison.' What was put in my condemnation is untrue, as I have written to your Lordship largely once before this. I judge and suppose, in your Lordship, such pity and compassion that you would of your own accord have besought the King to give me the liberty I desire, even had I been guilty, after so long imprisonment. I doubt not but that you will do so now, knowing, as you do, that I am innocent and have so great wrong. Therefore, I do not rehearse the diseases I have, nor my increasing misery, need, and poverty. I commit to you this little petition of going, to church and lying out of close prison.[190]

It was during the six years Abel was confined in the Beauchamp Tower that, probably due to boredom, he inscribed his name 'Thomas' and the letter 'A' within a bell upon the walls of this prison cell. This inscription epitomises Abel's strength and resilience in his defiance of the King of England. It also symbolises Henry's persecution of those who did not recognise his divorce to Katherine, his marriage to Anne and him as head of the Church of England. Katherine, the queen he championed, Anne Boleyn, the queen he defied, and even Thomas Cromwell, the man who he appealed for compassion, were dead before Abel was executed for committing treason against the King's Majesty. There was no purpose in Henry ordering the execution of Abel, except to use his death as an example to deter anyone who challenged him as sovereign. Thomas Abel would die a martyr when he was burnt at the stake at Smithfield on 30 July 1540. Abel was beatified by Pope Leo XIII in 1886.

Medieval Bishop's Palace, Lincoln

Henry VIII and Katherine Howard Visit During a Royal Progress

The medieval Bishop's Palace stands adjacent to Lincoln Cathedral and was built as the official residence of Bishop of Lincoln in the twelfth century. Henry VIII spent three days in this palace during the royal progress in 1541. The king ventured on a royal progress each year, touring various parts of the country for political purposes in order to reaffirm himself as sovereign, to allow his subjects accessibility so that they could see him and to remind them and the local nobles who controlled the country. In each of the northern towns and cities involved in the rebellion, the townspeople gave the king money. The people of Lincoln gave Henry 40 pounds (approximately £17,000 in 2019). There were also pleasurable reasons for embarking on such tours, for he was entertained at each stop with banquets and was able to pursue his passion for sports, such as hawking and hunting.

This progress was unique in that it was the furthest north Henry had ever ventured within his kingdom. There were several reasons why the king undertook a royal progress to this particular region. First, with the prospect of war with France, Henry wanted to ensure that Scotland remained neutral. When Henry left England to fight in France in 1513, Scotland invaded England, and therefore Henry invited his nephew, King James V, to meet in York in September 1541 to strengthen the now-friendly relationship between the two countries. Secondly, the progress deliberately passed through counties where there had been rebellion in 1536, and gave the king the opportunity of personally thanking those individuals in Lincolnshire and Yorkshire who had remained loyal to the Crown and receive submissions, appeals for forgiveness and money from those who had revolted.

Henry was fearful of another rising as well as being received negatively during the progress. There had been a minor revolt led by Sir John Neville at Pontefract during the spring of 1541. Although it was swiftly supressed, it reminded Henry of the dissension in the north of his realm and there was a risk a visit could potentially have an adverse effect, inciting further revolts. Henry needed to bring with him men with arms to ensure any further further rebellions could be supressed. The king was apprehensive to the extent that he arranged an escort of approximately 4,000 to 5,000 horses because, according to the French Ambassador, Charles de Marillac, 'the King wishes to go with more magnificence (as he has not yet been there) as to secure against seditious designs. They will be gentlemen of these quarters of King [Kent] whom he trusts most. The fifty gentlemen of the house will have tent and war equipment.' As the king and his entourage entered each town there were 'sixty or eighty archers with drawn bows behind'. Henry also sent artillery to be positioned within 10 miles of York.

The 1541 pilgrimage lasted four months and set off from London on 30 June. The king was accompanied by Queen Katherine, his fifth wife, and his daughters, Princess Mary and Princess Elizabeth. They were expected to reach Lincoln by mid-July, but the queen became ill during the journey and unseasonably inclement wet weather had made the roads muddy and therefore

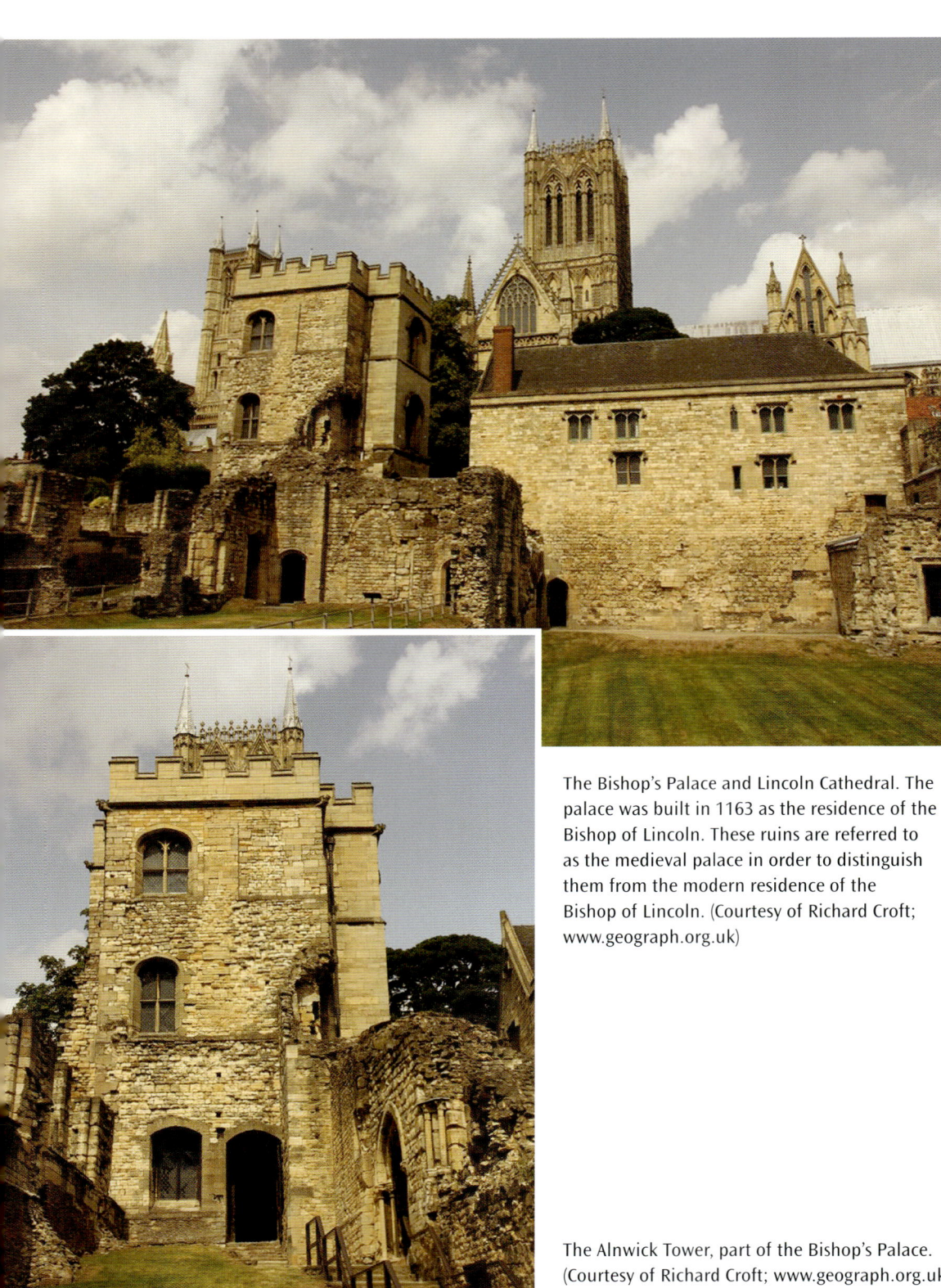

The Bishop's Palace and Lincoln Cathedral. The palace was built in 1163 as the residence of the Bishop of Lincoln. These ruins are referred to as the medieval palace in order to distinguish them from the modern residence of the Bishop of Lincoln. (Courtesy of Richard Croft; www.geograph.org.uk)

The Alnwick Tower, part of the Bishop's Palace. (Courtesy of Richard Croft; www.geograph.org.uk)

difficult to pass which delayed their arrival. They eventually entered Lincoln on 9 August and the entourage was welcomed by the sound of church bells. They passed through the western entrance to Lincoln Cathedral where the Bishop of Lincoln, John Longland, gave the crucifix to the king and queen for them to kiss and then they prayed while the choir sang *Te Deum*. At the end of the service they made their way to their lodgings at the medieval Bishop's Palace, which was adjacent to the cathedral, and the king retired to his bedchamber early that night. Although he had surrounded himself with men that he could trust and armed archers as a safeguard against any insurgency or betrayal, they could not prevent the personal betrayal of Queen Katherine when she engaged in an illicit relationship with Thomas Culpepper, a junior member of the Privy Council. Throughout the progress, the king and queen slept in separate chambers. Assisted by Lady Jane Rochford, sister-in-law of Anne Boleyn and George Boleyn's widow, the queen and Culpepper had been in an intimate relationship for several months, for Culpepper later confessed to 'many stolen interviews with the Queen at Greenwich, Lincoln, Pomfret, York, &c., since Maundy Thursday last, when she sent for him and gave him a velvet cap. Lady Rochford contrived these interviews. The Queen would "in every house seek for the back doors and back stairs herself".'

Culpepper admitted to an adulterous encounter in Lincoln which had happened when Henry and Katherine stayed at the Bishop's Palace. Lady Jane Rochford confirmed that plans for a liaison between the queen and Culpepper were thwarted when one of the king's guard locked the back door to the queen's chambers at the palace which meant that Culpepper had to pick the lock in order to gain access. In the interview notes relating to the questioning of Lady Rochford, her answers were recorded:

> One night at Lincoln she and the Queen were at the back door waiting for Culpepper, at 11 pm, when one of the watch came with a light and locked the door. Shortly after Culpepper came in, saying he and his man had picked the lock. Since her trouble the Queen has daily asked for Culpepper, saying that if that matter came not out she feared not. At Lincoln, when the Queen was with Culpepper, she was asleep until the Queen called her to answer Lovekyn [Mistress Lufkyn]. She thinks Culpepper has known the Queen carnally.[191]

The chronicler Edward Hall refers to the salacious incidents that took place in Lincoln:

> Since her marriage, she was vehemently suspected with Thomas Culpepper, which was brought to her chamber at Lincoln, in August last, in the progress time, by the lady of Rochford, and were there together alone, from eleven of the clock at night, till four of the clock in the morning, and to him she gave a chain and a rich cap.

The Bishop's Palace was set on fire and sacked during the English Civil War in the 1640s, but the ruins of the building which accommodated Henry VIII and Queen Katherine during the royal progress in 1541 still stand and are now administered by English Heritage.

83

Pontefract Castle, Yorkshire

Henry VIII Confronts the Rebels

Henry VIII arrived at Pontefract Castle on 24 August 1541 and stayed there for twelve days. Pontefract Castle was regarded as the key to the north and the French Ambassador, Marillac, described it as 'one of the finest castles in England'. Henry used the visit to put down the rebels who had threatened his position five years previously.

Pontefract Castle, spelled 'Pomfret' in the state papers, was captured by the rebels who supported the Pilgrimage of Grace in 1536. Five years later, during the royal progress, Marillac intimated that the king felt vulnerable and was concerned for his own safety as he made the journey from Doncaster to Pontefract:

> The day before yesterday this King sojourned near Doncaster where the river passes which, in the insurrection, separated the rebels' camp from that of Norfolk; and because he exceeded the programme of his journey which, till then, he had not infringed by a single half day, some said he feared to proceed and would turn back; but that proved false, for he has since come hither, where is one of the finest castles of England, and where he will sojourn ten or twelve days.[192]

Although Henry was fearful of the rebellious factions in Yorkshire, he wanted to directly confront the issue by asserting his presence, with the hope that it would discourage further revolts. Marillac accompanied the royal entourage on this progress and reported how the king welcomed those that loyally supported him and attempted to demean those that opposed him during the 1536 insurrection:

> The King has entered Yorkshire and been received in divers places by the gentlemen of the country, coming by bailiwicks and stewardships, to the number of 5,000 or 6,000 horse. Those who in the rebellion remained faithful were ranked apart, and graciously welcomed by the King and praised for their fidelity. The others who were of the conspiracy, among whom appeared the Archbishop of York, were a little further off on their knees; and one of them, speaking for all, made a long harangue confessing their treason in marching against their Sovereign and his Council, thanking him for pardoning so great an offence and begging that if any relics of indignation remained, he would dismiss them. They then delivered several bulky (*grosses*) submissions in writing. Receiving a benign answer, they arose and accompanied the King to his lodging; and after staying a day or two about the Court, were commanded to retire home.[193]

According to Edward Hall, 200 noblemen and 4,000 yeomen got on their knees and made a submission in the presence of the king and gave him 900 pounds (approximately £380,000 in 2019). Henry wanted to look into the eyes of the insurgents when they presented themselves in person to confess their part in the rebellion

ABOVE and BELOW: Two views of the ruined north wall of Pontefract Castle. (Author's Collection)

and declare their treachery. The Yorkshire rebels' declaration:

> We your humble subjects, the inhabitants of this your Grace's county of York, . . . confess that we wretches, for lack of grace and of sincere and pure knowledge of the verity of God's words . . . have most grievously, heinously and wantonly offended your . . . Majesty . . . in the unnatural, most odious and detestable offences of outrageous disobedience and traitorous rebellion.[194]

While Henry was dealing with matters of state, Lady Rochford continued to assist Queen Katherine with meeting her alleged lover, Thomas Culpepper, during their stay at Pontefract Castle. On one evening, Henry had sent his servant named Dane with a message and found the queen's bedchamber door locked: 'Margaret Morton confirmed in a letter to Sir Anthony Brown that: at Pomfret, every night, the Queen, being alone with lady Rochford, locked and bolted her chamber door on the inside, and Mr. Dane, sent to the Queen from the King, one night found it bolted'. This caused concern for the queen and Lady Rochford because they felt that the king's suspicions that something irregular was going on would be aroused. The notes relating to the interrogation of Thomas Culpepper reveal that:

> At Pomfret she feared the King had set watch at the back door, and Lady Rochford made her servant watch in the court to see if that were so. . . . Once she said that 'she doubted not that he knew that the King was supreme head of the Church, and therefore the Queen bade him beware that whensoever he went to confession he should never shrive him of any such things as should pass betwixt her and him; for,

if he did, surely, the King being supreme head of the Church, should have knowledge of it.' Replied, 'No, Madam, I warrant you.' Lady Rochford provoked him much to love the Queen and he intended to do ill with her.[195]

The king was preoccupied with trying to subdue further insurrection in Yorkshire and to persuade King James V to meet him in York. However, other members of the queen's

Another small section of the ruins of Pontefract Castle. (Author's Collection)

household were curious why she kept her chamber locked and only permitted Lady Rochford to enter the room. Margaret Morton and Mistress Lufkyn tried to find out what was happening in the queen's chambers during the night, but their curiosity was reprimanded by the queen. At the trial of Thomas Culpepper, his alleged crimes committed at Pontefract Castle were listed and Lady Rochford was cited as an accomplice:

> On the 29 August 1533, Henry VIII, at Pomfret, and at other times and places before and after, with Thomas Culpepper, late of London, one of the gentlemen of the King's privy chamber, falsely and traitorously held illicit meeting and conference to incite the said Culpepper to have carnal intercourse with her; and insinuated to him that she loved him above the King and all others. Similarly, the said Culpepper incited the Queen. And the better and more secretly to pursue their carnal life they retained Jane lady Rochford, late wife of Sir George Boleyn late Lord Rochford, as a go-between to contrive meetings in the Queen's stole chamber and other suspect places; and so the said Jane falsely and traitorously aided and abetted them.[196]

Queen Katherine not only had problems conducting and concealing her adulterous relationship with Culpepper, but on the day after their arrival at Pontefract Castle Francis Dereham, previously her lover, arrived and was seeking a position within the queen's household. Dereham was taking advantage of the young queen to further his own situation. Katherine may have felt compromised and compelled to give Dereham a position, in order to keep him quiet and ensure that the king did not hear about it. Katherine was aware of the fatal consequences if the king learnt that she had had carnal relations with another man. On 25 August the queen retained him in her service in a vague position which involved sending errands or writing letters in the absence of her secretary. At Dereham's trial it was alleged that:

> At Pomfret, and at other times and places, practised that the said Francis should be retained in the Queen's service; and the Queen, at Pomfret, 27 August, did so retain the said Francis, and had him in notable favour above others, and, in her secret chamber and other suspect places, spoke with him and committed secret affairs to him both by word and writing, and for the fulfilling of their wicked and traitorous purpose, gave him divers gifts and sums of money on the 27 August and at other times.[197]

84

King's Manor, York

Henry VIII Visits King's Manor During a Royal Progress

Henry VIII and his entourage were welcomed by the Archbishop of York on their arrival on 14 September 1541 in York, where they spent twelve days during the royal progress. Marillac alludes to the fact that reaction to the king was not joyous or celebratory, but maybe the people were curious because it was the first time the king had ventured that far north. Also, they may have been afraid of reprisals against the people of this county for taking part in the Pilgrimage of Grace uprising. Marillac reported: 'This King having made his entry into York . . . with like solemnity as at Lincoln and elsewhere'.

Henry and Katherine were lodged at the suppressed St Mary's Abbey in York, in the abbot's residence. The abbey had been established in about 1270 and surrendered to Henry VIII on 29 November 1539. In order to erase its history

King's Manor, York. The building was extensively renovated prior to the arrival of Henry VIII during his progress in 1541. It was used by King James I and King Charles I during the following century. The coat of arms of Charles I adorns the entrance. (Author's Collection)

The southern facade of King's Manor, York. (Author's Collection)

as a Benedictine abbey, the building was renamed King's Manor and during the following month it was used as the headquarters of the Council of the North. In 1541, approximately 1,500 craftsmen worked day and night to refurbish King's Manor in order to prepare for Henry's visit to York. King James V of Scotland was still expected to meet Henry so additional tents and pavilions were erected in the grounds of King's Manor. Henry was determined to impress his nephew and ordered that his richest tapestries, plates and cloths be sent from London to York. The finest food from all across the kingdom was ordered to be brought to York for this extravagant conference. The purpose of refurbishing King's Manor was kept secret. Marillac speculated that 'this seems to betoken some extraordinary triumph, like an interview of kings or a coronation of this Queen, which is spoken of to put the people of York in hope of having a Duke if she were to have a son'.

The Cardinal of Scotland and ministers dissuaded James V from meeting Henry. By 26 September, Henry realised that James V was not coming to York and two days later the royal progress began its long return journey to London.

The Chapel Royal, Hampton Court Palace

Archbishop Cranmer's Letter Detailing the Alleged Affairs of Katherine Howard

Renovations upon Wolsey's old chapel took place between 1535 and 1536 and one of the main transformations was the installation of an oak fan-vaulted ceiling, which was carved and painted gold and blue. Droplets descend from the ceiling with carved, gilt images of cherubs playing musical instruments. The royal motto Dieu et mon Droit *(God and my Right) appears thirty-two times within the design of the chapel and reinforces King Henry VIII's belief that the Tudor dynasty was endorsed by divine authority. Known as the Chapel Royal at Hampton Court, there*

Both sides of the western entrance to the Chapel Royal are adorned with the painted stone heraldic arms of Henry VIII and Jane Seymour held up by two angels. When Jane died in 1537, Henry ordered that the walls of the Chapel Royal be draped with black cloth for the period of mourning. (Author's Collection)

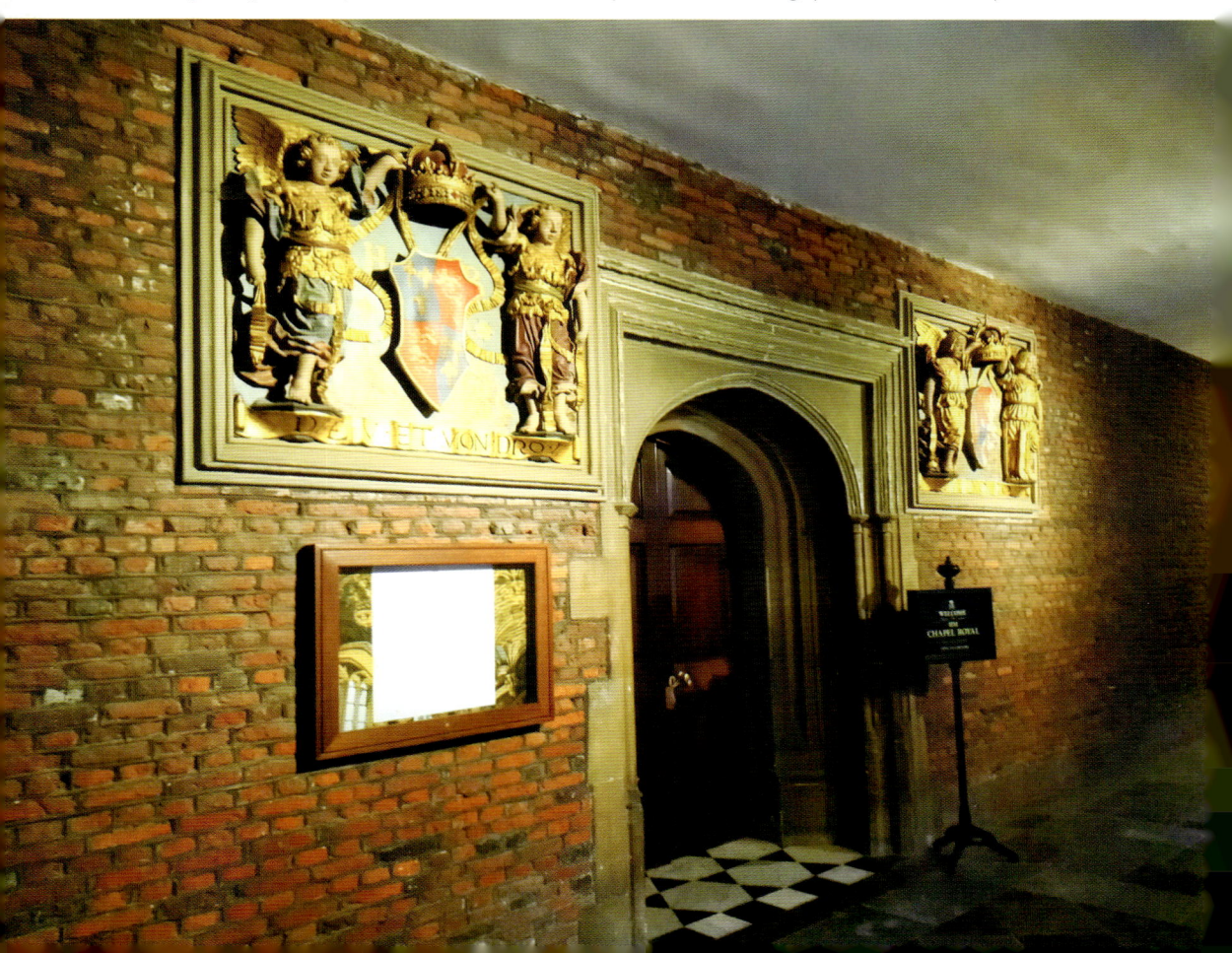

THE CHAPEL ROYAL, HAMPTON COURT PALACE

Detail of the painted stone arms of Jane Seymour. (Author's Collection)

A painting showing the Chapel Royal at Hampton Court Palace. Cardinal Wolsey began construction of the Chapel Royal during the late 1520s on the site of a chapel that had been patronised by the Knights Hospitaller from 1136. After Wolsey's fall, Henry VIII ordered renovations at the chapel. The far end of the chapel contained a stained-glass window featuring the images of Henry VIII, Queen Katherine of Aragon and Cardinal Wolsey. This window was later bricked up.

is a Chapel Royal at St James's Palace and the Tower of London. The Chapel Royal was not only a building, but represents a department within the monarch's household known as the Chapel Royal, which was an ecclesiastical ensemble of priests, singers and musicians that accompanied the sovereign and served their spiritual needs. Prince Edward, only legitimate son of Henry VIII, was baptised by Archbishop Thomas Cranmer in the Chapel Royal at Hampton Court Palace on 15 October 1537. Four years later, Cranmer would leave a letter in the Chapel Royal for Henry VIII that would have disastrous consequences for his fifth marriage.

The royal progress concluded on 29 October 1541 when Henry VIII and the court arrived at Hampton Court Palace. As preparations were made to celebrate All Saints Day on 1 November and All Souls Day on 2 November, rumours about the queen's behaviour over the summer were beginning to circulate among the court. Henry was oblivious to the alleged indiscretions of his wife, Katherine Howard, during the royal progress. It was not until 1 November 1541, All Saints Day, while in the pew in the Holyday Closet, which overlooked the Chapel Royal at Hampton Court Palace, at Mass that Henry read certain allegations alluding to his wife's infidelity in a sealed letter left on his chair by Archbishop Cranmer. The archbishop had received reports from the courtier John Lascelles, whose sister Mary Hall, née Lascelles, who attended upon the Norfolk family home in London, claimed that Katherine was a woman of loose morals who lived a promiscuous life. Lascelles confirmed that 'Frans. Derham [*sic* Dereham] had lain in bed with her in his doublet and hose between the sheets a hundred nights' and that Mannock 'knew a privy mark on her body'.

Cranmer was disturbed and perplexed after he had listened to Lascelles' allegations against Queen Katherine. He sought advice from Thomas Audley, the Lord Chancellor, and the Earl of Hertford and 'by their advice reported to the King in writing, as he had not the heart to tell it by word of mouth'.

Henry refused to believe the damning allegations set out in the letter and initially confided in William Fitzwilliam, Lord Privy Seal, the Lord Admiral Sir Anthony Brown and Sir Thomas Wriothesley that he believed the document to be forged. The king ordered an investigation in order to exonerate the queen. He dispatched the Lord Privy Seal to London to interview Lascelles to ascertain whether there was any truth in these serious allegations. He also sent the Duke of Suffolk to interview Lascelles' sister, Mary, to speak to her about Queen Katherine's conduct. Wriothesley was ordered to interrogate Mannock and Dereham. Henry left Hampton Court Palace for London on 5 November in order to reflect on what he was to do with his Privy Council. Rumours were rife in Hampton Court, Chapuys reported:

> Wrote last Lent that this King, feigning indisposition, was ten or twelve days without seeing his Queen, or allowing her to come in his room, during which time there was much talk of a divorce; but owing to some surmise that she was with child, or else because the means for a divorce were not arranged, the affair slept till the 5th inst., when the King went into the Council room and remained there till noon. Suddenly, after dinner, he entered his small barge and came here from Hampton Court, where the rest of the Privy Council remained sitting, to assist whom the Chancellor and Norfolk were sent for in haste the night before at midnight. After the King had left, the archbishop of Canterbury entered the Queen's chamber two or three times,—to interrogate and admonish her, as is supposed, on the part of the Council, but he did not make much out'.[198]

Ruins of Winchester Palace, Southwark, London

The Fate of Queen Katherine Deliberated at Winchester Palace

The visible remains of Winchester Palace were once part of the Great Hall which was situated along the southern bank of the River Thames. Within the gable wall there is a door, which led to the pantry, buttery and kitchen, and the impressive rose window. Beneath these ruins there was a vaulted wine cellar. The palace was transformed into warehouses and it was not until the redevelopment of the area in the 1980s that these ruins were discovered. It was here in 1541 that Henry and the Privy Council considered the evidence against Katherine Howard.

Henry VIII spent 5 November 1541 in London and travelled to Hampton Court Palace the next day. On 7 November he returned to London and decided upon his course of action while waiting for news of the investigation. Chapuys reported that Henry consulted with the Privy Council at the Bishop of Winchester's home in Southwark:

> On the evening of the 6th, the privy councillors returned [to Hampton Court], and stayed nearly all night deliberating in the King's apartments, and again the day after, night and day, at the house of the bishop of Winchester, where it was resolved to make most of those who were at Hampton Court with the Queen leave the palace, seals being put on all the coffers and chests, and the doors being guarded.[199]

Queen Katherine and Lady Rochford were placed under house arrest at Hampton Court Palace while the investigation took place. Henry would never set eyes upon his fifth wife ever again.

Dereham and Mannock confessed to their relationships with the queen and corroborated the allegations made by Mary Hall. The queen's maids were also interrogated and irrefutable evidence was found that confirmed that the queen had had carnal relationships with Dereham and Culpepper before and during her marriage to the king. It was reported that: 'Wriothesley found from Mannock's confession that he used to feel the [secret parts] of her body before Derrham [was familiar] with her; and Derrham confessed that he had known her carnally many times, both in his doublet and hose between the sheets and in naked bed, alleging three women as witnesses'.

Henry was distraught, heartbroken and reduced to tears when this evidence was put before him, probably at another Privy Council meeting held within Winchester Palace. 'On learning this the King's heart was pierced with pensiveness, so that it was long before he could utter his sorrow; "and finally, with plenty of tears (which was strange in his courage), opened the same".'

Queen Katherine was interviewed by Thomas Cranmer, Archbishop of Canterbury, and her uncle, Thomas Howard, Duke of Norfolk, about the matter. Initially she protested her innocence, however, when it became apparent to her that the charges against her would certainly be proven, she confessed that she had had a relationship with Francis Dereham before marrying the king. She also admitted that Culpepper had been brought to her bedchamber in Lincoln, but stated that she had not violated her marriage vows to the king.

Marillac reported:

> That this King has changed his love for the Queen into hatred, and taken such grief at being deceived that of late it was thought he had gone mad, for he called for a sword to slay her he had loved so much. Sitting in Council he suddenly called for horses without saying where he would go. Sometimes he said irrelevantly (*hors de propoz*) that that wicked woman had never such delight in her incontinency as she should have torture in her death. And finally, he took to tears regretting his ill luck in meeting with such ill-conditioned wives, and blaming his Council for this last mischief.[200]

Henry VIII was once smitten with Katherine and felt more pain than he did at the loss of his previous four wives. Chapuys wrote: 'This King has wonderfully felt the case of the Queen, his wife, and has certainly shown greater sorrow at her loss than at the faults, loss, or divorce of his preceding wives.'.

On 13 November 1541, Sir Thomas Wriothesley, Secretary to the King, went to Hampton Court Palace, assembled all Queen Katherine's household in the Great Watching Chamber and 'declared certain offences that that she had done in misusing her body with certain persons before the King's time'. He pronounced that she was no longer to be addressed as

These ruins are all that remain of Winchester Palace in Southwark, London. (Author's Collection)

queen. Wriothesley then dismissed the Queen's Household. Katherine was taken to Syon Abbey where she spent three months awaiting her fate. Lady Rochford, Dereham and Culpepper were taken to the Tower of London.

87

Guildhall, City of London

The Alleged Lovers of Queen Katherine Tried for Treason Against King Henry VIII

Construction of Guildhall, in the City of London, began in 1411 and was completed in 1440 when it became the second largest building in London, after St Paul's Cathedral. It is the only non-ecclesiastical stone building to have survived since the fifteenth century, which is remarkable considering the destruction following both the Great Fire of London in 1666 and the bombs of the German Luftwaffe during the Blitz in 1940. Thomas Culpepper and Francis Dereham were tried for treason in the Guildhall on 1 December 1541. Lady Jane Rochford was also due to be tried at the same time, but the stress of interrogation and incarceration had affected her mental state and she was excused from the trial. Henry Mannock was questioned, but no further action was taken against him.

Michael Dormer, Lord Mayor of London, Lord Chancellor Audeley, the Duke of Suffolk and Katherine's uncle, the Duke of Norfolk, were on the bench that sat to judge Culpepper and Dereham. Although Katherine was not present, one would think as the charges were read out to the court that she was being tried in her absence.

That Katherine, queen of England, formerly called Kath. Howard, late of Lambeth, Surrey., one of the daughters of Lord Edmund Howard, before the marriage between the King and her, led an abominable, base, carnal, voluptuous, and vicious life, like a common harlot, with divers persons, as with Francis Dereham of Lambeth and Hen. Manak [*sic* Mannock] of Streatham, Surrey, 20 and 24 May 1532, Henry VIII, and at other times, maintaining however the outward appearance of chastity and honesty. That she led the King by word and gesture to love her and (he believing her to be pure and chaste and free from other matrimonial yoke) arrogantly coupled herself with him in marriage. And the said Queen and Francis, being charged by divers of the King's Council with their vicious life, could not deny it, but excused themselves by alleging that they were contracted to each other before the marriage with the King; which contract at the time of the marriage they falsely and traitorously concealed from the King, to the peril of the King and of his children to be begotten by her and the damage of the whole realm. And after the marriage, the said Queen and Francis, intending to renew their vicious life, 25 August, Henry VIII., at Pomfret [*sic* Pontefract], and at other times and places, practised that the said Francis should be retained in the Queen's service; and the Queen, at Pomfret, 27 August Henry VIII., did so retain the said Francis, and had him in notable favour above others, and, in her secret chamber and other suspect places, spoke with him and committed secret affairs to him both by word and writing, and for the fulfilling of their wicked and traitorous purpose, gave him divers gifts and sums of money on the 27 August and at other times.

Also, the said Queen, not satisfied with her vicious life aforesaid, on the 29 August, Henry VIII., at Pomfret, and at other times

The Guildhall, City of London, was used as a place to try traitors and dissenters throughout the reign of Henry VIII. (Author's Collection)

and places before and after, with Thomas Culpepper, late of London, one of the gentlemen of the King's privy chamber, falsely and traitorously held illicit meeting and conference to incite the said Culpepper to have carnal intercourse with her; and insinuated to him that she loved him above the King and all others. Similarly, the said Culpepper incited the Queen. And the better and more secretly to pursue their carnal life they retained Jane lady Rochford, late wife of Sir George Boleyn late Lord Rochford, as a go-between to contrive meetings in the Queen's stole chamber and other suspect places; and so the said Jane falsely and traitorously aided and abetted them.[201]

Eustace Chapuys sent a clerk to observe the proceedings of the trial of Thomas Culpepper and Francis Dereham, and was able to provide the following details in his report to Charles V:

All the privy councillors witnessed the trial, which, after a long discussion lasting six hours, ended in the condemnation of the two abovementioned gentlemen, who were sentenced to be hung and quartered as traitors. Dereham did confess having known the Queen familiarly before she was either betrothed or promised to the King; but said he did not know that there was any wrong in that, inasmuch as they were then engaged to each other. Culpepper persisted in denying the guilt of which he was accused, maintaining that he never solicited or had anything to do with her; on the contrary, it was she who had importuned him through Madame de Rochefort, requesting him (Culpepper) to go and meet her in a retired place in Lincolnshire, to which she appointed him, and that on that occasion he (Culpepper) having kept the appointment, she herself told him, as she had on the first instance sent him word through Madame Rochefort, that she pined for him, and was actually dying of love for his person. It is thought that both will be beheaded to-day. Dame de Rochefort would have been sentenced at the same time had she not, on the third day after her imprisonment, been seized with a fit of madness by which her brain is affected.[202]

Culpepper and Dereham were found guilty and their punishment involved being returned to the Tower of London, from where they would be drawn through the streets of London to the gallows at Tyburn where they were to be hanged, cut down alive, disembowelled, and while still living their bowels burnt, heads decapitated and their bodies quartered. Culpepper appealed to the king for mercy and Henry commuted his sentence from the traitor's death of being

Inside Guildhall, where Culpepper and Dereham were tried. (Courtesy of David Diliff)

hung, drawn and quartered to beheading, but Dereham was executed as a traitor. Their heads were then set upon London Bridge, where they remained until 1546. Thomas Culpepper's decapitated corpse was buried at St Sepulchre-without-Newgate Church near Holborn Viaduct.

Queen Katherine was incarcerated in Syon Abbey for three months before she learned her fate. An Act of Attainder was introduced in Parliament on 21 January 1542 and passed on 11 February, which meant that it was treasonous for a woman to marry the king if she had led an unchaste life before the marriage. The king offered her the opportunity to defend herself in Parliament, but she declined, succumbing entirely to the king's mercy. Katherine was destined for execution.

Model of the Medieval London Bridge, St Magnus the Martyr Church, London

Katherine Howard's Final Journey
Katherine Howard saw the heads of Culpepper and Dereham as she passed under London Bridge on her journey by barge to the Tower of London on 10 February 1532. The old medieval bridge that spanned the River Thames during the Tudor period was built between 1176 and 1209. It was positioned 30yd east of the current bridge. The Church of St Magnus the Martyr was located at the northern end of the old bridge; a model of the bridge is on display there.

London Bridge was supported by twenty piers which were reinforced by nineteen arches. Wooden piles made of elm were driven into the riverbed in an elliptical shape, and masonry was constructed above them. Houses and shops were built upon the bridge. A chapel dedicated to St Thomas Becket was built in the middle of the bridge. On the approach from Southwark, pedestrians would cross two arches, before reaching a stone gate, which was fortified. After crossing a further four arches, pedestrians would arrive at another strongly fortified tower, where there was a drawbridge that could be raised for tall ships. It was upon the battlements of this fortification that the heads of traitors were stuck on pikes and displayed as a warning to Londoners and visitors of the consequences of treachery. In 1536, the heads of Bishop John Fisher and Sir Thomas More were without dignity positioned on pikes and, in 1540, the head of Thomas Cromwell received the same humiliating treatment. Their heads would be boiled and tarred to ensure that birds did not peck at them.

When Parliament passed the Act of Attainder Act on 11 February 1542, Katherine's fate was sealed. Two days later, Marillac reported that:

> Parliament has condemned this Queen and the lady of Rochefort to death. Her execution was expected this week, for last night she was brought from Syon to the Tower, but as she weeps, cries, and torments herself miserably, without ceasing, it is deferred for three or four days, to give her leisure to recover, and 'penser au faict de sa conscience'.[203]

As Queen Katherine was being transported from Syon Abbey to the Tower of London by barge during the afternoon of 10 February 1532 she saw the heads of her alleged former lovers, Thomas Culpepper and Francis Dereham, stuck on pikes. It must have been a disturbing sight for the young queen and an ominous warning of her impending fate. Chapuys' report indicates that she might have had to be physically manhandled into the barge:

> She was, with some resistance, conveyed by river to the Tower. The lord Privy Seal, with a number of Privy Councillors and servants went first in a great barge; then came the Queen with three or four men and as many ladies, in a small covered barge; then the

MODEL OF THE MEDIEVAL LONDON BRIDGE

A part of the model of the Old London Bridge which was created by David T. Aggett, a Liveryman of The Worshipful Company of Plumbers, in 1987. Though depicting the bridge as it would have appeared around 1400, it had not changed much by the reign of Henry VIII. The heads of traitors who had been executed were placed upon pikes on the battlements of the gatehouse to London Bridge, which also included a drawbridge, that can be seen here on the left. (Author's Collection)

A depiction of the Old London Bridge from an oil painting entitled *View of London Bridge* by Claude de Jongh, 1632. Henry VIII passed over London Bridge on 21 June 1509, on his journey from Richmond Palace to the Tower of London where he was to reside until his father's funeral. (Google Art Project)

Duke of Suffolk, in a great barge, with a company of his men. On their arrival at the Tower, the lords landed first; then the Queen, in black velvet, and they paid her as much honour as when she was reigning.[204]

Having passed under London Bridge, Katherine would have seen the Tower of London and shortly afterwards disembarked at Queen's Stairs, following in the footsteps of her cousin, Anne Boleyn.

A Blue Plaque at St Magnus the Martyr Church. The medieval London Bridge stood about thirty yards east of where the current bridge is positioned. The churchyard of St Magnus the Martyr formed part of the roadway approach to the bridge from the north. The model of the bridge can be viewed inside this church. (Author's Collection)

Masonry from the medieval Old London Bridge on display outside St Magnus the Martyr Church. (Author's Collection)

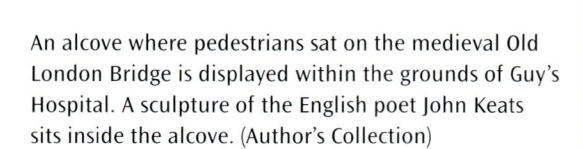

An alcove where pedestrians sat on the medieval Old London Bridge is displayed within the grounds of Guy's Hospital. A sculpture of the English poet John Keats sits inside the alcove. (Author's Collection)

89

Block and Axe Postcard

The Executions of Margaret Pole, Countess of Salisbury, and Queen Katherine Howard

Henry VIII is reputed to have sent more men and women to their deaths than any other British monarch. Prisoners of noble birth who were condemned as traitors were executed using an axe. This block and axe, seen here in this pre-war postcard, symbolises his tyrannical reign and although the block was used for the last public beheading on 9 April 1747, to execute Simon Fraser, Lord Lovat, it is typical of those used for executions during the Tudor period.

This axe is believed to have originated in the sixteenth century and may have been used during high-profile executions. The axe weighs 3.2kg (7lb) and as it was wielded to strike a victim's neck, the force of the swing would be absorbed by the block, which weighed 56.7kg (125lb). Beheading was believed to be a swift and humane punishment, which was reserved for the nobility and distinguished persons of stature. It was considered to be honourable and merciful. Sir Thomas More, Bishop John Fisher and Thomas Cromwell were publicly executed by axe on Tower Hill.

The execution would take place on a wooden scaffold that would be covered with straw, in order to soak up the blood. The top of the block was carved at a curve on both sides, to accommodate the victims head and chest and to ensure that as the head was placed comfortably on the block with the neck exposed. A minister was present on the scaffold

The pre-war postcard of the block and axe on display at the Tower of London. (Author's Collection)

to provide spiritual comfort to the condemned prisoner, if required. The prisoner was expected to pay the executioner and offer forgiveness for what he was about to conduct. The prisoner was allowed to address those who observed the execution, before placing their neck upon the block. A skilled executioner with a sharpened axe would conduct the beheading swiftly within seconds. If the executioner was not experienced, had a blunt axe or the prisoner moved, then it would take several strikes and minutes to detach the head from the body, as was the case with the execution of Thomas Cromwell.

Once the head had been decapitated, the executioner raised the severed head to the crowd, shouting 'behold the head of a traitor!'. The purpose was not to show the spectators the head, but to allow the head to see the crowd and its own decapitated body. Despite the head being severed, the brain still functions for a further eight seconds until the oxygen supply is exhausted and the head loses consciousness and dies. On some occasions, the features on the decapitated head moved.

The execution of Margaret Pole, 8th Countess of Salisbury, was a completely botched affair. She was the last member of the Plantagenet line and had been imprisoned for two years for alleged treason, which she denied. Henry probably wanted her dead for political purposes so after being imprisoned for two years in the Tower of London, she was executed on 28 May 1541. Despite being frail and ill, Margaret Pole, who was aged 67, resisted execution to the last moment. Chapuys reported:

> [The] lamentable execution of Madame de Salisbury, the daughter of the duke of Clarence, and mother of Cardinal Pole, took place at the Tower in the presence of the Lord Mayor of London and about 150 persons more. ... She was told to make haste and place her neck on the block, which she did. But as the ordinary executor of justice was absent doing his work in the North, a wretched and blundering youth (*garçonneau*) was chosen, who literally hacked her head and shoulders to pieces in the most pitiful manner. May God in His high grace pardon her soul, for certainly she was a most virtuous and honourable lady, and there was no need or haste to bring so ignominious a death upon her, considering that as she was then nearly seventy years old, she could not in the ordinary course of nature live long.[205]

Within a year of Margaret Pole's death there were other high-profile executions using the block and axe within the walls of the Tower of London. On 13 February 1542, Queen Katherine and Lady Jane Rochford were executed. Chapuys reported:

> On Sunday the 12th, towards evening, she was told to prepare for death, for she was to die next day. That evening she asked to have the block brought in to her, that she might know how to place herself; which was done, and she made trial of it. Next morning, about seven, those of the Council except Suffolk, who was ill, and Norfolk, were at the Tower, accompanied by various lords and gentlemen, such as Surrey (Norfolk's son and the Queen's cousin), and she was beheaded in the same spot where Anne Boleyn had been executed. Her body was then covered with a black cloak and her ladies took it away. Then Lady Rochford was brought, who had shown symptoms of madness till they told her she must die. Neither she nor the Queen spoke much on the scaffold; they only confessed their guilt and prayed for the King's welfare.[206]

Both Queen Katherine and Lady Rochford were buried in the Church of St Peter ad Vincula immediately after their execution.

Queen Elizabeth's Hunting Lodge

The 'Great Standing'

Although refurbished during the reign of his daughter and named Queen Elizabeth's Hunting Lodge, it was Henry VIII who ordered its building at Chingford in 1543. It was called the 'Great Standing' and used as a viewing platform.

From this lodge royal guests would observe and take part in the hunting of fallow deer in Epping Forest. There was a kitchen on the ground floor, which provided food, including roast meats and poultry, that would be served to guests in the upper floor viewing galleries as they watched the

ABOVE and RIGHT: Queen Elizabeth's Hunting Lodge is in Chingford in Epping Forest and was commissioned by Henry VIII in 1543. (Author's Collection)

View from Queen Elizabeth's Hunting Lodge looking towards Epping Forest. (Author's Collection)

hunt. It is believed that there was no glass in the window openings and that wooden shutters in hinges hung over these windows.

Henry had been a keen huntsman throughout his life. Secretary to the King, Richard Pace wrote to Wolsey on 12 August 1520 discussing the king's daily hunting rituals: 'The King rises daily, except on holy days, at 4 or 5 o'clock, and hunts till 9 or 10 at night. He spares no pains to convert the sport of hunting into a martyrdom'.

Henry was aged 52 when this lodge was built. If he visited this place during his final years, he was obese, infirm and suffering from an ulcerated leg, which would have prevented him from mounting a horse and participating in the hunts. He perhaps took part by shooting crossbows from the open windows on the first-floor level.

91

Katherine Parr's Closet Chamber, Hampton Court Palace

Henry VIII's Wedding to Katherine Parr

Katherine Parr came to the attention of Henry VIII during March 1543. She was already in a relationship with Sir Thomas Seymour, but that did not stop the king from pursuing her. Henry dispatched Seymour as English Ambassador to Mary of Hungary, Regent of the Netherlands in March 1543, clearing the path for him to marry Katherine Parr. He also appointed her brother, Lord William Parr, to the Privy Council. Henry VIII was aged 52 and looking for companionship and stability from his next marriage. Parr, aged 31, was over twenty years younger than the king and was twice widowed. She became a faithful companion of the king and remained by his side for the last five years of his life.

Katherine Parr became Henry's sixth wife on 12 July 1543 when they married in the queen's Privy Closet Chamber at Hampton Court. The ceremony was presided over by Bishop Stephen Gardiner and attended by eighteen people including the king's two daughters, Princess Mary and Princess Elizabeth. The notarial attestation produced by Richard Watkins, witnessing the wedding, stated:

> On 12 July 1543, 35 Hen. VIII., in an upper oratory called 'the Quynes Pryevey closet' within the honour of Hampton Court, Westminster. dioceses., in presence of the noble and gentle persons named at the foot of this instrument and of me, Richard Watkins, the King's prothonotary, the King and lady Katherine Latymer *alias* Parr being met there for the purpose of solemnising matrimony between them, Stephen, Bishop of Winchester proclaimed in English (speech given in Latin) that they were met to join in marriage the said King and Lady Katherine, and if anyone knew any impediment thereto he should declare it. The licence for the marriage without publication of banns, sealed by Thomas Archbishop of Canterbury and dated 10 July 1543, being then brought in, and none opposing but all applauding the marriage, the said bp. of Winchester put the questions (recited) to which the King, *hilari vultu*, replied 'Yea' and the lady Katherine also replied that it was her wish; and then the King taking her right hand, repeated after the Bishop the words, 'I, Henry, take thee, Katherine, to my wedded wife, to have and to hold from this day forward, for better for worse, for richer for poorer, in sickness and in health, till death us depart, and thereto I plight thee my troth.' Then, releasing and again clasping hands, the lady Katherine likewise said 'I, Katherine, take thee Henry to my wedded husband, to have and to hold from this day forward, for better for worse, for richer for poorer, in sickness and in health, to be bonayr and buxome in bed and at board, till death us depart, and thereto I plight unto thee my troth.' The putting on of the wedding ring and proffer of gold and silver (described) followed; and the Bishop, after prayer, pronounced a benediction. The King then commanded the prothonotary to make a public instrument of the premises.[207]

Henry VIII and Katherine Parr were married in the queen's Privy Closet Chamber at Hampton Court Palace on 12 July 1543. (Author's Collection)

The attractive and charming Katherine Parr was declared queen on the day of the wedding at Hampton Court Palace. There was no procession into London and there were no plans for a coronation because the Treasury was unable to bear the cost of the pageantry. 'To be useful in all I do' was the motto that she adopted and she fulfilled the role of being the devoted, submissive wife that Henry wanted. Katherine was able to nurse the ailing king and she was instrumental in inviting all the royal children to court whenever possible, in an effort to reunite the family and improve the the king's relationship with his children. Katherine was a loving stepmother to Prince Edward, Princess Mary and Princess Elizabeth, and she also encouraged Henry to restore his daughters to the line of succession. An Act of Parliament in 1543 returned the two princesses to the line of succession after Prince Edward.

On 7 July 1544, Henry appointed Katherine Parr as Regent of England during his absence while he was in France during the siege of Boulogne. However, Katherine was an independent thinker and, on 29 May 1545, Katherine's book *Prayers or Meditations* was issued, making her the first Queen of England to have a book published. She revelled in debating theological matters and was an advocate of religious reform which was in conflict with the king's ideology. When discussing religion with the king in 1546, Bishop Stephen Gardiner, who represented conservative religious factions within the country, encouraged Henry to charge her with heresy, but she escaped punishment by submitting before the king, appealing for forgiveness and promising to follow his guidance on all matters. Katherine Parr outlived Henry VIII and married a fourth time to her previous lover, Sir Thomas Seymour, but died prematurely aged 36 on 5 September 1548.

Debased Groats

Henry VIII's Currency Debasement Policy

The dissolution of monasteries impacted upon the workers at the Mint within the walls of the Tower of London because they received an influx of silver that needed to be transformed into coins. The French Ambassador, Marillac, reported on 20 June 1542 to King Francis I that 'nothing is done in the Tower, but dress bows, iron arrows and pikes, mount artillery, prepare waggons and coin money, day and night of the silver plate obtained from the spoil of the Abbeys'.

The coins produced from the profits of the dissolution of the monasteries was not sufficient to sustain the coffers of the Treasury. By 1544, the prospect of war with France and Scotland and the need to maintain an extravagant lifestyle meant that Henry VIII needed to find ways to increase revenue to fund this expenditure. Stripping the wealth and assets and, in particular, silver from religious institutions during the dissolution of the monasteries had helped to raise income for the Treasury. Items could be sold and silver could be used to produce coins, however it was

Henry VIII debased groat dated 1544–7. (Courtesy of the Royal Mint)

Henry VIII debased groat dated 1544–7. (Courtesy of the Royal Mint)

not enough. Henry needed to find other ways to raise income and found a solution by introducing the currency debasement policy in 1544. The principal aim of this was to raise revenue for the Crown, by implementing savings in the cost of currency production by using less bullion to mint new coins. It meant that the amount of gold and silver was reduced in the production of coins, and these metals were substituted with cheaper base metals such as copper. Henry became known as 'Old Coppernose' because as the coins wore down copper appeared through the king's image.

There was a surge in demand for more coins and the increased workload exhausted the workers in the Mint at the Tower of London. It was recorded by Holinshed in his chronicles that William Foxley, a pot maker, fell asleep on 27 April 1546 and remained asleep for the following fourteen days and fifteen nights.

Although the cost of materials had been reduced by using inferior metals, the value of the currency was maintained at pre-debasement level. The policy of debasement was implemented several times during the last years of the reign of Henry VIII which meant the mint had to be expanded within the Tower of London, with the Upper Mint established close to the Salt Tower. After Henry's death the debased silver coins had to be withdrawn from circulation.

An English Cannonball Fired During the Siege of Boulogne, 1544

Capturing Boulogne

The French had been providing Scotland with assistance and this spurred Henry VIII to capture Boulogne in retaliation. Henry VIII arrived in Calais with an army of 40,000 English soldiers on 15 July 1544 and from there proceeded to Boulogne to begin a siege that lasted two months. In Sandgate Road, Folkestone, there is an English cannonball that was fired during the siege of Boulogne.

Henry VIII encamped half a mile north of Boulogne. Edward Hall wrote that Boulogne:

> Was assaulted and so besieged with an abundance of great ordnance that never was there a more valiant assault made, for beside the undermining of the castle, tower and walls, the town was so beaten with ordnance that there was not left one house whole therein: and so sore was laid to the charge of the Frenchman that after the King had assaulted them by the space of a month, they sent forth of the town to the King two of their chief captains, called Monsieur Semblemound and Monsieur de Haies, which declared that the chief captain of the town, with his retinue was contented to deliver the town unto his grace, so that they might pass with bag and baggage, which request the King's majesty mercifully granted them.[208]

On 13 September 1544, Boulogne capitulated when Charles Brandon, Duke of Suffolk, rode into the town and received the keys. During the following day 4,454 soldiers and civilians vacated the town passing the English victors. The last to leave was Vervin, the Governor of Boulogne. Edward Hall wrote that Vervin, 'when he approached near the place where the King stood, he alighted from his horse, and came to the King. And after he had talked with him a space, the King took him by the hand and he reverently kneeling upon his knee, kissed his hand and afterwards mounted upon his horse and so departed.'

Vervin was regarded as a coward by his countrymen for surrendering the town and was later beheaded as a consequence. Henry VIII entered Boulogne triumphantly, like a valiant conqueror, on 18 September 1544 when English trumpeters, standing on the town ramparts, welcomed him with a fanfare. The Duke of Suffolk presented him with the keys of Boulogne. After riding through the town Henry VIII ordered the demolition of Our Lady Church of Boulogne. He remained in Boulogne for the following two weeks during which time he established a garrison before leaving for England. Henry arrived in Dover at midnight on 30 September.

English engineers fortified Boulogne and, in June 1546, Henry VIII signed the Treaty of Ardres where he agreed to eventually return the town to the French for 2,000,000 crowns. The French built a fortification at Marquise, which was able to blockade the port from the north. Boulogne was still under English control when Henry VIII died, but it was returned to France in 1550.

An English cannonball which was used during the siege of Boulogne in 1544. (Author's Collection)

An explanatory plaque with the cannonball. (Author's Collection)

The plaque on the English cannonball in Folkestone reads, 'THIS CANONBALL FIRED BY THE ENGLISH DURING THE SIEGE OF BOULOGNE IN 1544 HAS BEEN RETURNED TO US BY THE PEOPLE OF BOULOGNE AS A GESTURE OF FRIENDSHIP NOW EXISTING BETWEEN US, 1976'.

94

Queen Elizabeth's Pocket Gun, Dover Castle

A Gift to Henry

Despite its name, Queen Elizabeth's Pocket Gun displayed at Dover Castle was not intended for a queen. Its name was probably originated during the English Civil War when similar guns were named 'Queen's Pocket Gun'. This gun was constructed by Jan Tolhuys in Utrecht in the Netherlands during 1544 and was presented to Henry VIII by his friend, Maximilian of Egmon, Count of Buren and Leerdam and Stadholder. The coats of arms of Henry and Maximilian adorn the top and rear of the gun.

Henry VIII purchased guns and armaments from abroad, commissioned Continental gunmakers and created an armaments industry within England in which cast iron was used, which was a much stronger material than bronze and was used to make this pocket gun. Guns similar to this one were used during the siege of Thérouanne in 1513 and at Boulogne in 1544. It is believed that this gun stood on the black bulwark on the pier at Dover harbour. It was used during the English Civil War, 1642–6 and was captured by the Royalist Army at Lostwithiel, Cornwall. The gun was eventually returned to Dover Castle where in 1827 a cast-iron frame was built to support it. The letters ER (Elizabeth Regina) were inscribed upon it, further supporting the myth that this gun was built for Henry VIII's daughter, Elizabeth I.

On the rear of the barrel are inscribed the words 'Jan Tolhuys of Utrecht 1544'. Elaborate designs featuring flowers, vases and eagles are engraved on the gun alongside the figures of the goddesses Victory and Liberty, together with Scalda, the god of the River Scheldt. The following poem is also inscribed on the gun:

> As breaker of ramparts and walls
> Am I known,
> Over mountain and valley fly balls
> By me thrown.

This is a medium calibre gun, measuring 4.75in in diameter. Its long barrel, measuring 7.3m, stabilised the gun and enhanced its accuracy

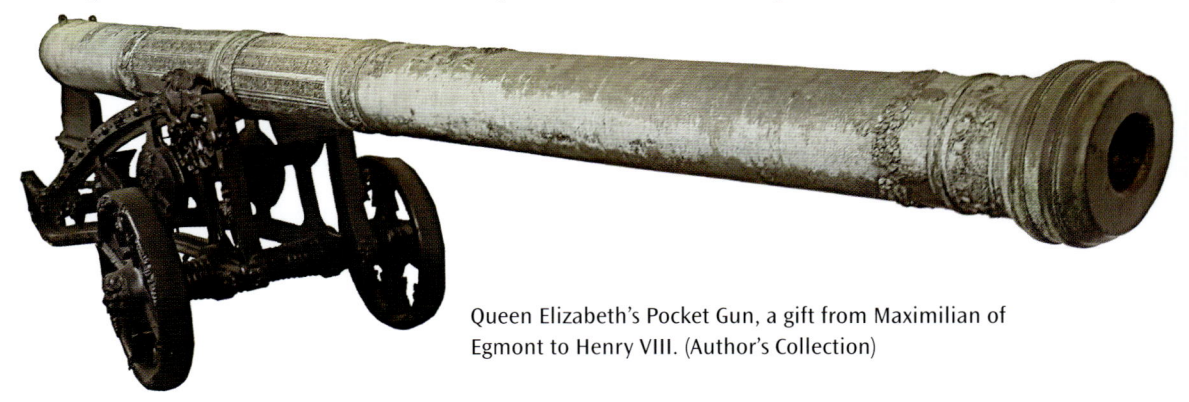

Queen Elizabeth's Pocket Gun, a gift from Maximilian of Egmont to Henry VIII. (Author's Collection)

The rear of Queen Elizabeth's Pocket Gun. (Author's Collection)

when firing at a target. It fired a solid circular ball, propelled by a charge of gunpowder. A small trail of gunpowder was ignited in a narrow vent at the top rear of the barrel.

The gun was tested in 1613, 1617 and 1622 and it was recorded that when elevated at 45 degrees, it fired a 4.5kg ball a distance of 1.8m with great accuracy.

95

Southsea Castle, Portsmouth

Defending City and Dock

Henry VIII ordered the construction of Southsea Castle during the spring of 1544 in anticipation of a French assault upon Portsmouth and its dockyard facility. It has been renovated over the centuries, but the square keep was part of Henry VIII's original castle.

Southsea Castle was specifically built in a position to guard the deep-water channel into Portsmouth at the point where it brought vessels closest to the shore. Sir Anthony Knyvet, Governor of Portsmouth, supervised the work together with John Chaderton, Captain of the Portsmouth garrison.

Work was temporarily hindered for ten days during June 1544 because of bad weather, which prevented the transportation of building supplies from the Isle of Wight. Construction resumed, but numerous sails of unidentified vessels were seen on the horizon. Also, it seems that the king had been misinformed about progress and

The eastern wall of Southsea Castle looking south towards the Solent and Spitbank Fort, which was built during the reign of Queen Victoria between 1859 and 1878. The *Mary Rose* sank to the right of Spitbank Fort in 1545, witnessed by Henry VIII who was encamped close to Southsea Castle. The square keep is the most prominent part of the castle and the walls, built of rough stone bonded with clay, are 3m thick and contain the original Tudor stonework. (Author's Collection)

believed that the castle was already defensible. Kynvet wrote the following progress report to the Privy Council on 8 July 1544:

> Has received their letter dated the last of June, and perceives the King is informed that the fortress now making at Portsmouth is defensible, 'the which is not'. The forepart of the barbican towards the sea is come to the vaudmure and some of the 'ventes' are up, but the North part is not so far forward; however, it will shortly be defensible. The square tower is at the second floor. As for furnishing Mr. Chaderton with ordnance; of the proportion for which the writer sued to their Lordships only 2 brass sakers are come, and, unless he were to disgarnish the town, he cannot furnish the fortress, which would need 12 great pieces and 24 'bassys and hagbuttes a crok'. Only half a last of powder is come, but good store of bows, arrows, bills and pikes. Begs them to consider the work is chargeable, and is best defence for the 'Isley' of Portsmouth and the town. Begs them to move the King for the ordnance. It is necessary; for on Saturday and Sunday last they saw three score sail of ships lying off and on the coast, but could not see what they were, so Knyvet sent word along the coast for good watch to be kept.[209]

It was important that construction of Southsea Castle was finished as soon as possible, but there was a lack of money to finance the project and pay the workforce. Sir Anthony Knyvet made repeated appeals for money to ensure

The northern wall of Southsea Castle. (Author's Collection)

the completion of the castle and workmen either left or were discharged. On 8 October, Knyvet reported to Lord Wriothesley, the High Chancellor, that he had to 'discharge six score workmen and paid all men for September, and some money remains. . . . There was never such a piece of work brought up with so little cost. When the King sees the work, which was of his Majesty's own device, I trust your Lordship, and we here, shall have thanks.' In this report, Knyvet confirmed that the king played an important role in the design of Southsea Castle. It took six months to complete the work. There were reports of English fisherman being molested and taken for ransom during French raids along the southern coast of England.

On 22 October 1544, Sir Anthony Knyvet wrote to Henry VIII:

> Begs licence to come to the King to show the state of the fortress, which may be called a castle, both for size, strength and beauty, and is praised of all who see it. Begs he may come for three days. Has at the King's command, by a letter from the Council, placed John Chaderton chief captain of the said new fortress, with twelve gunners, eight soldiers and a porter, which is of the fewest, considering the greatness of the place. Has also given over to Chaderton the ordnance he received from the master of the King's ordnance, which is too little for half the place.[210]

A detail from the Cowdray engraving showing the Battle of the Solent, 19 July 1545. This section shows Henry VIII close to Southsea Castle and the masts of the *Mary Rose* protruding from the sea. (Author's Collection)

The construction costs totalled £3,000, of which £1,300 was funded through the proceeds of items requisitioned as part of the dissolution of the monasteries. The building of Southsea Castle was groundbreaking and marked a departure from previous designs of fortifications in England. The style of the castle is different in comparison with the fortresses built along the south-eastern coastline at Deal, Walmer, Sandgate and Camber. Rounded circular towers were vulnerable to direct canon fire and there was scarce flanking cover. The curvature of the walls meant that there were blind spots. Henry adopted Italian architectural design in fortifications with square keeps, instead of circular keeps. Rectangular gun platforms were constructed east and west of the castle providing 360-degree cover and sloping bastions on the north and south sides reduced the size of the target. There were eight gun-ports built within the curtain wall facing the Solent which could fire upon enemy ships with devastating effect as they passed close to the shore.

It is believed that Henry VIII may have witnessed the sinking of the *Mary Rose* from the castle ramparts on 19 July 1545. In the Cowdray illustration, he is depicted on horseback close to the castle as the vessel sunk. When Henry VIII died in 1547, Southsea Castle was armed with seventeen guns and was regarded as a formidable fortress.

The Mary Rose

Henry VIII's Favourite Warship Sinks in the Solent

From 23–4 June 1545, the Mary Rose *and other English warships were anchored off the Downs, overlooked by Deal Castle and Walmer Castle in Kent, for the purpose of supporting the English army's occupation of Boulogne. When a French fleet, commanded by Admiral Claude D'Annebault, set sail on 6 July to attack Portsmouth, this English fleet was ordered to leave the Downs and confront them. On 19 July 1545, Henry VIII's favourite vessel, the* Mary Rose, *sank during the Battle of the Solent. On 11 October 1982, 437 years later, the wreck was raised from the seabed and transported to No. 3 Dock, Portsmouth harbour where she has been on display to visitors.*

A French invasion fleet, commanded by Admiral Claude d'Annebault, sailed towards the eastern approach to the Solent on 19 July 1545 and anchored close to St Helen's Point on the Isle of Wight. The English fleet, comprising sixty ships, under the flag of High Admiral Dudley Lord Lisle departed from Portsmouth dockyard to confront them. The *Mary Rose*, commanded by Captain Sir George Carew, was part of that fleet. It was estimated that the French fleet comprised between 225 and 324 warships, transporting 30,000 soldiers, and was intent on invading England to reverse the English Reformation. This fleet was much larger than the Spanish Armada which threatened England forty-three years later during the reign of Henry's daughter, Elizabeth I.

Henry had assembled his soldiers close to Southsea Common and they were encamped around the castle where he expected to oppose a French landing. The king held a banquet aboard the *Henry Grace à Dieu* the previous day with Admiral Sir John Dudley, Viscount Lisle and Sir George Carew, the commander of the *Mary Rose*. During that feast, Henry appointed Carew Vice Admiral.

By late afternoon both fleets were at anchor, the English fleet close to the entrance to Portsmouth, the French fleet close to St Helen's Road anchorage off the north-east corner of the Isle of Wight. Four French galleys proceeded towards the English fleet firing their guns forward. During this engagement the *Mary Rose* sank, a mile from Southsea, close to where Spitbank Fort is situated in the Solent. King Henry VIII observed the events from Southsea Castle in the company of Lady Carew, the wife of the captain of the *Mary Rose*.

The Anthony Roll confirmed that the crew aboard the *Mary Rose* included 200 mariners, 185 soldiers and 30 gunners, amounting in total to 415 men. Most of the crew drowned as the *Mary Rose* sank and there were only 35 survivors. The French were convinced that they had sunk her by their guns, but the cause of the catastrophe is uncertain. The English believed that the *Mary Rose* sank as a result of negligence. However, various theories have been cited, including that the vessel was overladen with ordnance which made her unstable and a gust of wind blew her over, and that the gun-ports were too low causing her to sink and capsize. A Flemish sailor, one of the survivors, reported that guns were fired from one side of the *Mary Rose* and as she turned to fire the guns on the other side,

The wreck of the *Mary Rose*, on display in Dock No. 3 in Portsmouth harbour. (Shutterstock)

The main decks of the *Mary Rose*. The gun-ports which were believed to be responsible for her sinking are clearly visible at the top. The Tudor warships were the first vessels of their kind to have gun-ports on hinges, enabling a broadside to be fired. It was a great innovation in warship design and a new tactic for naval warfare which would be used for the next 300 years. (Shutterstock)

water entered through the open gun-ports and she subsequently sank. Wriothesley wrote that, 'the *Mary Rose*, one of the King's great ships, by great misfortune by leaving the port holes open, as she turned and sank'.

The account of the Flemish sailor was contained in a report written by François van der Delft, the ambassador representing Emperor Charles V at the English court. He had replaced Chapuys, who had requested to be relieved as ambassador owing to ill-health. Van der Delft was introduced to Henry VIII aboard the *Henry Grace à Dieu*, where he was dining, on 18 July 1545, shortly before the French fleet had arrived and the Battle of the Solent had begun.

On 24 July 1545, van der Delft reported to Charles V:

> Next day, Sunday [19 July 1545] while the King was at dinner on the flagship, the French fleet appeared. The King hurriedly left the flagship and the English sailed to encounter the French, shooting at the galleys, of which five had entered the harbour while the English could not get out for want of wind. Towards evening the ship of Vice Admiral George Carew foundered, all the 500 men on board being drowned save about 25 or 30 servants, sailors and the like. Was told by a Fleming among the survivors that when she heeled

over with the wind the water entered by the lowest row of gun ports which had been left open after firing. They expect to recover the ship and guns.[211]

Edward Hall also confirmed this theory. He recorded that 'a goodly ship of England called the *Mary Rose*, was by too much folly, drowned in the midst of the haven, for she was laden with much ordinance, and the ports left open, which were very low, and the great ordinance, unbreached so that when the ship should turn, the water entered and suddenly sank'.

Martin de Bellay, a French eyewitness, offered a different explanation for the sinking of the *Mary Rose*, attributing it to French gunfire. He wrote:

> In the morning with the help of the sea which was calm, without wind or force of current, our galleys could be steered and manoeuvred at will to the detriment of the enemy, who, not being able to move through lack of wind, lay openly exposed to the fire of our artillery, which could do more harm to their ships than they could do to the galleys, more so because they are higher and bulkier, and also by their use of oars, our galleys could run away, avoid danger, and gain the advantage. Fortune supported our force in this way for more than an hour. During this time, among other damage suffered by the enemy, *la Marirose*, on their main ships, was sunk by gunfire, and out of five or six hundred men who were sunk by gunfire, only thirty-five were saved.[212]

As the masts of the *Mary Rose* protruded from the sea, the Battle of the Solent continued throughout the following day. Van der Delft reported: 'On Monday firing on both sides

Detail from the Cowdray engraving showing the sinking of the *Mary Rose*. This image was based on an original painting created between 1545 and 1548 for Anthony Browne, Master of the Horse, which was lost in the fire that destroyed Cowdray House in 1793. (Author's Collection)

lasted all day and at nightfall one of the French galleys was damaged. The French had over 300 sail, besides 27 galleys; but the English seem determined to give battle when they get their ships together and the wind is favourable'.

On 21 July 1545 French galleys continued to fire upon the English fleet in the Solent. The lack of wind frustrated the English vessels and Admiral Lord Lisle withdrew his fleet inside Portsmouth harbour. The French landed 2,000 soldiers on the Isle of Wight at Bembridge, but they were opposed. Van der Delft wrote, 'On Tuesday [21 July 1545] the French landed in the Isle of Wight and burnt ten or twelve small houses; but they were ultimately driven to take refuge in a small earthwork fort, and a large force, 8,000, is now opposed to them'.

Admiral d'Annebault received intelligence from captured English fishermen that Henry VIII was present in Portsmouth with an army and decided to withdraw his soldiers from the Isle of Wight and the French fleet from the Solent. It sailed for Dover, attacking coastal towns during the passage, but these assaults were strongly resisted and the French fleet eventually headed home. Ironically, Admiral d'Annebault returned to England during the following year in August 1546 as Lord High Admiral of France to ratify a peace treaty between England and France at Hampton Court Palace.

Although the French invasion had been deterred, the sinking of the *Mary Rose* was a tragedy in terms of loss of life as well as a financial disaster because a vessel such as this was an economic asset. The loss of the *Mary Rose* symbolised Henry's failure to achieve naval supremacy at sea and in his quest for military triumph. He had strengthened his navy and coastal fortifications, debased coinage, caused inflation and bankrupted the country for nothing. Within weeks of the sinking, thirty Venetian mariners were commissioned to attempt to recover the *Mary Rose* from the seabed of the Solent. Sails and rigging were salvaged by 5 August 1545, but the foremast was broken and the attempt to raise the ship was abandoned. The wreck was rediscovered in 1836 by John Deane and William Edwards who were diving at Spithead in search of HMS *Royal George*. Armaments from the wreck were recovered, but it became too expensive to continue to excavate the vessel. The *Mary Rose* was eventually raised on a cradle on 11 October 1982 in the presence of HRH Prince Charles and was returned to Portsmouth Historic Dockyard and placed in No. 3 Dock. Conservation work has continued over the decades following and a museum housing the ship and numerous artefacts is located in the dockyard.

97

Bronze Culverin from the Mary Rose

Defending England

The bronze muzzle-loading gun, on display at the Tower of London, was built by Arcangelo Arcana in London during 1542. Arcangelo belonged to a gun-making family from Cesena, Italy which migrated to England in 1523 and established a foundry in Salisbury Place, London.

This gun was aboard the *Mary Rose* when she sank in the Solent in 1545. It measured 3.5in in diameter and could fire a cast-iron shot weighing 6lb a distance of 330m.

The *Mary Rose* carried seventy-one guns, of which thirty-nine were large guns positioned on wooden carriages at gun-ports at the sides of the vessel. There were two types of gun used aboard the *Mary Rose*. The wrought-iron breach-loading gun was larger and surmounted upon wooden stock, and could be manoeuvred on a single axis by a pair of wheels. It had several

Examples of the wrought-iron breach-loading gun found aboard the *Mary Rose*. (Shutterstock)

This bronze culverine is adorned with a Tudor rose, surrounded by the garter with a royal crown above it. The double layer of petals on the Tudor rose symbolises the union of the Houses of York and Lancaster after the Wars of the Roses. The Latin inscription translates: 'Henry VIII, King of England, France and Ireland, Defender of the Faith, most unconquered'. There were similar inscriptions on other guns and this was another way of emphasising the king's power and prowess. The initials 'H I', for 'Henricus Invictissimus' – 'Henry most invincible', were inscribed on over 12,000 cast-iron shots found on the wreck of the *Mary Rose*. (Shutterstock)

chambers and there was no requirement to withdraw the gun to reload.

The other type of gun was the bronze muzzle-loading gun which was built upon an elm carriage, supported by four wheels, enabling it to be withdrawn for reloading. The purpose of this type of gun was to take down the rigging or damage the superstructure of an enemy vessel. It could not be moved and relied upon the ship aligning its muzzle to the target.

98

The Rack

Anne Askew Tortured on the Rack

The rack was used as an instrument of torture during the reign of Henry VIII. The purpose of it was to extract confessions through the dislocation of joints and the severing of tendons and to reduce the resolve of a prisoner through extreme pain and disablement. This replica, displayed in the Tower of London, was similar to the rack used to torture Anne Askew in 1546.

The rack was a commonly used instrument of torture during the Tudor period to obtain declarations of guilt from prisoners. It comprised an iron frame containing three wooden rollers. A warder could operate the rack by pulling a wooden lever, causing the ropes that were connected to the other rollers at the head and foot of the rack to pull in opposite directions. The central roller had an iron ratchet and teeth, which stabilised the rack, held it in position and kept the prisoner stretched.

The prisoner was placed on the frame and his or her hands were raised open and tied to the upper rollers of the rack. The feet were tied in a similar way to the lower roller. The device then pulled the feet and hands in opposite direction causing excruciating pain to the prisoner. By pulling hard on the wooden levers, the torturer lifted the prisoner's body off the ground using the ropes and stretched the limbs of the body apart, causing dislocation to the arms and legs.

Anne Askew was a poet and writer who practised her Protestant faith while the Reformation was taking place. She preached in London and attempted to convert several ladies in the court by providing them with Protestant literature. On 13 June 1546 Anne Askew was indicted by the Act of the Six Articles for speaking words against the sacrament and brought to the Guildhall in the city for questioning, but she was acquitted. Five days later Askew was arrested for heresy and taken to the Guildhall for a further trial. Askew confessed her heresy without the presence of a jury and was condemned to be burnt. She was then sent to Newgate Prison to await her execution. Henry VIII wanted to know which ladies had been converted to the Protestant faith and as a result Anne Askew was tortured on the rack on 29 June 1546. Charles Wriothesley wrote that, 'Anne Askew was had to the Tower of London and their set in the rack where she was sore tormented, but she would not convert for all the pains.' Sir Richard Rich and Sir Thomas Wriothesley not only witnessed her torture, but participated in the process, increasing her pain. Anne Askew wrote of her experience in the Tower of London and her torture in a letter to an anonymous friend:

> On Tuesday I was sent from Newgate to the sign of the Crown, where Master Rich and the bishop of London with all their power and flattering words went about to persuade me from God; but I did not esteem their glosing pretences. Then came to me Nic. Shaxton who counselled me to recant as he had done. I told him it had been good for him never to have been born, with many other like words. Then Master Rich sent me to the Tower, where I remained till 3 o'clock, when Rich and one of the Council came,

THE RACK

The replica of the rack on display at the Tower of London. (Brian Kenney/Shutterstock)

charging me upon my obedience to show them if I knew any man or woman of my sect. Answered that I knew none. Then they asked me of my lady of Suffolk, my lady of Sussex, my lady of Hertford, my lady Denny and my lady Fitzwilliam. Answered that if I should pronounce anything against them I could not prove it. Then they said, the King was informed that I could name, if I would, a great number of my sect. Answered 'that the King was as well deceived in that behalf as dissembled with in other matters'. Then they bade me show how I was maintained in the Compter, and who willed me to stick to my opinion. 'I said that there was no creature that therein did strengthen me, and as for the help that had in the Compter, it was by means of my maid,' who as she went abroad in the street, 'made moan to the prentices, and they by her did send the money; but who they were I never knew.' Then they said that there were divers gentlewomen that gave me money; but I knew not their names.

Then they said that there were divers ladies that had sent me money. I answered that there was a man in a blue coat who delivered me ten shillings and said that my lady of Hertford sent it me; and another in a violet coat gave me eight shillings, and said my lady Denny sent it me; whether it were true or no, I cannot tell, for I am not sure who sent it me, but as the maid did say. Then they said, there were of the Council that did maintain me: and I said No. Then they did put me on the rack, because I confessed no ladies or gentlewomen to be of my opinion, and thereon they kept me a long time; and because I lay still, and did not cry, my lord Chancellor and Master Rich took pains to rack me with their own hands, till I was nigh dead. Then the lieutenant caused me to be loosed from the rack. Incontinently I swooned, and then they recovered me again. After that I sat two long hours reasoning with my lord Chancellor upon the bare floor; where he, with many flattering words, persuaded me to leave my opinion. But my lord God (I thank his everlasting goodness) gave me grace to persevere, and will do, I hope to the very end. Then was I brought to a house and laid in a bed, with as weary and painful bones as ever had patient Job, I thank my lord God therefor. Then my lord Chancellor sent me word, if I would leave my opinion, I should want nothing: if I would not, I should forthwith to Newgate, and so to be burned. I sent him again word, that I would rather die than break my faith.

'Thus, the Lord open the eyes of their blind hearts, that the truth may take place! Farewell, dear friend, and pray, pray, pray.'[213]

Although Askew was disabled and unable to use her limbs as a consequence of being tortured on the rack, she never revealed any names and maintained her faith and integrity until the end. On 12 July 1546, Askew, who could not walk, was taken by boat from the Tower of London to Blackfriars where she was placed in a chair and returned to Newgate Prison, where she was incarcerated for a further four days before her execution.

Anne Askew is one of two women (the other being Margaret Cheyney) who is recorded as having been tortured in the Tower of London and burnt at the stake.

99

Statue of Henry VIII at St Bartholomew's Hospital and Smithfield Execution Site

Henry VIII's Gift of St Bartholomew's Hospital to the Corporation of London

The only statue of Henry VIII in London stands above the northern gatehouse of St Bartholomew's Hospital. The hospital was originally founded at Smithfield, in the suburbs of the City of London, along with the Priory of St Bartholomew in 1123 during the reign of Henry I. It is the oldest hospital in England and has provided continuous patient care for five centuries. This was jeopardised when the Priory of St Bartholomew was closed on 25 October 1539, when Robert, Abbot of Waltham, surrendered the priory with all its possessions to Henry VIII during the dissolution of the monasteries.

Henry VIII allowed the hospital to continue, but removed its ability to earn an income, which enabled it to function. Sir Richard Gresham, Lord Mayor of London, petitioned the king to help save the hospital. Henry bestowed the hospital on the Corporation of London in December 1546: 'The King vested the Hospital of St. Bartholomew in the mayor, commonalty, and citizens of London, and their successors, for ever, in consideration of a payment by them of 500 marks a year towards its maintenance.' This money has been paid by the Corporation of London annually for over 500 years since 1546.

In January 1547, shortly before his death, Henry bequeathed to the hospital properties and income entitlements that would allow it to continue to operate and therefore secured its future.

Also grant that the said late hospital of St. Bartholomew shall be a place and house for the poor, to be called The House of the Poor in West Smythfelde of the foundation of King Henry VIII., and that the church within the site of the said hospital shall be a parish church, called the church of St. Bartholomew the Little, the parish church for all inhabitants within the site and close of the said late hospital.[214]

The statue of Henry VIII stands majestically above the entrance to St Bartholomew's Hospital and overlooks the place of execution at Smithfield, where those who opposed or defied his rule were executed. Traitors were hung, drawn and quartered and heretics were burnt at the stake here. Among those that were executed at Smithfield was Richard Roose. On 5 April 1531, he was taken to Smithfield where he was lowered into a cauldron and boiled to death in public (see Object 44). Thomas Abel, chaplain to Henry's first wife, Katherine of Aragon, would die a martyr when he was burnt at Smithfield on 30 July 1540 together with five other priests (see Object 81). Richard Hilles wrote to Henry Bullinger:

Soon after the dissolution of Parliament, viz., 30 July last year, were executed six of the

The statue of Henry VIII stands above the northern entrance to St Bartholomew's Hospital, which is named the Henry VIII gate. He overlooks the site where those condemned as traitors and heretics during his reign were mercilessly executed in public. (Author's Collection)

Detail of the only statue dedicated to King Henry VIII in London. (Author's Collection)

The information panel at the entrance to the park, north of St Bartholomew's Hospital, confirms that 'this open space occupies part of the original "Smethefelde" or "Smoothfeld", which from ancient times was used for jousts, tournaments and executions as well as a market'. Sir William Wallace is the most notable person to have been executed here on 23 August 1305 during the reign of Edward I. A memorial panel commemorates his execution on the north wall of the hospital facing the park. (Author's Collection)

men excepted from the pardon. Three were popish priests, Abell, Powell, and Fetherston, who refused to acknowledge the King's new title and authority over the clergy. The other three were preachers of the Gospel, of no mean order, Barnes, Gerrard, and Jerome. They were brought from the Tower on a sledge to Smithfield, tied to one stake and burned where the others were executed.

The place had never been used before for the execution of any persons but heretics. They remained in the fire as quiet as if they had felt no pain. Could never learn why these three gospellers were exempted from the general pardon. Thinks it was to gratify the clergy and the ignorant, and that there would not have been more than one, or at most two, holocausts in the year, were it not to get the clergy and others to pay more readily. They were not condemned for their preaching by due course of law; and I know that from the 12 July 1539 (from which day the bill by which the truth was condemned took effect) until they were apprehended, they never spoke expressly against the Statute except in private. They were committed to prison in Easter week, 1540, even after submitting to the King in many things in their sermons at Easter. Thus, they could not have been justly condemned. Many others of those excepted from the pardon were executed the week following, for reasons unknown to me. But, to say the truth, people did not inquire much, as it is no new thing to see men hanged, quartered, or beheaded, for one thing or another, sometimes for trifling expressions construed as against the King.[215]

On 12 July 1546, Anne Askew was brought to Smithfield to be burnt at the stake along with three other heretics who were condemned by the king's laws of heresy against the sacrament of the altar. The execution was carried out in the presence of the Lord Mayor of London and the Duke of Norfolk who saw Askew suffer among the flames (see Object 98).

Today an information panel reminds visitors of the purpose of this site as a place of execution during the medieval and Tudor periods, which stands in a quiet, secluded park in between St Bartholomew's Hospital and Smithfield Meat Market.

100

King Henry VIII's Tomb, St George's Chapel, Windsor

The End of Henry's Reign

Throughout 1546, Henry VIII suffered a series of illnesses. The king was nursed attentively by his sixth wife, Katherine Parr, during these periods of ill-health. However, his health was clearly failing and on 8 January 1547 Henry VIII died of septicaemia at Whitehall Palace.

François van der Delft, Imperial Ambassador to the English court, reported that the king had suffered a fever for three days in early March. The king was by this time immobile. His obese frame could not allow him to climb stairs and he required assistance with various tasks. While at Oatlands Palace, the king suffered a bout of fever, but recovered during early December. Later that month he returned to London.

Within a month of the death of Henry VIII, the reign of terror continued. The Duke of Norfolk and his son, Henry, the Earl of Surrey, were arrested in 12 December 1546 and imprisoned in the Tower of London. Three days later on 15 December, William Harpin, an ale brewer from Southwark, was tried and found guilty of counterfeiting silver coins. He was drawn from Newgate Prison to Tower Hill where he was hung for this crime on 20 December 1546. The Duke of Norfolk and the Earl of Surrey languished in the Tower of London during Christmas and on 13 January 1547 they were brought to trial at the Guildhall and convicted of high treason. The Earl of Surrey became the last victim of Henry VIII's tyrannical reign when he was led to the scaffold on Tower Hill and beheaded on 20 January 1547. The day before he died, Henry ordered the execution of his father, the Duke of Norfolk, but when he died the order was revoked by the king's ministers on the grounds that they did not want to begin the new reign with bloodshed.

Henry VIII spent Christmas at Whitehall Palace where he suffered a further bout of fever on New Year's Day, 1547. He rallied and was well enough to receive the French and Spanish ambassadors on 17 January. At 2am on 28 January 1547, Henry VIII died at the palace. Due to the secrecy maintained around his illness and passing the exact cause of death is difficult to ascertain, but it is believed that he died from septicaemia.

Henry VIII stipulated in his last will that he wanted his son, Edward, to succeed him as sovereign and had appointed the Earl of Hartford and the boy's uncle, Edward Seymour, Earl of Hertford, as Lord Protector and Governor until the young king reached 18 years of age.

During the afternoon of 7 February 1547, from 2–6pm, at Leaden Hall and St Michael's in Cornhill, alms amounting to 1,000 marks were distributed to the poor in accordance with his last will with 'injunctions to pray for his soul'. His will also instructed that 'common beggars, as much as may be, avoided'.

Each man, woman and child who was there was given a grote. According to Charles Wriothesley, 21,000 people received these alms. Church bells within the City of London and the suburbs rang through the day and night in honour of

St George's Chapel, Windsor Castle.
(Courtesy of Aurelien Guichard)

The plaque marking the grave of Henry VIII, Jane Seymour and Charles I.

Henry VIII, and a requiem Mass for his soul was held in every church throughout England.

Charles Wriothesley recorded that the '14th day of February, the corpse of King Henry the Eighth was solemnly with great honour conveyed in a chariot, with his image lying on it, toward Windsor, and rested that night at Syon, where was a rich hearse made of wax of nine stories high'.

The king's remains arrived at Windsor on 15 February 1547 and were received by the Dean of Windsor and the Eton College choir, before being taken to Windsor Castle. Henry's wish, in accordance with his will, was to be 'laid in the choir of his college of Windsor, midway between the stalls and the high altar, in a tomb now almost finished in which he will also have the bones of his wife, Queen Jane'. He was buried next to his third wife, Jane Seymour, the following day in St George's Chapel, within Windsor Castle.

St George's Chapel was built during the reigns of four monarchs. A chapel had existed on this site since the reign of King Henry III, but when King Edward III established the religious college named St George's at Windsor in 1348, this chapel was rededicated as St George's Chapel. King Edward IV commenced major renovation work building the current chapel at Windsor Castle in 1475. The nave and stone vaulted ceiling were constructed by Henry VII and Henry VIII completed the work in 1528. Henry VIII planned an elaborate tomb but he died before it could be finished. His sarcophagus survives but the remains of Admiral Lord Nelson were entombed within it at St Paul's Cathedral in 1806. Henry VIII was buried in the vault beneath the nave of St George's Chapel with a black marble slate that just bears his name, alongside his third wife, Jane Seymour, King Charles I and an infant child of Queen Anne.

Notes

1. *Letters and Papers, Foreign and Domestic, Henry VIII*, Volume 2, 1515–18, pp. 1376–7.
2. R.W. Chambers, *Thomas More* (London: Jonathan Cape, 1935), pp. 70–1.
3. Edward Hall, *The Triumphant Reign of King Henry VIII, Volume 1* (London: T.C. & E.C. Jack, 1904), p. 149.
4. *Letters and Papers, Foreign and Domestic, Henry VIII*, Volume 1, 1509–14, p. 37.
5. *Letters and Papers, Foreign and Domestic, Henry VIII*, Volume 2, 1515–18, p. 116.
6. St Clare Byrne, *The Letters of King Henry VIII* (London: Cassell, 1936), p. 9.
7. Edward Hall, *The Triumphant Reign of King Henry VIII, Volume 1* (London: T.C. & E.C. Jack, 1904), p. 5.
8. *Letters and Papers, Foreign and Domestic, Henry VIII*, Volume 1, 1509–14, p. 59.
9. Edward Hall, *The Triumphant Reign of King Henry VIII, Volume 1* (London: T.C. & E.C. Jack, 1904), p. 5.
10. ibid.
11. ibid., p. 7.
12. ibid.
13. Edward Hall, *Hall's Chronicle* (London: 1809, originally published 1548), p. 513.
14. See *Letters and Papers, Foreign and Domestic, Henry VIII*, Volume 1, 1509–14.
15. *Letters and Papers, Foreign and Domestic, Henry VIII*, Volume 16, 1540–1, p. 481.
16. *Letters and Papers, Foreign and Domestic, Henry VIII*, Volume 1, 1509–14.
17. *Letters and Papers, Foreign and Domestic, Henry VIII*, Volume 2, 1515–18, pp. 1406–7.
18. *Letters and Papers, Foreign and Domestic, Henry VIII*, Volume 4, 1524–30, p. 762.
19. *Letters and Papers, Foreign and Domestic, Henry VIII*, Volume 1, 1509–14.
20. Edward Hall, *The Triumphant Reign of King Henry VIII, Volume 1* (London: T.C. & E.C. Jack, 1904), p. 245.
21. *Letters and Papers, Foreign and Domestic, Henry VIII*, Volume 3, 1519–23, p. 975.
22. *Letters and Papers, Foreign and Domestic, Henry VIII*, Volume 2, 1515–18, p. 116.
23. *Letters and Papers, Foreign and Domestic, Henry VIII*, Volume 1, 1509–14, pp. 3–4.
24. ibid.
25. ibid.
26. ibid.
27. Edward Hall, *The Triumphant Reign of King Henry VIII, Volume 1* (London: T.C. & E.C. Jack, 1904), p. 75.
28. *Letters and Papers, Foreign and Domestic, Henry VIII*, Volume 1, 1509–14.
29. ibid.
30. ibid.
31. ibid.
32. *Letters and Papers, Foreign and Domestic, Henry VIII*, Volume 1, 1509–14, p. 789.
33. George Cavendish, *Life and Death of Cardinal Wolsey* (Boston: Houghton, Mifflin and Company, 1905), pp. 15–16.
34. ibid., pp. 53–4.
35. *Letters and Papers, Foreign and Domestic, Henry VIII*, Volume 4, 1524–30, p. 2683.
36. Charles Wriothesley, *The Chronicle of England During the Reign of the Tudors, Volume 1* (London: The Camden Society, 1875), p. 16.
37. *Letters and Papers, Foreign and Domestic, Henry VIII*, Volume 4, 1524–30, p. 3035.

38. *Letters and Papers, Foreign and Domestic, Henry VIII*, Volume 1, 1509–14.
39. ibid.
40. *Letters and Papers, Foreign and Domestic, Henry VIII*, Volume 2, 1515–18, p. 789.
41. *Letters and Papers, Foreign and Domestic, Henry VIII*, Volume 1, Part 1, Letter 1.
42. *Letters and Papers, Foreign and Domestic, Henry VIII*, Volume 2, 1515–18, p. 1100.
43. Edward Hall, *The Triumphant Reign of King Henry VIII, Volume 1* (London: T.C. & E.C. Jack, 1904), p. 165.
44. *Letters and Papers, Foreign and Domestic, Henry VIII*, Volume 2, 1515–18, p. 1102.
45. Edward Hall, *The Triumphant Reign of King Henry VIII, Volume 2*, pp. 24–5.
46. Letters and Papers, Foreign and Domestic, Henry VIII, Volume 10, January 1536, p. 71.
47. *Letters and Papers, Foreign and Domestic, Henry VIII*, Volume 2, 1515–18, p. 1372.
48. ibid., pp. 1376–7.
49. ibid.
50. *Letters and Papers, Foreign and Domestic, Henry VIII*, Volume 3, 1519–22, p. 402.
51. Edward Hall, *The Triumphant Reign of King Henry VIII, Volume 1* (London: T.C. & E.C. Jack, 1904), p. 188.
52. ibid., pp. 188–9.
53. *Letters and Papers, Foreign and Domestic, Henry VIII*, Volume 3, 1519–22, pp. 328–9.
54. Edward Hall, *The Triumphant Reign of King Henry VIII, Volume 2* (London: T.C. & E.C. Jack, 1904), p. 198.
55. *Calendar of State Papers Relating to English Affairs in the Archives of Venice*, Volume 3, 1520–6.
56. Edward Hall, *The Triumphant Reign of King Henry VIII, Volume 2*, p. 199.
57. *Calendar of State Papers Relating to English Affairs in the Archives of Venice*, Volume 3, 1520–6.
58. ibid.
59. ibid.
60. *Letters and Papers, Foreign and Domestic, Henry VIII*, Volume 3, 1519–22, p. 312.
61. Brett Dolman, Suzannah Lipscomb, Lee Prosser, David Souden and Lucy Worsley, *Henry VIII: 500 Facts* (London: Historic Royal Palaces, 2009), p. 77.
62. *Calendar of State Papers Relating to English Affairs in the Archives of Venice*, Volume 3, 1520–6, Antonio Giustinian report, 7 September 1520.
63. Edward Hall, *The Triumphant Reign of King Henry VIII, Volume 2* (London: T.C. & E.C. Jack, 1904), p. 214.
64. *Letters and Papers, Foreign and Domestic, Henry VIII*, Volume 3, 1519–23, p. 491.
65. ibid., p. 492.
66. ibid., p. 506.
67. Henry VIII, *Assertio Septum Sacramentorum adversus Martinum Lutherum* (1521), p. 100.
68. *Calendar of State Papers: Spain*, Volume 2, 1509–25, p. 437.
69. ibid., p. 427.
70. ibid.
71. ibid., p. 437.
72. ibid., p. 427.
73. Edward Hall, *The Triumphant Reign of King Henry VIII, Volume 1* (London: T.C. & E.C. Jack, 1904), pp. 319–20.
74. Anon., *A Collection of Ordinances & Regulations for the Government of the Royal Household* (London: Society of Antiquities, 1790), p. 148.
75. *Letters and Papers, Foreign and Domestic, Henry VIII*, Volume 4, January 1524–30, p. ccclxxviii.
76. ibid., p. 1960.
77. Clare M. St. Byrne, *The Letters of King Henry VIII* (London: Cassell and Company Ltd, 1936), p. 82.
78. *Letters and Papers, Foreign and Domestic, Henry VIII*, Volume 4, 1524–30, p. 639.

79. George Cavendish, *Life and Death of Cardinal Wolsey* (Boston: Houghton, Mifflin and Company, 1905), p. 69.
80. *Calendar of State Papers: Spain*, Volume 3, Part 2, 1527–9.
81. ibid.
82. Edward, Hall, *The Triumphant Reign of King Henry VIII, Volume 2* (London: T.C. & E.C. Jack, 1904), p. 145.
83. George Cavendish, *Life and Death of Cardinal Wolsey* (n.p.: R. & T. Washborn, 1901), p. 121.
84. *Letters and Papers, Foreign and Domestic, Henry VIII*, Volume 4, 1524–30, p. 2593.
85. Giles Tremlett, *Catherine of Aragon, Henry's Spanish Queen* (London: Faber & Faber, 2011), p. 340.
86. *Letters and Papers, Foreign and Domestic, Henry VIII*, Volume 5, 1531–2, p. 60.
87. J.R. Tanner, *Tudor Constitutional Documents, A.D. 1485–1603* (Cambridge: Cambridge University Press, 1922), p. 381.
88. *Calendar of State Papers Relating to English Affairs in the Archives of Venice*, Volume 4, 1527–33.
89. *Letters and Papers, Foreign and Domestic, Henry VIII*, Volume 6, 1533, p. 224.
90. ibid., p. 230.
91. *Calendar of State Papers: Spain*, Volume 4, Part 2, Henry VIII, 1531–3.
92. *Letters and Papers, Foreign and Domestic, Henry VIII*, Volume 6, 1533, p. 240.
93. Edward Hall, *The Triumphant Reign of King Henry VIII, Volume 2* (London: T.C. & E.C. Jack, 1904), pp. 230–1.
94. *Letters and Papers, Foreign and Domestic, Henry VIII*, Volume 6, 1533, p. 583.
95. ibid., p. 244.
96. *Letters and Papers, Foreign and Domestic, Henry VIII*, Volume 5, 1531–2, p. 563.
97. ibid., p. 567.
98. Edward Hall, *The Triumphant Reign of King Henry VIII, Volume 2*, p. 231.
99. Charles Wriothesley, *The Chronicle of England During the Reign of the Tudors, Volume 1* (London: The Camden Society, 1875), p. 36.
100. *Letters and Papers, Foreign and Domestic, Henry VIII*, Volume 6, 1533, p. 266.
101. *Calendar of State Papers: Spain*, Volume 4, Part 2.
102. *Letters and Papers, Foreign and Domestic, Henry VIII*, Volume 7, 1534, pp. 164–5.
103. *HLRO Original Journal*, H.L., Volume 1, pp. 174–5 (30 March 1534).
104. *Letters and Papers, Foreign and Domestic, Henry VIII*, Volume 7, 1534, p. 240.
105. *Calendar of State Papers: Spain*, Volume 5, Part 1, 1534–5.
106. William Roper, *The Life of Sir Thomas More* (London: Burns & Oates, 1905), p. 22.
107. ibid., pp. 71–2.
108. ibid., p. 49.
109. *Letters and Papers, Foreign and Domestic, Henry VIII*, Volume 4, 1524–30, p. 2684.
110. *Letters and Papers, Foreign and Domestic, Henry VIII*, Volume 5, 1531–2, p. 467.
111. William Roper, op. cit., pp. 71–2.
112. ibid., p. 106.
113. ibid., p. 72.
114. ibid., p. 73.
115. *Letters and Papers, Foreign and Domestic, Henry VIII*, Volume 7, 1534, p. 73.
116. ibid., p. 200.
117. ibid., pp. 201–2.
118. William Roper, op. cit., p. 81.
119. John Bailey, *History and Antiquities of the Tower of London* (London: Jennings & Chapman, 1830), p. 132.
120. William Roper, op. cit., p. 165.
121. ibid., p. 170.
122. J.R. Tanner, *Tudor Constitutional Documents, A.D. 1485–1603* (Cambridge: Cambridge University Press, 1922), p. 47.

123. ibid., pp. 47–8.
124. ibid., p. 323.
125. William Roper, op. cit., p. 78.
126. *Calendar of State Papers: Spain*, Volume 5, Part 1, 1534–5.
127. *Letters and Papers, Foreign and Domestic, Henry VIII*, Volume 8, 1535, p. 394.
128. ibid.
129. ibid., pp. 394–5.
130. William Roper, op. cit., p. 86.
131. *Letters and Papers, Foreign and Domestic, Henry VIII*, Volume 8, 1535, p. 395.
132. William Roper, op. cit., p. 176.
133. ibid., p. 99.
134. John Bailey, *History and Antiquities of the Tower of London* (London: Jennings & Chapman, 1830), p. 365.
135. *Letters and Papers, Foreign and Domestic, Henry VIII*, Volume 9, 1535, p. 331.
136. *Letters and Papers, Foreign and Domestic, Henry VIII*, Volume 10, 1536, p. 3.
137. *Letters and Papers, Foreign and Domestic, Henry VIII*, Volume 9, 1535, p. 355.
138. ibid., p. 356.
139. *Letters and Papers, Foreign and Domestic, Henry VIII*, Volume 10, 1536, p. 49.
140. ibid., p. 22.
141. ibid., p. 51.
142. ibid.
143. ibid., p. 52.
144. ibid., p. 102.
145. ibid., p. 134.
146. ibid., pp. 10–32.
147. ibid., p. 334.
148. ibid., pp. 341–2.
149. ibid., pp. 361–2.
150. ibid., pp. 377–8.
151. Charles Wriothesley, *The Chronicle of England During the Reign of the Tudors, Volume 1*, p. 42.
152. Edward Hall, *The Triumphant Reign of King Henry VIII, Volume 2* (London: T.C. & E.C. Jack, 1904), pp. 268–9.
153. *Letters and Papers, Foreign and Domestic, Henry VIII*, Volume 10, 1536, p. 377.
154. ibid.
155. *Letters and Papers, Foreign and Domestic, Henry VIII*, Volume 11, 153, p. 65.
156. Madeline Dodds and Ruth Hope, *The Pilgrimage of Grace 1536 to 1537 and The Essex Conspiracy 1538* (Cambridge: Cambridge University Press, 1915), p. 95.
157. *Letters and Papers, Foreign and Domestic, Henry VIII*, Volume 11, 1536, p. 229.
158. ibid., p. 217.
159. ibid., p. 346.
160. ibid., pp. 302–3.
161. ibid., p. 242.
162. Edward Hall, *The Triumphant Reign of King Henry VIII, Volume 2* (London: T.C. & E.C. Jack, 1904), p. 278.
163. *Letters and Papers, Foreign and Domestic, Henry VIII*, Volume 11, 1536, p. 302.
164. ibid., p. 272.
165. ibid., p. 288.
166. *Letters and Papers, Foreign and Domestic, Henry VIII*, Volume 11, 1536, p. 216.
167. ibid.
168. *Letters and Papers, Foreign and Domestic, Henry VIII*, Volume 12, Part 2, 1537, p. 121.
169. ibid.
170. *Letters and Papers, Foreign and Domestic, Henry VIII*, Volume 12, Part 1, February 1537, pp. 226–7.
171. Anon., *A Collection of Ordinances & Regulations for the Government of the Royal Household* (London: Society of Antiquities, 1790), p. 156.
172. Raphael Holinshed, *Holinshed Chronicles of England, Scotland and Ireland, Volume III* (London: 1808), p. 809.
173. *Letters and Papers, Foreign and Domestic, Henry VIII*, Volume 14, Part 1, 1539, p. 502.
174. ibid., p. 107.

175. *Letters and Papers, Foreign and Domestic, Henry VIII*, Volume 14, Part 2, 1539, pp. 345–7.
176. ibid., p. 234.
177. ibid., pp. 60–1.
178. ibid., pp. 70–1.
179. ibid., p. 9.
180. ibid., p. 34.
181. Charles Wriothesley, *The Chronicle of England During the Reign of the Tudors, Volume 1* (London: The Camden Society, 1875), pp. 109–10.
182. Alison Weir, *Henry VIII, King & Court* (London: Vintage, 2008), p. 435.
183. Martin Hume, *Chronicle of King Henry VIII of England* (London: G. Bell & Sons, 1889), p. 90.
184. *Letters and Papers, Foreign and Domestic, Henry VIII*, Volume 15, 1540, pp. 77–8.
185. Edward Hall, *The Triumphant Reign of King Henry VIII, Volume 2* (London: T.C. & E.C. Jack, 1904), pp. 306–7.
186. Arthur Galton, *The Character & Times of Thomas Cromwell* (Birmingham: Cornish Brothers, 1887), p. 156.
187. *Letters and Papers, Foreign and Domestic, Henry VIII*, Volume 15, 1540, p. 458.
188. *Letters and Papers, Foreign and Domestic, Henry VIII*, Volume 5, 1531–2, p. 546.
189. *Letters and Papers, Foreign and Domestic, Henry VIII*, Volume 6, 1533, p. 622.
190. *Letters and Papers, Foreign and Domestic, Henry VIII*, Volume 12, 1537, p. 255.
191. *Letters and Papers, Foreign and Domestic, Henry VIII*, Volume 16, 1541, p. 619.
192. ibid., p. 532.
193. ibid.
194. ibid., p. 534.
195. *Letters and Papers, Foreign and Domestic, Henry VIII*, Volume 16, 1541, pp. 618–19.
196. ibid., p. 646.
197. ibid.
198. ibid., p. 611.
199. *Calendar of State Papers: Spain*, Volume 6, Part 1.
200. *Letters and Papers, Foreign and Domestic, Henry VIII*, Volume 16, 1541, pp. 665–6.
201. ibid., pp. 645–6.
202. *Calendar of State Papers: Spain*, Volume 6, Part 1.
203. *Letters and Papers, Foreign and Domestic, Henry VIII*, Volume 17, 1542, p. 44.
204. ibid., p. 50.
205. *Calendar of State Papers: Spain*, Volume 6, Part 1, 1538–42.
206. *Letters and Papers, Foreign and Domestic, Henry VIII*, Volume 17, 1542, p. 50.
207. *Letters and Papers, Foreign and Domestic, Henry VIII*, Volume 18, Part 1, 1543, p. 483.
208. Edward Hall, *The Triumphant Reign of King Henry VIII, Volume 2* (London: T.C. & E.C. Jack, 1904), p. 349.
209. *Letters and Papers, Foreign and Domestic, Henry VIII*, Volume 19, Part 1, 1544, p. 541.
210. ibid.
211. *Letters and Papers, Foreign and Domestic, Henry VIII*, Volume 20, Part 1, 1545, p. 627.
212. A. McKee, *How We Found the Mary Rose* (London: Souvenir, 1982), pp. 25–6.
213. *Letters and Papers, Foreign and Domestic, Henry VIII*, Volume 21, Part 1, 1546, pp. 589–90.
214. ibid., p. 416.
215. *Letters and Papers, Foreign and Domestic, Henry VIII*, Volume 16, 1541, pp. 271–2.

Bibliography

Anon., *A Collection of Ordinances & Regulations for the Government of the Royal Household*, London: Society of Antiquities, 1790

Bailey, John, *History and Antiquities of the Tower of London*, London: Jennings & Chapman, 1830

Borman, Tracy, *The Story of the Tower of London* London: Merrell, 2015

Byrne, M. St Clare, *The Letters of King Henry VIII*, London: Cassell, 1936

Cavendish, George, *Life and Death of Cardinal Wolsey*, Boston: R. & T. Washborn, 1901

Cavendish, George, *Life and Death of Cardinal Wolsey*, Boston: Houghton, Mifflin and Company, 1905

Chambers, R.W., *Thomas More*, London: Jonathan Cape, 1935

Clephan, R. Coltman, *The Tournament: Its Periods and Phases*, London: Methuen & Co. Ltd, 1919

Dodds, Madeline and Hope, Ruth, *The Pilgrimage of Grace 1536 to 1537 and The Essex Conspiracy 1538*, Cambridge: Cambridge University Press, 1915

Dolman, Brett, Lipscomb, Suzannah, Prosser, Lee, Souden, David and Worsley, Lucy, *Henry VIII, 500 Facts*, London: Historic Royal Palaces, 2009

Galton, Arthur, *The Character & Times of Thomas Cromwell*, Birmingham: Cornish Brothers, 1887

Hall, Edward, *Hall's Chronicle*, London: 1809, originally published 1548

Hall, Edward, *The Triumphant Reign of King Henry VIII, Volume 1*, London: T.C. & E.C. Jack, 1904

Hall, Edward, *The Triumphant Reign of King Henry VIII, Volume 2*, London: T.C. & E.C. Jack, 1904

Holinshed, Raphael, *Holinshed Chronicles of England, Scotland and Ireland, Volume III*, London: 1808

Hume, Martin, *Chronicle of Henry VIII*, London: G. Bell & Sons, 1889

Moorhouse, Geoffrey, *Great Harry's Navy: How Henry VIII Gave England Seapower*, London: Weidenfeld & Nicolson, 2005

Pettifer, Ernest, *Punishments of Former Days*, Hook: Waterside Press, 1992

Roper, William, *The Life of Sir Thomas More*, London: Burns & Oates, 1905

Souden, David and Worsley, Lucy, *The Story of Hampton Court Palace*, London: Merrell, 2015

Starkey, David, *The Reign of Henry VIII: Personalities and Politics*, London: Vintage Books, 2002

Tanner, J.R., *Tudor Constitutional Documents, A.D. 1485–1603*, Cambridge: Cambridge University Press, 1922

Weir, Alison, *Henry VIII, King & Court*, London: Vintage Books, 2008

Wriothesley, Charles, *The Chronicle of England During the Reign of the Tudors, Volume 1*, London: The Camden Society, 1875